PAIN PEACE
&
PROSPERITY

The Greatest Story Never Told

(Book 1)

PAIN PEACE & PROSPERITY

The Greatest Story Never Told

(Book 1)

BRIAN D. CARENARD

Copyrighted © 2020 by Brian D. Carenard

Point Blank MG Publications

All rights reserved.

No part of this book may be reproduced or used in any manner without written permission of the copyright except for the use of quotations in a book review.

In Loving Memory of

Harvey James & Mary Elizabeth Sampson –
Josephine Sampson - Stephen Sampson

My best friend and mentor Sharieff "AC" Clayton

Introduction

I wrote this book when we were all locked in our homes because of an order issued by the governor of NY. We were in the first phase of a deadly pandemic known as Covid-19, and I had my youngest daughter, Milan Amor, staying with me. She was doing virtual school and remote learning because all the schools had shut down until further notice. I noticed I was having the hardest time getting my daughter to read books, so I made a deal with her. I told her if she would read a book, I would WRITE a book. My initial purpose was to show by example that sometimes we have to do things we may not want to do to get ahead in life. I had zero intention of writing a book before this, but I wanted to show her I would join her in putting in some work. I figured I'd write a few paragraphs, give them some chapter titles, to keep my end of the bargain… 3 months and 210,000 words later, I was sitting on an autobiography so lengthy I had to split it up into 3 books. This is a real and honest story of my life as vividly as I can remember it. I hope not to offend, disappoint or discredit anyone as I am only telling my story. I used this opportunity to show how sometimes it takes PAIN to find PEACE, and overall gain some PROSPERITY... I hope you all enjoy this journey as you learn all that it took to get me to the space I am in today... Thank you kindly...

Brian "Saigon" Carenard

Table of Contents

Introduction vii
Chapter 1: Light Up 1
Chapter 2: 7/13/77 9
Chapter 3: They Loving The Crew 26
Chapter 4: Kingsborn Ma Justice 39
Chapter 5: That Nasty Lake 54
Chapter 6: Child on Trial 69
Chapter 7: This Moment In Time (Say His Name) 91
Chapter 8: Choke and Slide 100
Chapter 9: Watch Out For Your Friends 118
Chapter 10: Bulls vs Lakers 133
Chapter 11: Unhappy Meal 150
Chapter 12: Crack is Wack 172
Chapter 13: Boy to a Man 196
Chapter 14: What the Lovers Do 222
Chapter 15: King Cabrini 245
Chapter 16: Same Ol' Me 263
Chapter 17: Drive Slow 284

Chapter 18: Young and Sprung 304
Chapter 19: Wild Animalescents 316
Chapter 20: Southern Hospitality 346

CHAPTER 1

Light Up

As far back as I can remember, I was always told that I differed from most other children. Whether it was from the teachers at school, adults in the park, other parents at the playground, or just from the elders in and around whatever neighborhood I lived in, I was often reminded of this. Whenever an adult got a chance to have some dialogue with me, they made it their business to tell me how different and special I was.

I used to think maybe it was because I could fluently read at the tender age of three. And I don't mean like cat, rat and hat, Dr. Seuss-type books. I mean, I could read and *comprehend* what I was reading, like someone in junior high school. My grandmother, Mary Elizabeth Sampson, who was affectionately known around the neighborhood as Mama Sampson, would gather her friends from church inside her small living room and scream out to me, "Brian, get in here and read the Book of Genesis!" And just like that, with my lisp and all, I would read. *"In the beginning, God created the Heavens and the Earth..."*

Mama Sampson had nine daughters and two sons, so as one would probably guess, I had a gang of cousins. Until my grandma passed away in 2003, she would always let me know that I was one of her favorite grandchildren. There was me, my cousin Angela, and her ultimate favorite, my older cousin Buttercup. We were in the top three favorites out of at least twenty-plus grandchildren. This alone made me feel very special because whenever all the cousins got together, which was more often than not, we would all vie for Mama Sampson's attention and affection, and I always got it. *A lot* of it.

One person didn't seem so happy about me being called 'special' every day, or always seeming to win Mama Sampson's attention; this was my mother's only other child. My then arch-nemesis, my big sister, LaDedra. Over the years, LaDedra and I would have sibling battles like you wouldn't believe. Yet in time, she also eventually grew to be one of my best friends, and one of the only people I trust 'til this very day. But let's get back to this whole me being special thing.

Even as a small child, I could remember being fascinated by how one could plug things into the wall, and they would LIGHT UP, or come to life. Whether it was my Aunt Doshia Lee's tape recorder, my mother's stereo, or one of Mama Sampson's lamps. That one could take this wire, plug it into the wall and things had life, fascinated me on so many levels. I would sit next to a socket when no adult or older person was around, and plug and unplug any appliance that had lights, or would LIGHT UP. It fascinated me to think that whatever is in this wall can make these appliances LIGHT UP, and to a 3-year-old, this was very intriguing.

I can distinctly remember the day I asked myself what would happen if I could get some of this magic from this wall that makes things LIGHT UP. Would *I* LIGHT UP? Which part of me would LIGHT UP? My nose? My eyes? My belly? I had no idea what would happen, but I was tempted to discover. My only dilemma at the time was, I had no wire connected. How and what would I do to generate some of whatever was in this wall so I could somehow LIGHT UP?

My fingers didn't fit in those little holes. It didn't work by just touching it. I clearly had something to figure out. I knew if I brought my idea to my big sister LaDedra, she would probably just say, "Oooohhh Mommy, Brian is messing with the outlet again!" I had gotten caught a few times plugging and unplugging different appliances and I was scolded and warned many times to 'stay away from the outlets.'

"If I see you playing with that outlet again, Imma beat yo ass," my mother would say. Yeah, I had one of those mothers. I had to figure out a way to get some of this magic from this wall on my own. Why didn't they want me next to these outlets anyway? Were they trying to get this magic out of the walls for themselves? Did they just not want me to LIGHT UP? In my 3-year-old mind, I gave myself all these variables of why they were keeping me away from this magic. I would get to this magic no matter what it took. Nothing was gonna stop me. I was destined to LIGHT UP, just like these other things I was plugging into the wall.

One day, while the evil LaDedra sat between my mother's legs getting her hair done, it came to me. As she scooped a glob of that black Dax grease (which I couldn't stand the smell of), I saw her spread a bobby pin to use to lay down one of the big doo-doo braids she was administering to my sister's hair. That was it; I had figured it out! I would steal one of these bobby pins, spread it like my mom was doing, and insert it into the wall. Tonight, I was most certainly going to LIGHT UP. Now that my plan was figured out, I had to plot on how to get one of those bobby pins. I knew I would get in trouble if I was caught fiddling around in the blue tin cookie can my mom used to hold all my sister's hair supplies, so I figured I'd just wait it out. Yep, just wait until LaDedra fell asleep and take the bobby pin straight from her doo-doo braid.

I don't quite remember what city or town we lived in at this time as we moved around quite often, but I remember this was still when LaDedra and I shared a bed. This would make my maneuver easy as ever. I had only to wait until she fell asleep. The issue was, 99% of the time, I fell asleep before she did, so I would have to tough this one out and stay awake tonight.

"Get y'all asses in there and go to bed!" I recall my mom yelling from the living room where she would drink beer and smoke joints with her sisters, whom are also my aunties. On this evening, I believe it was my Aunts Lorraine, Teen and Janet at our house. I didn't care who was there; this was is it. Tonight was the night, and it was almost closer to the time to make my move. Tonight, LaDedra and I would be alone in that room, and all I would have to do was outlast her and I would be able to steal the bobby pin, insert it into the wall, and finally LIGHT UP. If I remembered correctly from the one or maybe two times I had stayed up longer than she did, after The Honeymooners went off, and that M.A.S.H theme song started rolling on the TV, she was knocked out cold. Nothing was gonna make me fall asleep first on this night... absolutely nothing.

As she laughed at Ralph Kramdon belittling his poor friend Ed Norton, or verbally abusing his wife Alice, even threatening that one of these days he would 'Bang Zoom' and punch her to the moon, I laid there pretending to be enjoying the episode knowing I was just patiently waiting for her to fall asleep; and not before long—I heard it!

"*Din nin nin nin niiiiin.* —" there it was. This was my cue. This was the theme song to the show M.A.S.H., a stupid show about some guys in the Army or something. Remember, I had never ever seen LaDedra still awake while the notes of that theme song were playing. Sometimes, that stupid ass song would actually wake me, or just be playing on the TV as I got up to use the bathroom, and LaDedra would always be asleep. That night, just like on any other night when I was awake to hear that theme song, I looked over to find my sister knocked out with her mouth open as she slept.

LaDedra was always a hard sleeper, so I knew me playing in her hair looking for that pin wouldn't wake her. That was the least of my concerns. My real concern was not finding the pin in all that hair she had. Right at the end of the big doo-doo braid my mother had neatly done, was the U-shaped end on the bobby pin. Taking that pin out of my sister's hair was as easy as taking a pacifier from a sleeping baby.

There I was, bobby pin in hand, sitting next to the wall just anticipating which part of me would LIGHT UP when I inserted this pin into this outlet. I remember spreading the bobby pin exactly enough to where both ends would slide into the socket perfectly. I rechecked to make sure my sister was still asleep. Through the cracked door, I could hear my aunts and my mother in the living room chatting loudly while blasting 98.7 KISS FM on the radio. It was my time to shine, literally, or so I thought. *Okay, here goes nothing*, I said to myself while trying to curb my enthusiasm about finally seeing which part of my body would LIGHT UP once I did this. And, just like that... I stuck the pin inside the wall. *Zzzzzzzzzzzzzzzaaaaaapppppppp...* Out!

The last thing I remember seeing was a flash, almost like a flash from a camera. When I had regained consciousness, I was in a hospital on a stretcher with my mother and my eldest aunt, Doshia Lee, (who wasn't at the house with the other sisters) crying and looking very concerned. I looked over to notice my right hand had swole up to almost 3 times its normal size. I didn't remember any of my body parts lighting up. I also didn't feel like I gained any kinda magic power either. All I felt was extreme pain in my swollen right hand and complete disappointment.

Laying on that stretcher, my three-year-old self came to the conclusion that this might've not have been the best of ideas. That I actually *didn't* care to wanna LIGHT UP anymore. That maybe the wall did not have the magic; maybe it was the appliance itself. I just knew that I wasn't happy. And seeing my mama cry was always something I hated, even as a three-year-old. We stayed at the hospital the whole day, I'm guessing for observation or whatever. They finally put my little arm in a tiny sling and sent us on our way.

As I got in the back seat of the car, I remember my mother scolding me. "What I tell you about fucking around with those outlets?" she said. "When we get home, I'm gonna LIGHT that ass UP!" How ironic.

I don't know if it was that JOLT of electricity that went through my small young three-year-old body, or the teachers and older people who always told me how special I was. Maybe it was the looks of amazement on the faces of my grandmother's church friends as I would read out of the King James version of the Bible; or the proud look on my mother's face while a cigarette dangled from her lips as she showed her sisters how I could retrieve albums by reading the names of the artists in her collection. I can't pinpoint exactly what it was, but something led me to believe from a very early stage of my life I was destined to be great and do great things.

What I couldn't and certainly didn't anticipate was the suffering, the pain, and the agony I would endure along the way. My life has been a series of very extreme highs, as well as VERY extreme lows, which you will notice as you continue to read my story. I wrote this book just in case I leave this earth in an untimely fashion. I will tell my OWN story, in my OWN words. NOBODY else can, or will.

CHAPTER 2

7/13/77

As my life would go on, every time my mother, Ms. Josephine Sampson, would have to come pick me up after me being suspended, expelled or arrested, it was the same old song. "Boy, don't you know I almost died bringing your ass into this world!?" She would be yelling while almost always simultaneously crying. "Without those damn generators, I wouldn't have made it."

This was a story I had heard my whole entire childhood. She never tired of telling it, but I most certainly tired of hearing it. It got to where I would cut her off before she could even finish. "Boy, don't you know that I almost...." I would interject before she could complete her sentence. "...yeah, you almost died because I was born during a major blackout, I get it, I get it." She would either then curse me out or smack me on the back of my head for what she deemed "getting fresh" with her.

What my mother was referencing all of these times was the infamous 1977 New York City Blackout. Which was also the day I came into this world. On July 13th, 1977, New York City endured a 25-hour blackout after lightning struck the power lines. This blackout resulted in widespread riots, looting, and chaos around the entire city. I always wondered if my fascination with the outlets in the wall had any correlation with me being born during this blackout. A blackout started by lightning striking nuclear plants. Did I come here through one of those lightning bolts? Was this why I was so adamant about sticking that bobby pin in the wall to LIGHT UP at three years old? As absurd as it sounds, these were some of the things I would think about later on in life while being locked in solitary confinement 23 hours a day. I would look at the bruise I still have on my right hand from sticking that damn bobby pin in the wall and ask myself, *Am I actually like, "Electricity Man"? Can I zap my way outta this prison?* These are some of the insane thoughts your mind concocts while you're going through the inhumane experience of solitary confinement. But I will expound on that much later on.

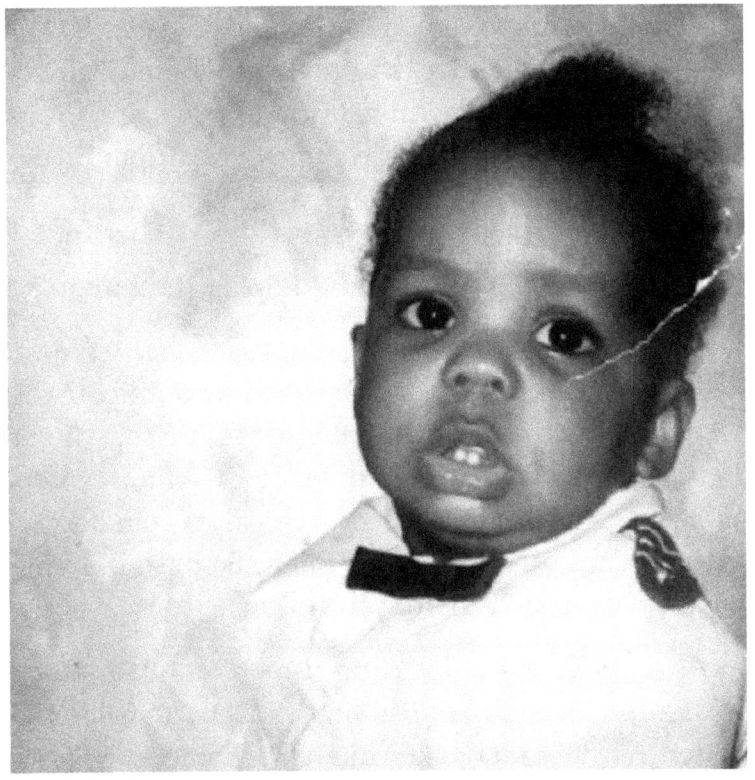

Me at 8 months old

Let's rewind for a second and get back to my birth. I didn't know exactly where I was born until I tried getting a driver's license at twenty-two years old. I had been told so many stories growing up that eventually, I stopped asking. I had been moved around to so many places and households as a child, I didn't know what exactly the truth was. I used to look back and wonder why people would want to keep the truth from me. Was it because they didn't want me to look at my mother in a weird way? Was it the fact that my father, a Haitian immigrant named Roland Carenard, was twenty-one years older than my mother, and had his own wife and family at home while I was being born? I had heard so many stories about the origin of my existence I didn't know what was fact, and what was fiction. Not until I was of legal age, and had been through hell and hot water, did I ever even care to go find out the facts for myself.

Through talking to people around my family in the seventies, I learned that my mother and a few of her siblings had been placed in Juvenile Detention centers as teenagers. This resulted from my grandfather, Harvey Sampson, husband of Mama Sampson, having developed a serious heroin addiction.

As an outcome of his drug use, my mother, along with a few of her many siblings, mostly female, had gotten in trouble and taken out of the home and placed in Juvie. Juvie is short for Juvenile Detention. If I'm correct, my mother, along with my Aunts Geraldine, Lorraine, Celestine (or Teen), Melanie and Uncle Bobby, were all placed in different Juvenile Detentions centers around the State of New York. I was told that during my mother serving her time, she had gotten pregnant with my older sister LaDedra. LaDedra is two years older than me and we share the same father; the Haitian immigrant named Roland. I was once even told that one of my aunts had dated him prior to my mother dating him, and the only reason either of them even liked him was because there were rumors that the

Haitian immigrants had "money" and would spend it on the younger American women. One reason I resented my father early on was simply because he was Haitian, which made me Haitian. I would get teased by my own full black American cousins, classmates and just anyone who knew. They would say we had H.B.O., and not the network. But an acronym for Haitian Body Odor. As a child, I hated I had to put up with this, it made me very angry, and I blamed him for it.

I can remember being told how my mother ended up in a battered women's shelter in Jamaica, Queens, after being released from the Juvenile Detention center. I was supposedly born in there while my mother was admitted there. I would later ask my mother about this and she would say, "That wasn't me pregnant in there. That was Geraldine," and the baby who was born in the shelter wasn't me, but my cousin Buttercup. He was the cousin who I earlier explained was Mama Sampson's ultimate favorite grandchild.

Then I was told I was born in East Flatbush at a house I would later live in with one of my "aunts" on the Haitian immigrant's side of the family. When I would ask my grandmother where I was born, she would say, "Right there up the road," no matter where we happened to be at the time. I figured she just said this because who would wanna tell their grandchild they were born in a battered women's shelter? Or maybe somewhere even worse. This all left me to where I just stopped asking or caring altogether.

In all honesty, I would say from about the age of five until adulthood. I felt unloved by everyone besides my grandmother. I didn't actually feel that my mother didn't love me, I just think she didn't know HOW to show me she loved me. Anybody who knows me will attest that I practically raised myself from the age of about eight or nine until, well, until the age I am today. I once wrote a heartfelt song dedicated to my mother titled, *My Mommy*. This was a song I wrote while I was incarcerated. I had planned to record and play it for my mom once I got released. Some lyrics of the songs are:

> *I wonder how it would be if you had the chance to raise me/Would I still NOT know how to romance a lady/Is it cause you made me a Cancer baby/That I stay on some crab shit so nobody get the chance to betray me.*

In the year 2005, I got the chance to play this song for my mother one day and we both cried. We cried for about five minutes straight, like babies. For the first time in my life, my mother apologized to me. She apologized for not knowing HOW to raise me, for loving me, but not knowing HOW to show me the love. She told me she would use Anita Baker songs to try to describe the way she felt about me. She told me she was never good at expressing herself through talking, so she used songs. I reflected as she was telling me this. I remember her always singing the words to Anita

Baker's song 'No One in the World' to me, but I never noticed she had changed the lyrics to fit and make it a Mother to Son anthem,

> No one in the world's gonna hold you/No one in the world's gonna need you/No one in the world's gonna love you like I do baby.

I didn't realize until many years later those weren't the actual lyrics to the song. She had altered Anita's lyrics to tell ME how much she loved me because she didn't know how to find the words to tell me any other way. This same day in 2005, after I played my song for my mother; after we cried; we had the most heart to heart conversation we have ever had. She expressed things I had never known and I did the same to her. Like I stated earlier, I raised myself from the age of eight or nine, and by eleven, the streets had gotten a hold on me like you wouldn't believe. My official criminal history dates to 1991, to when I was a mere thirteen years old. And there had been many run-ins with the law even prior to that.

During this same lengthy conversation with my mother, she told me something I had never known about her. She said, "Brian, I never wanted children." I responded with, "So why did you have a whopping *FIVE* of us?" and we both busted out in laughter. One thing I can tell you about my mother, Ms. Josephine Sampson, is she had the sense of humor of every funny comedian you can name, put together, times ten. She had this gift of turning even the harshest of situations into a funny joke. I can remember not having any food in the house, and asking what was for lunch, and she would say, "Wish sandwiches. Just slap two pieces of bread together and WISH you had something in between 'em." Or when my sister LaDedra and I would say, "Ma, we're hungry!" knowing her food stamps hadn't come yet, to which she'd reply, "Well if y'all would take your hungry asses to bed, you can have some nice good ol' sleep for dinner!" People who know me will tell you, I have a keen sense of humor and I absolutely get it from my mother. Yes indeed.

As our heart to heart conversation went on, I also expressed some things to her I had never expressed before. Again, my mother had nine sisters, all of which who had children, so there were a lot of first cousins around. I'd probably say out of twenty-plus or more of my first cousins, maybe 1% of us graduated high school. So, it's not like her sisters were experts at raising children, but for some reason, I felt my mother had always gotten the brunt of the blame for my stupid actions. I really hated this more than anything.

My mother would always try and tell me the right things to do. I just refused to listen. What more could she have possibly done when she had a son willing to suffer the consequences of his actions? It's not like her sisters, who were blaming her for MY actions, were raising scholars. I felt like my aunts were picking on my mother and that made me resent them. I eventually got over it, but for a while, I harbored animosity towards many for blaming my mother for MY fuck ups.

A lot of this fueled my desire to succeed in life. I wanted to eventually redeem myself, not just for me, but so my mother would have her own redemption against her siblings. I wanted her to be able to brag about her son for once. I wanted instead of her always having to say, "Yeah, Brian is locked up again" to be able to say, "Turn on the radio, Brian's new song is on again!" or "Turn on the television, my son is on again!" So, I decided during one of my stints of incarceration, that I would bust my ass, and work my ass off to make this a possibility, even if it was just a pipedream to most of the people around me. I believed in me. And when I believed in me, she believed in me as well...

During one of my many stints in a Juvenile Detention center, my mother had moved to the City of Newburgh in New York. By this time, my little sister Tyeshia, and my youngest twin siblings, Stephen and Stephanie had been born. This now made five of us. I remember receiving a letter while I was placed in St. Cabrini school, which was a residential school for juvenile delinquents. The letter read:

"Son, I found place in Newburgh that has rent that I could afford, so the kids and I will be moving there soon."

As I read this, my heart dropped. Two things automatically stuck out in my head. One, as long as my mother was living in Newburgh, I would never live with her again. And two, my little brothers and sisters wouldn't stand a chance at a fair shot at life if they were being raised in Newburgh. By this time, I had grown up in multiple places — some better than others. I had the experience of living in the Seth Low Houses in Brownsville, Brooklyn with extended family and Nyack, New York with my grandmother Mama Sampson. One was one of the most dangerous places in NYC, while one was a multi-faceted NYC suburb twenty minutes outside of The Bronx, where millionaires lived only blocks away from us. I lived in Spring Valley, N.Y. during the 80s, where crackheads would try and climb through your window while your family was still awake watching television. I even lived in East Flatbush where I was the only person in the whole household who spoke any English.

Until that point, I had seen it all as far as neighborhoods and living conditions go. The ONE place of all in which I lived where I told myself I would, or could *never* live again no matter what, was Newburgh N.Y. The City of Newburgh has the highest crime rate per capita in the entire state of New York. There is a new rapper named Pardison Fontaine, who is mostly famous for writing *Bodak Yellow, Be Careful,* and other hit songs for N.Y. superstar Cardi B, who was born and raised in Newburgh. When this guy says he is from the absolute bottom, he isn't bullshitting. AT. ALL.

I remember during my childhood of bouncing from home to home, my sister LaDedra and I went to live with my Aunt Geraldine in Newburgh. At this time, I say I was around seven, so my sister was nine. We were too young to understand the level of poverty we were living in at this stage. I mean, we were always living poor unless we were with our father's side of the family, so we didn't quite understand the concept of NOT being poor. But Newburgh, this was a different level of poor.

We befriended two young boys named David and Charles. Everyone who knew them called them "The Rat Kids." At the time I thought it was a really cool name. I related being a Rat Kid to being like, a Bat Man. One day I asked my cousin Mister, who is also my Aunt Geraldine's son and had been living in Newburgh for most of his life, why they called David and Charles the Rat Kids and he explained it. He said that where they lived was so infested with rats that these kids had developed relationships with the rats and damn near treated them like pets. Hence the name, The Rat Kids...

Now in Flatbush, we had mice. In Spring Valley, we lived in a shithole with even bigger mice. But as poor and run down as those other places were, compared to

Newburgh, they were fucking paradise. Newburgh was just different.

One summer, after sending us there, my mother decided she wanted my sister and I back living at home with her. She had gotten back on her feet and wanted us to come from Newburgh, where we were sent to stay with our aunt and wild crazy cousins. I loved it. My sister hated it. But it was family, so we made the most of it, nonetheless.

I remember returning and playfully walking into my mother's house with my sister, and she looked at us and immediately picked up the phone to call my aunt. "What the hell are these marks all over my babies' bodies!?" she screamed into the phone. I couldn't hear what my Aunt Geraldine said on the other end, but I knew it was nothing nice. Out of all of my mother's sisters, Geraldine was the O.G. of them all. She wasn't the oldest, but she was by FAR the toughest. My mother screamed into the phone a few more times and slammed the phone down. I remember thinking to myself. *I highly doubt mama love would have this same energy if Aunt Geraldine were right here.*

My mother wasn't a punk at all, but my Aunt Geraldine was just a different level of toughness. She used to literally beat up all of her boyfriends. To the point we would feel sorry for these dudes. Not surprisingly, her two sons, Buttercup, (yeah... Mama Sampson's ultimate favorite grandchild) and Mister, are two of the toughest dudes I've ever been around in my entire life. And I've been around some tough dudes. We'll also get more into that much later.

As soon as my mother slams the phone down, she immediately calls us over to inspect these marks on my sister and me from head to toe. At first, she assumed we had chicken pox but quickly ruled it out because we had already had chicken pox before and had been vaccinated. She then questioned us, and I remember telling my mother that all the kids who lived in the house had these marks. We actually believed these marks were normal because all the kids walked around scratching and itching the marks all over their bodies just like we were. After hanging up with my aunt, my mother quickly dialed to schedule an emergency doctor appointment for my sister LaDedra and me.

The doctor broke the news to my mother. "Ma'am, I'm afraid to tell you that these are not chickenpox, measles or anything like that. These are actually flea bites." Her response? She looked at him in pure disbelief.

"Flea bites?" she asked.

"Yes, they either came from fleas or some other similar insect of the sort."

"You gotta be fucking kidding me!" she said. He prescribed us some kinda special lotion and sent us on our way. "Good luck with that," he said to my mother as he looked at her in disgust. Thinking back, I remember the dog that would sleep on the couch during the day while we were out playing. That same couch was our bed at night while he was out catching fleas, I guess. We all had those damn marks on our bodies. We were young kids at the time, and back then, it was just about having fun. The dog was actually my cousin Mister's dog. He loved that damn dog, and my aunt loved her son, that's why she had let him keep that mutt that had brought all these fleas around.

As I stated earlier, my Aunt Geraldine was a tough one. She had four children. Two girls and two boys. Now the girls, my cousins Doretha and Beatrice, aka LuLu and Beatt, they were tough too, but pretty normal. The boys, Edward and Jean, aka Buttercup and Mister, these guys were just built differently from birth. Mister and I were only a year apart, so a lot of the shit he was getting into, when I was around him, I was right there with him. He was older, so he was the leader when we were together, and he was very good at leading us straight into trouble. If we weren't breaking into bread factories, stealing old thrown-out donuts, fighting (each other most of the time), we were trying to sell crack, smoking weed or doing some other shit ten and eleven-year-olds had NO business doing.

Now Buttercup, he was different. Cup was a light-skinned pretty boy who just acted like a dark-skinned, ugly gorilla ass dude. He was such an anomaly. You hear the name "Buttercup," and you think a sweet, delicate guy. He was the complete opposite of this. Guns, fists, knives, bats… you name it, he was all about it. He wouldn't back down from anything or anyone. The six hundred or so stitches and staple marks that decorated his head and face were a testament to this. Buttercup was eight or nine years older than us, but this didn't stop him from treating us like we were in his age group.

One day, while Mister and I were playing in front of his house on West Parmentar Street, my cousin Buttercup comes running up the street and says, "Mister and Brian, come on! Y'all coming with me right now." Now Mister never questioned his big brother, and I never questioned my big cousin Mister. I looked up to these guys so whatever it was time to do, I was all in. I knew by the look on Buttercup's face that wherever he was taking us, it was to do something kids our age shouldn't be doing.

As we followed him down the street and around the corner, I noticed a group of older guys and younger kids gathered around. Buttercup comes around the corner, screaming, "Yeah, I got my little brother and my little cousin and they'll fuck any of these little niggas up!" I look over at Mister and he's looking like this is something he does regularly. Mister rolled up his sleeves and was getting ready for physical combat, so I followed his lead and did the same thing. As the other kids also looked like they were preparing for combat, I noticed Buttercup and the other guys pulling out wads of cash. At first, I thought he had known these guys, but it quickly dawned on me that Mister and I were about to fight some complete strangers in exchange for money. They were making us fight and betting on us like one would bet on Pit bulls or cockfights. As wrong as it felt, I loved every second. Mister and I both won our fights, and for winning, Buttercup gave us each a dollar and we excitedly ran to Pete's store to get penny candy and quarter waters.

From that day on, I would sit around and wait for Buttercup to come get us to fight some other unfamiliar kids; not necessarily because I wanted to fight, that was more my cousin Mister's thing, but I enjoyed making that dollar. I realized early on how much I enjoyed making my own money; therefore, I was with it... Every. Single. Time.

As I laid back in my bed reading this letter my mother wrote me about moving up to Newburgh, all these things were playing out in my mind. The flea bites, the robbing of the bread factories, the kid prizefighting, the Rat Kids, all of the negative things I knew about that place. I got scared and concerned for my younger siblings. LaDedra had lived there before, so she would know how to handle it. But Tyeshia, Stephen and Stephanie, my younger siblings, were babies. I wanted to write my mother back so badly and say, "Whatever you do, DON'T move to Newburgh." But as I re-read her reasoning for moving there in the first place, it made me realize she had no choice...

As the letter stated, she had found a place she could actually afford. *This can't be life*, I thought to myself as I stood for a standing head count...

CHAPTER 3

They Loving The Crew

By the time I was 5 years old, I had already experienced some good times, as well as some hardships in my life. Aside from living in and OUT welfare Motels, moving from aunt to aunt, Haitian family members, or with whoever would take me in, I was still one of Mama Sampson's favorites, and that made me happy. Before kindergarten, I had already been born in a blackout, electrocuted to where I had to be hospitalized, while being deemed a baby genius because of my reading comprehension at such an early age. It was also around that tender age of five that another aspect of my personality developed. My mother once told me it was around this time she noticed that I had a very quick temper. While at first, she thought it was kind of cute, my quick temper quickly became a major cause for concern.

My mother Josephine, my sister LaDedra and me circa 1981

I remember the first time my evil big sister LaDedra did this evil, evil thing to me. I mean, it literally terrified me at this stage of my life. Whenever she would do it, I would run to my mother crying uncontrollably, "Tell her to stop!"

"LaDedra, leave your brother alone!" she would say nonchalantly to my sister. Did my mother not realize how scared I was? This wasn't just like any of the many other times my evil sister would harass me. When she did THIS in particular, it terrified me, and boy did she know it. She always could beat me up, so that became kind of normal to her. I'd try to fight back, get my ass kicked and it was the same old thing. But when she discovered THIS... Oh, man. She had found a way to scare me to the point I would go running to our mother and LaDedra absolutely loved this. Probably even more than beating me up. "To Your Brain!" she would say as she pointed it to my head.

Depending on what mood my mother was in, I would either get her support when my sister started her evil doings, or I would get yelled and cursed at for being a damn "tattletale." And boy oh boy, LaDedra loved those moments as well.

"Get yo ass in there and hit her back and stop being a damn tattletale!" my mother would scream at me as I would attempt to state my case. That no tattle-telling mantra would be something I would go on to live by for the rest of my life. Even 'til this very day. When someone does something to you, stab you, shoot you, punch you or even *kill* you: YOU DON'T TELL. You either retaliate, or you let it be.

Much later in life, again, while sitting in solitary confinement, I wondered if black mothers around the world realized they invented the "No Snitching" street code within their own households. There would be times my sister would do something bad, and I'd be the one who got punished for telling on her. Oddly enough, I can't recall one time where she got in trouble for telling on me when I was misbehaving. Was it because I was a boy? Did my mother understand the code of the street was different for a male than it was for a female? I mean, she had been in juvenile detention centers herself. Was she hipped to the code? So many unanswered questions.

"To Your Brain!" LaDedra yelled as she once again did the ONE thing she knew not only terrified me, but as I stated earlier, always sent me running to our mother for safety. She had it down to a science. She knew that at least seven out of ten times I ran to my mother with a grievance, I still was the one that got yelled at. So, whether it was me being horrified by her actions, or me getting yelled at for telling about her actions, she was satisfied with the 70% odds of her being the victor overall.

I don't know where LaDedra learned this evil thing, but it seemingly came out of nowhere. She would take a rubber band, place one end on the tip of her pointer finger, pull it back to where its elasticity was at its limit, and then hold the other end down with her thumb and point it at my head as she yelled "To Your Brain!" I can still remember the feeling I got as I thought about the pain I would be in if she ever released her thumb and let that rubber fly against my head. I mean, in hindsight, it probably wouldn't have hurt nearly as much as I imagined in my head, but as a five-year-old child, I just thought it would probably be a pain I couldn't endure.

I later wondered if it was just for terrorizing purposes she did this, because she actually never shot me with the rubber band. Not even once. Maybe it was just another one of her 'instill fear in me tactics,' but this tactic in particular would go on to backfire on her.

"To Your Brain!" I heard her say as I sat in my mother's tiny living room watching my favorite cartoon. I quickly jumped up ready to run to find my mother, but this day was different. Something inside me told me if I didn't do something about this, this would continue way longer than I would like it to. I could deal with getting beat up by her every now and then, but this rubber band gun shit had to STOP. I can't recall if it was because my mother was in a bad mood and I knew I would get cursed out if I told, or if I had just come to my breaking point, but this day things went down differently. Instead of running toward my mother's room, I turned around and bolted toward LaDedra. In that split second, I can remember pushing her with such force, it thrust her into a 180 turn and she fell and hit her face on the corner edge of the coffee table. Not even having time to feel vindicated or victorious, LaDedra let out the loudest blood-curdling scream, and with the amount of blood I seen, I knew my ass was in BIG TROUBLE.

My mother appeared in the living room, seemingly out of nowhere. "Brian, what the fuck did you do!?" she yelled. Before I could explain myself, *POW!* My mother had smacked me across the face. It was common for my mother to curse at me or threaten to hit me, but it was very, very, *very* rare for her to actually do it. I knew, at this point, I had messed up. She sent me to go sit down as she catered to my screaming, bleeding and crying sister; and then picked up the phone to call my Aunt Lorraine (her closest sister) to come bring LaDedra to the hospital. My other Aunt Janet would babysit me as they were away accommodating my sister's medical needs.

"You gonna get your ass beat when they get back," my Aunt Janet repeated over and over. But something inside of me felt good. Not that I hurt my sister, but the fact I defended myself against something that had me absolutely petrified.

As my mother, sister and aunt walked into the house after returning from the ER, I noticed my sister with a big bandage between her chin and bottom lip. "You gave her stitches, you little nappy head son of a bitch." my mother stated. "I should whoop your ass!" So, I wasn't getting a beating after all? I wanted to look at my Aunt Janet and stick my tongue out but decided against it. Maybe my mother decided the slap was enough. My mother was very heavyset at the time, so her slaps had serious impact. Maybe LaDedra had confessed about doing that "To Your Brain" thing she knew scared me so much. Whatever it was, I seemed to be in the clear. At least with my mother I was, but with the evil LaDedra, that was a different story.

That night, as we ate our dinner of Oodles of Noodles with chopped up hot dogs in it, I noticed LaDedra was a lot less vocal. She even seemed a little timid with the eye contact. Was she still in pain? Had I earned some of her respect for not only not backing down, but also sending her to the hospital? Whatever happened that day, it was a shift in the dynamic of our relationship. I started to be the one who would talk louder to her. I started to be the one who would change the TV channel when I wanted to. I had fought her back before, but never did I win. Not only did I win this time, I did damage. I had finally won the upper hand in our sibling rivalry. I guess she understood I was becoming a man because from that point on, she seemed to fall in line. She might've won a few more fights after that, but she was less eager to start them. And I most certainly never heard those words "To Your Brain" again until I was an adult. And at that time, the gun wasn't rubber; it was made of steel.

Until this very day, my sister still shows me the small scar under her lip and reminds me of that day. Gladly we can laugh and joke about it now. But from then until today, my sister has become accustomed to the level of violent behavior her baby brother would exude over the years. I would scare my sister in many, many more ways than one after that incident. That was the start of something that would be a constant with me.

When I was around eight, we had gotten evicted from somewhere again and went to live with my Aunt Lorraine in Spring Valley, N.Y. During dinner time, the adults would usually eat in the living room while they watched TV, but the children didn't have this same privilege. My Aunt Lorraine was a little stricter than my mother, and when you lived under HER roof, it was HER rules whether you liked it or not. Kids were to eat dinner at the dinner table and that was that. As all of us kids sat eating dinner, my little cousin Benita had done something that really angered me. Now Benita was two years younger than me. And when I say this kid had a way of getting on my nerves... Man! I couldn't stand this kid. Now between me, my sister LaDedra, and my Aunt Lorraine's children, there were five of us kids living there altogether. Us being my mother's two kids, and my aunt's three children. From oldest to youngest, there was my cousins Angela, Jamie, and of course, the baby of her three, little annoying ass Benita.

When I say spoiled, Benita was one of the most spoiled kids I've ever encountered, probably until today. No matter what the situation, Benita had only to cry or pretend to be crying and my aunt would come running to give her whatever she wanted. Attention or otherwise. Her son Jamie was like a freaking man child. He was four years older than me so when we moved in with them, I was around seven or eight, so he was about eleven. He had a full goatee at this age.

Like, literally, a beard at eleven or twelve. Chest hair and all. I idolized this guy for many, many years of my life.

Jamie was the ultimate dog lover, and at one point, even tried to convert me into loving dogs like he did. I mean, this guy used to have four or five dogs tied up to trees in the woods at any given time. If you hung around with us, he would assign a dog to you, whether you wanted the dog or not. I had a dog named Sam that was literally a stray that Jamie made me claim. I had never even as much as pet the dog in my entire life, but he was "MY" dog, according to Jamie. He became the big brother I never had. I was literally his shadow during these times. My first experience with humping girls, was with Jamie. My first experience having a fist fight, was with Jamie. First time getting chased by a dog (one of his dogs), shoplifting, vandalizing, strong armed robberies, all were with my cousin Jamie. If my big cousin Buttercup was like God in my eyes, Jamie was Jesus. Period!

Then there was Angela. Angela was pretty much like everybody's mother when our real mothers were out drinking, smoking weed, partying or just not paying attention to us in general. My mother was never much of a party person. That was until she got around my Aunt Lorraine. I mean, she would smoke a little weed here and there, but when she got around her big sister Lorraine, she pretty much fell in line with whatever Lorraine wanted to do. This would leave

Angela in charge of us younger kids a lot of the time. That would also be the time when Jamie and I would run amuck.

Angela was super strict like her mother. I can recall one time my sister LaDedra and her got into an argument and Angela pushed my sister into a wall. Literally into the wall. Left a hole the size of her entire body. I remember being so mad because LaDedra was too small to defend herself. Also, it seemed like ever since the incident a few years earlier where I gave her those stitches, she kind of lost a lot of her toughness. I kind of subliminally blamed myself, and for this reason, I didn't like Angela for a very long time.

This evening at the dinner table, my quick temper and violent behavior were again put on display. As I stated before, my little spoiled cousin Benita had done something that angered me. I had just finished my fried pork chop and was waiting for Jamie to finish so we could go outside and throw rocks at cars or some other mischievous activity he would have us doing. I can't quite remember what she did, but I remember getting mad to the point a tear dropped from my eye, and I bit my bottom lip. The tears and the biting of the bottom lip would become the telltale signs I was about to do something extremely crazy. My mother would pinpoint this many years later. "When you bite your lip and do that little silent cry you do, I know you're about to do some crazy shit," she would say to me.

Whatever Benita had done that evening had compelled me to grab my pork chop bone as if it were a shank, and slash her across the arm with it as if I were in a prison knife fight... "Oh, my God!" Angela yelled. "Ma!" As I watched the blood begin to gush out of my cousin's arm, I automatically knew I fucked up. My mother and aunt came storming into the dining area as my little cousin Benita screamed out in pain. "Brian cut her with the bone!" Angela yelled. As my nervous little eyes looked around the room, I noticed LaDedra with the 'here we go again' look. My cousin Jamie had a not too concerned look, and Angela was looking as if she was about to be the one who was gonna give me the ass whooping. I focused on Angela's face. *Payback for pushing LaDedra into the wall*, I thought to myself.

I knew I was getting not just one, but *two* ass whooping's that day. One from my mother, and one from my Aunt Lorraine. Just two, I don't know what Angela was thinking. While the adults were home, Angela had no seniority. None. And although Jamie would beat me up occasionally, he didn't seem to care too much about me slashing his baby sister with the bone. I think he had gotten what I had gotten years later when my little sister was born. That little jealous trait you get when you're not the baby of the house anymore.

Surprisingly enough, I only got one ass whooping that night and it wasn't from my Aunt Lorraine. It was from my mother, and that was all to my benefit. Even though what I did was extremely bad, my mother used to take it easy on me when she whooped my ass. I could count the times on one hand when she went hard on me for doing something bad. The only real, real bad ass whooping I got from my mother was for stealing a spiked belt from one of my friends' homes. My mother would always say, "I ain't raising no damn thieves!" And judging by the leniency I got in the ass whooping for slashing my little cousin's arm open, compared to the one I got for stealing from someone's home, she was dead serious about that sentiment.

Living with my aunt in Spring Valley was some of the most fun times of my childhood, although it was a very dangerous place to live in the 1980s. I can remember walking outside the building and seeing thousands of assorted colored crack vials all over the floor. Shooting and killings became a very constant thing during this era because of this new drug called Crack that would not only infiltrate the neighborhood, but even make its way into our family. In this small town, about 15 miles north of The Bronx, everything that happened there seemed magnified by one hundred because it was such a small place. I had lived in the city for a short time prior to this, so I had the experience of living in a place where you hear about people getting shot and killed a lot and it's kind of not as big of a deal. But in a small town where everyone sort of knows everyone, the impact is a lot stronger.

When your friends are shooting and killing each other it.... it hits a lot different.

    I loved this place, though. Or maybe I just loved my big cousin Jamie because he taught me how to navigate through this place. I knew we wouldn't be living with my aunt forever, but while we were, I was determined to make the most of having a big brother around. It would take me a hundred years to sit here and write about all the episodes I went through while being under Jamie's tutelage. But I would also be doing myself a disservice if I didn't try. So here we go.

CHAPTER 4

Kingsborn Ma Justice

I didn't actually learn how to drive a car until I was about twenty-two or twenty-three years old. But somehow, I stole my first car at only twelve. I can remember like it was yesterday. Jamie walked into the living room where my family slept and says, "We ain't gonna be walking today B, we gonna get us some wheels!" The "we" he was referring to was him, myself, Chris Lowery, Caesar Dow and our cousin Tyrone. This was our little five-man crew. We had went by many names over the years, but at this time, we called ourselves The Prosecutors.

My Cousin Jamie circa 1989

Chris Lowery was a local kid who lived around the corner. This guy really believed in his mind he was Treach from Naughty By Nature. He wore the jail suits, he let his hair grow long braids, and sometimes would even walk around with a machete. The kid had a hell of an imagination. Whenever Chris would come over to our house, my mother and Aunt Lorraine would always say, "Something is really wrong with that little boy…" the second he would leave.

Caesar Dow was our friend who lived in a huge, beautiful house somehow placed directly on the same street we lived on. I say somehow because the street we lived on was the infamous Bethune Blvd. Now Bethune Blvd was a street known for nothing but drugs, prostitution, shootings and everything that involved negativity. It was also the street that led you directly to The Hill. The Hill was pretty much known for housing and producing mostly undesirables. It was one place where if the police saw a white person there, they automatically would pull them over because they knew they were most likely there to buy drugs or solicit prostitutes.

Imagine a bunch of torn down tenements, crack houses and dirty apartment complexes, with one big old nice, beautiful house smack dead in the middle of them. That was Caesar's house. Caesar was the first guy I had ever known who wasn't an actual rapper on the radio, that could actually *really* rap. My older cousin Buttercup would make up funny little raps about the neighborhood crackheads and things, but those were more like joke raps. Caesar was the real deal on the microphone, or so I thought, but that's another story. I always wondered that if his parents could afford that big, beautiful home, along with the fancy cars and exotic pets, why they lived amongst the filth. We were a part of that filth; we knew it, and we embraced it.

As Caesar and I became closer, I would question his desire to always be outside with us poor kids when he had that big, beautiful house to go home to. He had a mom *and* a dad in his household, which was a different dynamic and pretty rare to see amongst us. He had everything a child could want; the newest video game systems, the newest Air Jordan's that came out. You name it, he had it. Yet for whatever reason, he always chose to be out causing mischief with us. I would've traded places with him any day, and I always reminded him of that.

Then there was Tyrone. Now Tyrone I had known mostly all of my life because like Jamie and I, we were also first cousins. His mother was Mama Sampson's eldest daughter, my sweet Aunt Doshia Lee. As I stated before, my grandmother had nine daughters and two sons, so there were lots and lots of us as far as cousins go. Tyrone was unique, though. He was, lacking a better word, very "flamboyant" as we were growing up. Tyrone only seemed to care about how he dressed and making sure his hair was always laid greased perfectly to the side.

When we would have gatherings at Mama Sampson's house and all the cousins would get together, Tyrone always had to be the loudest person in the room. I remember when Mama Sampson would tire of his nonsense and yell to him, "Sit your sissified behind down somewhere!" This was when I knew nothing about sexuality or anything like that. To me, a sissy was just a weak man, or a male who acted more like a female than most boys. This word "sissy" would take on a whole different meaning a little later on in life. As things would unfold, I realized exactly what my grandmother was really saying.

My Aunt Doshia Lee also had three other children, but Tyrone was her youngest. It always seemed that she favored him over the others. I didn't know if it was because he was the youngest, or because of his condition. Tyrone had a severe case of epilepsy. He could go from just talking to you, directly into a seizure within the blink of an eye. When this would happen, it would literally scare the shit out of me. He'd be on the floor shaking, and then be right back up laughing and joking right afterward as if nothing had happened. Though Tyrone was at least five or six years my senior, we hung out together at times even though we didn't get along at all. It was always Jamie who would recruit Tyrone and allow him to join our little posse. Jamie and Tyrone got along pretty well although they were completely opposite; I figured it was because they were close in age, sort of like my cousin Mister and I. In case you forgot, Mister was Buttercup's little brother from Newburgh who had introduced me to the "Rat Kids."

Jamie's logic for always recruiting Tyrone into our small little posse was simple: he was the best fighter out of all of us, and this he was right about. When we would fight other guys across town, or further up on

"The Hill," as flamboyant or "sweet" as Tyrone was, he could take on two or three guys at a time. He loved the thrill of hand to hand combat. It's almost like he lived for it. I would argue with Jamie about allowing Tyrone to come along when it was time to do anything besides fight. I believe he picked up on this because he would complain to Jamie about me. Mind you, these guys are my older cousins. Like, *years and years* older than me. I shouldn't have been able to hang around them in the first place, but because my mother was forced to go live with Jamie's mother, he was forced to treat me like a little brother, and I loved every second of it.

As I stated, I was around ten or eleven years old when I started smoking cigarettes, drinking 40 oz of beer and doing things even Jamie hadn't even began doing yet. I can still hear him now telling me how I needed to slow down. One occasion, he had gotten into a fight with some other neighbor kids his age who had allowed me to drink so much alcohol, I was found passed out on the side of the road laying in my own vomit. The last thing I remember from that incident was an older white lady standing over me in tears crying out, "Whose child is this?" Jamie hated when I would sneak away and do shit. The thing was, his mother was very strict, and on the contrary, my mother was borderline negligent. And though we were living under my aunt's roof, I was my mother's child. If she didn't mind me doing something, I was doing it.

Period! It's also not that she didn't mind the shit I was doing, I guess she just wasn't fully aware so to speak.

On this hot day summer day, my cousin Jamie, Chris Lowery and I had gathered in front of our building to talk about these wheels we were supposed to be getting. I had no idea where these wheels were coming from and I didn't care. I was so excited about the idea of not walking as we usually did that I was ecstatic. At this time, I'm ten or eleven years old, hanging out with these fifteen and sixteen-year-old guys who I assumed knew how to drive a car. But this was what our gathering was all about.

"I can drive, but I don't have a permit yet," Jamie said.

"Why don't we call Tyrone and..."

"Hell no," I said. "I don't feel like being around that faggot today." As harsh as the word sounds now, this was a time where the word faggot wasn't as offensive as it is today. My grandmother used it. My mother used it. My aunts and uncles used it, almost as if it were absolutely normal. In our family, that word was thrown around as freely as the word nigga was. Like I stated before, at this stage of my life, I knew nothing about sex, so the word had nothing to do with sexuality. To me, it just meant a boy who acted feminine or didn't play sports. It had absolutely nothing to do with anything sexual.

"I don't know how to drive," Chris stated, looking dazed as he always did. Caesar was probably at football practice at the time because he hadn't yet linked up with us. I wasn't really up for hanging with Tyrone on this day so we had a bit of a dilemma.

"Whose car are we rolling in anyway?" I asked. Jamie looked at me with this devilish grin.

"You wanna tell him?" he asked Chris.

Chris, still looking spaced out, replied, "You remember Terrell? Well, he just stole the spare car keys from his uncle's house, and tonight we're going to go take his car."

I remembered Terrell because he was a guy who we tried to recruit a few weeks earlier. The recruitment didn't last because we had to beat him up. He had taken some crack from Jamie to sell a few weeks prior and never returned with the money. We not only beat him up, we reenacted the opening scene from the movie New Jack City and threw him off a bridge onto a stream with very shallow water and rocks. How he broke no bones is beyond me. I guess this was his way of getting back in Jamie's good graces. Chris pulled out a set of car keys. "I just know tonight we gonna be rolling!" he stated as Jamie nodded in agreement.

"So, all you gotta do Brian, is put the car in R, that means 'Reverse,' and the car will back up," Jamie said to me as I listened closely. "Once you're out of the driveway, put the car in D, that means 'Drive.' Once you drive up the street to where we are, I'll take the wheel from there." It never dawned on me to ask him why I should be taking the car, when I had no driving experience. I was so excited thinking about driving a car, I never even bothered to ask him. "You got it?" he asked.

"I got it," I replied. All sorts of thoughts went through my mind as I walked up the dimly lit driveway. What if someone was watching? What if I fucked around and made a mistake? I just kept repeating to myself, "R is Reverse and D is Drive. R is Reverse and D is Drive..."

I quickly jumped into the Subaru and cranked the engine. I didn't want the sound of the car to wake anyone so I moved swiftly. I put the car in reverse and stamped on the gas. Mind you, I had never even attempted to drive a car until this point, so I had no knowledge of the use of rearview mirrors or any of that stuff. The car abruptly sped out of the driveway backward and into the street. The impact of the car hitting a wired fence behind me is actually what stopped the motion. I quickly put my foot on the brake, put the car in D, turned the wheel and mashed on the gas headed towards the two figures I could see down the street waiting for me. *Oh shit*, I thought to myself. I was driving. Even if it was for only a couple seconds until I got the car to Jamie. I was driving. I was literally driving!

As the images got closer and closer, I realized the car was still speeding. I then noticed Jamie waving his hands in the air signaling for me to stop or slow down. The thing was, I didn't actually know how to. I quickly approached Jamie standing in the middle of the street. I had to be doing what I assume was about 50 or 60 MPH. I'd seen his body instantly jump, and tuck and roll to the right to avoid getting hit. I was still driving a little in control, but just like that, I panicked as I lost control of the vehicle. *Oh, my God!* I thought I was about to die on my first time trying to drive a car, which was stolen.

I immediately took my foot off the gas and let the car roll into a small shallow ditch. *At least I'm not gonna hit a wall where I will immediately die from the impact,* I thought. Luckily for me, when the car jumped the curb, it slowed the speed of it tremendously as it sank halfway into the ditch. "Yo, what the fuck man! You could've killed me B," I heard Jamie say as him and Chris ran down the street to where I had ended up. In my mind, I was thinking, *You're the only one who knows how to drive a car, you should've had the heart to take it from the get-go.* This is what I was thinking, yet I would never say this to Jamie out loud. Definitely not at that stage of my life.

"My fault," I said as I stepped out of the car, happy to be alive and not seriously hurt.

"Watch out," Jamie barked as he jumped in the driver seat and maneuvered the car out of the ditch. "Hop in fellas, we rolling," he said as Chris and I jumped in the vehicle and we sped off.

Stealing cars would become a frequent thing for Chris and I. It wasn't so much Jamie's thing at all. As with most of my illegal acts and activities, Jamie would introduce me to them, and I would just take them to the next level. Whether it was breaking into houses, stealing cars, robbing stores, etc., my first time would usually be with Jamie, and then I would sneak behind his back and do these things by myself or with other people.

As far as stealing cars, another local guy had showed Chris and I that in a nearby neighborhood called Monsey, N.Y., the Hasidic Jewish people who lived there would leave their keys in their cars overnight. Once we discovered this, we would steal a different car almost every other night. Neither Chris nor I could drive, so we would always have to find someone willing to drive for us. That was actually harder than finding which cars to take. It had gotten to where we would take the cars, drive them into the Bronx to see Chris's girlfriend, or to go play basketball against kids in Bronx River Projects, and then return the car to exactly where we took it from. I used to wonder how they wouldn't notice that their car had been gone all night. Did they not keep track of the gas they had in their cars? We would try to park as close to the spot we'd taken the car from as possible, but I'm sure it wasn't close enough not to ever notice. Who knows? Who cared at that time. As long as those keys were there, we were riding.

"It was a long time ago that I'd never forget/ Got my heart broken up by this girl names Yvette..."

***

Caesar rapped on the front porch of his family's mini-mansion smack dead in the ghetto. I remember standing there being mesmerized. Until that day, I had never heard anybody who rapped songs that weren't on the radio or on an album. Caesar was not only rapping, but he was a twelve-year-old kid rapping, and rapping really WELL.

I was so in awe of this. I couldn't wait to go home and tell Jamie what Caesar could do. In the back of my mind, I knew this was also something I wanted to learn how to do. Although Caesar was older than me, I was more experienced as far as being off the porch, or "outside" as they say. I drank, I smoked cigarettes, I stole cars, I did robberies, etc., and he knew this. I had this image I had to uphold as the younger "BIG" homie. I couldn't ask Caesar to teach ME how to do something. Hell nah. He was supposed to come ask ME how to do shit.

Caesar was a football player. I had no interest in playing football at all. But now I realized he had another talent. A talent I wanted to learn. Rapping. I would somehow get Caesar to teach me to rap... Somehow, some way. I was so in love with Hip Hop at this stage of my life. I mean, I was totally infatuated. I never thought I could be a rapper or anything at that point, but if he could do it, I could do it too. I still had a small dilemma. Even if I tried to make my own rap, I would still need Caesar to tell me if it was good or not. This guy could actually really rap! I couldn't ask Jamie; he couldn't rap. Couldn't ask Chris; he couldn't rap either. I most certainly couldn't ask Tyrone because we couldn't stand each other, and he couldn't rap. I would figure this out sooner or later, because rapping is something I wanted to learn how to do, and Caesar would teach me, whether he knew it or not.

That evening, after playing Combat with Caesar on his Atari 7800, his mom, who we all affectionately addressed as Mrs. Dow, called us upstairs and offered us sandwiches and Kool-Aid. Mrs. Dow was famous for her sweet Kool-Aid. Every day after Caesar would leave football practice at 5 P.M., I would make sure I would walk down the street to meet him to play his video game and to get some of that Kool-Aid. Caesar's dad, Mr. Dow, was one of those old school gangsters who had done well in life and had one of those 'never forget what made you' mentalities. This is probably why he built that large, beautiful house in the middle of the slums. It was either his way to stay true to his roots, or to rub it in everybody's faces he had done well. Either way, he was a cool guy. As kids, we were always kinda scared of Mr. Dow because of his large frame, and the fact he talked with one of those electronic voice boxes. I believe he had caught throat cancer at some point and it damaged his natural voice box, so he talked with that electric one. Before I knew him personally, I thought it was scary. But as I got to know him, I thought it was kind of cool.

After eating our sandwiches, Caesar asked his mother if we could go outside and play. Now playing to us meant probably throwing rocks at cars or going up the street to steal out of the corner stores, or beating up Ajax, the local bum and taking his last dollar, or some stupid shit like that. When he asked her, his mother immediately yelled at him.

"You need to take your black ass back downstairs and do some homework!" she screamed. "All you wanna do is run around in those damn streets and get in trouble," she continued. "You need to be more like your friend Brian here." As soon as she said that, Caesar looked at her as if was about to say, *'Like Brian? Do you have any idea what kinda shit this guy is into?'* And when he looked like he was gonna say something, I gave him this look like, *'Don't you even think about it,'* and he just burst out laughing.

"What the hell is so funny!?" she screamed.

"Nothing," he replied as I sat there with the most innocent face I could possibly muster up.

"I'm gonna let your black ass out to play today cause you're with Brian. I don't want you hanging out with nappy head ass Chris." If only she knew, the plan was, as always, to go meet up with Jamie and Chris, and get into some bullshit.

"Thank you, Mrs. Dow," I said, smiling with my innocent chubby face.

Much later, Mr. and Mrs. Dow would come to know I wasn't the innocent child they thought I was for all of those years. They would come to discover what my family and a lot of the people in the streets already knew. Little fat face Brian was an absolute terror.

CHAPTER 5

That Nasty Lake

That "innocent act" I mastered is actually what got me out of a lot of trouble during my life. I had mastered the art of playing the victim after I had done something to someone else. I also believe it was how I got all the way to the 9th grade without ever getting left back. I hardly ever completed any school or homework; certainly not enough to pass. Out of a 180-day calendar school year, I would be absent at least 70 or 80 of those days. If I had a dollar for each time a Caucasian social worker would come to our house threatening to take me out of the household for missing school, I'd have Jay Z money. Okay, maybe not Jay Z money, but it was very, very often. The only reason they weren't able to take me out of the home was that my mother's defense was rock solid. While I would miss 70 or 80 days of school per school year, my sister LaDedra, who lived in the same household, would have perfect attendance. I remember my mother telling this one lady, "He may not be going to school, but he leaves here every single morning."

I hated when they would come to our house because, for the next few weeks, the forged parent-signed absent excuse notes I would bring in wouldn't work because they would call my mother to verify them. I actually don't know what it was that I hated about school, but I knew I hated it. How I was able to pass doing no work was quite simple. I was always very smart, insightful and always had exceptionally good reading comprehension. My logic was, as long as I could pass the exams, it shouldn't have mattered if I did homework or took notes or not.

I felt like Allen Iverson comparing practice to an actual game. Notes and homework were practice, and the tests and exams were the actual game. I had enough insight to where I could cram for a test two hours before it was to be taken, and have all the key points locked in. My teachers would plead with me to just come to school and do the homework. I never obliged. My attitude was like A.I.'s. *"Homework, we talking about homework, not the test, Homework."* I had learned how to work the system. I also knew how to use my chubby cheeks to get on mostly all of my teachers' good sides.

'I will do the homework' I would tell Mr. or Mrs. whoever my teacher was. I knew as long as my cram skills worked and I was passing the necessary state exams, I had no intention of being present or doing any homework. I remember being threatened with getting left back because of the school days I was missing, but then teachers and counselors would always go to bat for me. "He shouldn't be punished for something going on in the home. He is bright and can do the work." I would hear this sentiment time and time again during my life. "Brian is one of my brightest students when he is actually present," they would say. And that was only one of the components that made my teachers side with me.

In every class, in every school I ever attended, there was always a class clown, a troublemaker, a loudmouth, and the one every teacher hated the most, the kid who would disrespect and challenge their authority. This always opened doors for me to get in good with any teacher I ever had. "Why don't you shut the fuck up and listen, don't you see she is here trying to teach us something!?" I would scream to the loudmouth student who talked during class. "Hey, tough guy, you're the bitch! Why don't you talk to *me* like that?" I would say to the disrespectful kid who would invite the teacher to suck his private parts and/or call her a bitch. Although they would warn me about the bad language, they would always keep me after class and thank me for sticking up for them. Once I realized how good this worked when it came to passing, I worked it like you would never believe.

This is also why when they did try putting me in advanced classes, I would always tell my mother to decline. I knew I could do the work if I applied myself, but I also knew those classes didn't have the knuckleheads and clowns that the regular classes had. I knew I would lose my edge. Looking back, I would have loved to have had challenged myself in those advanced classes just to see if I had what it took. Guess I'll never know.

One day, after one of the rare occasions I went to school, I came home only to find my mother packing up our belongings, seeming very happy, while my Aunt Lorraine was steaming mad. Jamie was nowhere to be found to tell me what was going on, so I immediately went to my mother to find out what was happening. "Baby, I found us an apartment, were moving out!" I immediately felt like someone had ripped my heart out of my chest, yet I was happy my mother was happy.

"You and LaDedra are even going to share y'all own room again," she added assuming that would be a good selling point. All I could think about was Jamie not being there every day. No more walking up the street to my boy Caesar Dow's house, playing his video games and drinking that sweet Kool-Aid. No more of Jamie's dogs chasing me. Life was about to change dramatically. I assumed my Aunt Lorraine was so upset because her sister was about to move out. They were the closest out of all of the sisters. But come to find out, this wasn't why my aunt was mad at all.

Before I could find out why my aunt was so angry, Jamie had come through the door with a quarter water, a bag of sour cream and onion potato chips, and a pack of filterless Pall Mall cigarettes. I knew those chips were his favorite, and I knew our mothers both smoked cigarettes, but they smoked Newports. *What the hell is going on?* I wondered.

I greeted Jamie with our secret crew handshake and gave him a tighter hug than usual. I was sad because I knew I was moving out and moving on. I hadn't even inquired about where we were moving because I didn't care. I wasn't ready to leave the big brother I never had. As soon as I let go of my big cousin, my aunt came storming in the room. "Did you get the ones I told you?" she asked.

"Yeah, I think so," he said as he passed her the pack of Pall Mall cigarettes.

"Get your ass in here, Benita!" she yelled. *What the HELL is going on!?* I wondered. Benita emerged from the back room with tears flowing down her face. Now let me remind you, Benita was my aunt's youngest. She was her baby, her pride and joy. As I said earlier, Benita was spoiled rotten. I just could not wrap my head around what was going on. "You wanna be a smoker?" my aunt asked my little cousin Benita as she cried out loud.

"No, Ma, no! I'm sorry!" she repeated.

"Well, today you gonna be a smoker. You're gonna sit here and smoke this whole damn pack!" I looked at Jamie with the confused look and he motioned me over.

"My moms caught Benita smoking a cigarette in the woods today," he informed me. Benita was eight years old. Eight years old and about to smoke a whole pack of Cowboy Killers. I remember her crying while she lit the first Pall Mall.

"Mommy I'm sorry!" she cried.

"Don't be sorry now!" my aunt screamed at her. "You wanted to be a smoker earlier, now you gonna smoke the whole damn pack." For the first time, probably ever, I felt sorry for little annoying Benita. I wondered what my mother would've done if she had caught me smoking. I literally smoked cigarettes every day. I believe Benita had gotten caught just experimenting, but I was a full-fledged smoker. I'm pretty sure she wouldn't have punished me like this, if at all. Besides, she would send me to the stove to light her cigarettes for her when she didn't have matches or didn't wanna get up from wherever she was. My Aunt Lorraine would do the same. I wondered where they thought we even got the idea of even wanting to smoke from.

Benita emerged from the back room after about ten minutes with dried tears on her face. No way she had smoked the whole pack that fast. I guess after two or three cigarettes, my aunt felt she had learned her lesson. Now that it was over, Jamie and I busted out laughing hysterically at her. We thought my aunt's method of punishing Benita was the funniest thing in the world. But soon after, our laughter had subsided and reality set in. I was moving out and he was losing his little brother. I believed we both cried that night. In fact, I'm sure we did.

The next day I remember the Haitian immigrant, A.K.A. my father, showing up. He rarely appeared at this place because he hated the crime in the neighborhood. Although he couldn't stand the hoodlums and hooligans who lined the streets of the ghetto, he didn't fear them at all. I can clearly recall him coming to pick me up in Brooklyn one day, and there were about five or six guys meddling on the corner. "You want to end up like these bum?" he screamed in his Haitian accent clearly loud enough for the guys to hear.

"Who the fuck you calling a bum?" one guy shouted back. My father ignored them and continued his rant.

"You see, dem fucking bum stand on da corner and sell dwug," he said. I remember thinking, *'If they come over here and start beating his ass, there is literally nothing I can do.'* I must've been about six or seven. My father would then look at the guys, smack his teeth and continue walking toward his car. Why was he here today, though? Were LaDedra and I going back to live with him and one of his "other" families? Even though I actually liked his official wife Luce, I didn't like all the other so-called "aunts" and/or "Godmothers" he would introduce me to and bring me to stay with.

Besides, my mother had just said LaDedra and I would be sharing our own room. *What the heck is going on?* I wondered yet again. WHY was my father here? "More good news! Your father is also going to help me get a new car," my mom said excitedly.

"But you don't even drive," I said to my mother, still confused and sad at the same time.

"I know, but Lorraine is going to teach me," she replied. That brought a little joy back. If Lorraine would be able to teach her how to drive, that meant we weren't going too far away, and I could still be around Jamie. "We're moving into our new place on the first of the month," she continued as my father grabbed my sister's hand.

I finally conjured up the courage to ask where exactly we were moving to this time around. I mean, until this point, the two or three years we were living here was the longest I had ever lived in one place. Although I felt settled in here, I was still used to the bouncing around, so that aspect of it was normal. Plus, if Lorraine would be close enough to teach her how to drive, Jamie would still be nearby, right? *Right?* "So where are we moving to?" I asked curiously.

"Oh, I found me a nice two bedroom down over there in Hyenga Lake."

When she uttered those two words, my whole entire universe came crumbling down. I didn't care about the distance away from Jamie. I didn't care about not being close to Caesar and the video games, the Kool-Aid, none of that. I was NOT going to live in Hyenga Lake. Over my dead body. Mama Sampson had since moved out of her big house in Nyack, N.Y., where the cousins would gather and had moved into a senior living complex. Now the idea of living in my father's house with his "other" family didn't seem like such a bad idea. Until this stage of my existence, I had lived in project houses, torn down apartment buildings, welfare motels even. Nothing was worse than the thought of living in Hyenga Lake.

I was one of the kids in school during recess who would play dozens or rank on any kid who lived in Hyenga Lake. No matter how funny the kid was, or how good his/her ranks or jokes were, once you mentioned the fact they lived in Hyenga Lake, you automatically won. Hyenga Lake was like the absolute poorest place in the world to live. There was a big dirty-ass lake on the property there that looked like a freaking swamp. It was horrible. There would be kids in homeless shelters saying, "At least I don't live in

Hyenga Lake!" It was *that* bad. I went into the back room and cried.

LaDedra would walk in the room a few minutes later to console me. "You know there is a McDonald's right across the street from there, Mom said," she uttered trying to make me feel better. She didn't understand this was another part of what made it so embarrassing to live there. It wasn't in a residential area of any sort. This place was a hub of broken-down bungalows that were directly off of a highway. No normal size school buses even went into Hyenga Lake. You automatically had to ride on the small little yellow school bus that had the stigma of being for only special education students. The potholes in the road that led to the bungalows were so big and deep that people with nice cars would expect you to walk all the way to the entrance to meet them. They wouldn't even drive inside. This was ALL bad in my mind. ALL bad. I was NOT moving to Hyenga Lake; and my plan was to get my father to take me to live with him and his "other" family. Fuck it, I wasn't moving to Hyenga Lake. No way!

The next day, my mother comes in from outside, screaming uncontrollably. "I got it, I got my new car!" she yelled in excitement. I didn't care about any car. I was looking to see if my father was with her. I was gonna try to chubby cheek my way into getting him to agree to letting me come stay with him. I knew this would be a long shot because the only time I would end up with my dad is when nobody else seemed to wanna take me in. My mother had just gotten a new car and a new apartment so there was NO reason whatsoever for my father to let me come stay with him.

So many other times while attempting to go live with my father, I would be only about a month in, and demand to go back to live with my mother or Mama Sampson. There was something about living in a Haitian household I hated. It most certainly wasn't the cuisine, because that was A-1. I had many other siblings and stepsiblings there, so it was usually fun. The main problem was, my father's wife Luce was super sweet, but also super strict. If I came to live with them, and I had a high-top fade or any other trendy haircut in style, it had to go. It not only had to go, she would be the one to cut it and usually fuck my hairline up. I never understood how my own mother would allow me to have any haircut I wanted, parts, designs and all, but a lady who wasn't my actual mother wouldn't allow it. I had to follow her rules and regulations though. She was the Queen of that castle.

I remember her son, my stepbrother McGregor and I would bring different clothes to change into before school. We'd leave the house with the cheap nonmatching outfits Luce would send us to school in and change clothes in the woods before school so the other kids wouldn't see us in the clothes she picked out for us. We would have to do this on the way to school and change again on the way back home. But I'd wear anything to school if it meant not having to live in Hyenga Lake.

"Where is Roland?" I asked her while everyone else ran out to see the new car. I had never addressed my father as "Dad" or even as my father as a child. That didn't begin until I was an adult.

"I don't know where the hell he is," she said. She only seemed excited to show Aunt Lorraine and Angela her new vehicle that she couldn't, or wouldn't, probably ever even drive. There went that chance. But I WOULD get my chance to ask him, one way or another.

Ring Ring Ring! "Hallow?" a deep female Haitian accent said on the other end of the phone. My half-sister Rolande had answered the phone on the third or fourth ring.

"Yeah. Hello, Rolande. Is Roland home?"

Rolande was my half-sister whom my father had just recently relocated from Haiti. She was now living with him and his wife Luce in their big two-family home in Rockland County, N.Y. I found it very weird that my father would give one of his daughters his same exact name with only an 'e' at the end differentiating the two from one another. Was the 'e' silent? According to them, that 'e' changed the sound of the 'a.' They would pronounce his name Roland, and her name Rolande or (row-lahnd).

Rolande wasn't the only child my father had moved from his native Haiti to the United States. Besides her, there would be many, many other siblings I would come to meet over the course of my life. But there were about five or six who had come from Haiti to settle in his home with his new wife Luce in the good old U S of A. I remember taking a trip to Kennedy airport to pick up my half-brother Jackson. We were all (besides my father) laughing at his dress code. He had on some funny looking sneakers we had never heard of. My stepbrother McGregor and I literally laughed all the way home.

Rumor has it my father has around eighteen or nineteen children altogether. If I'm not mistaken, I believe I even have a half-sister who is older than my mother. Out of all of my half-siblings, I myself have met about eight or nine. I also, to my surprise, have had pretty decent relationships with most. As much as I don't like the term half-sister or half-brother, I have so many siblings I figured it would make it a little less confusing to follow along with my story as you read this.

I can remember thinking to myself, *if there is a Rolande who is a female, there has to definitely be a Roland Jr. somewhere out there.* What man would give his daughter his namesake, and not his son? The other half-siblings that I actually met who had come from Haiti were named Margarlie, Jackson, Frank, Ronald, Rolande and Guy. The only child he had with his wife

Luce was my younger sister Linda. Linda was born here in the states. I don't know where exactly, but I know she was born in America.

Linda was my heart growing up. She and I were only three months apart, so whenever I would live with them, we were like a team in everything we did. We would attend the same schools, while being in the same grade. We would watch the same cartoons, listen to the same music, etc. It was almost like having a twin sister. It never dawned on me that my father was actually married to her mother, yet her and I were pretty much the same exact age. That must've meant he was probably just creeping with my mother. Was my mother a side chick? My sister LaDedra once explained that she herself was born before our father married Luce, and that when I was born, my father denied me and claimed I wasn't his until a blood test proved otherwise. She would remind me of times when he would come pick her up and leave me behind because, as he had put it, to him, I wasn't his.

But now he knew I was his child, so I was calling for him to rescue his son from moving into Hyenga Lake. A place where in my mind, would've added up to a lifetime of torment. If they thought I was missing a lot of school already, I was *never* going to school on that small little yellow bus that picked up the kids from Hyenga Lake. I would not stand on the side of a highway across the street from a McDonald's to catch a bus to a school I didn't wanna be at anyway. I would have rather been in a group home than to live in Hyenga Lake. If they thought I was bad already, they had seen nothing yet. I told myself if I had to live in Hyenga Lake, I was gonna be so bad, I'd have to get placed in juvenile detention. My mother couldn't say much if I ended up there because she was in one when she was young, right? These different variables went through my mind as I waited for my half-sister Rolande to get our father on the phone.

Two minutes later, after what had seemed like an eternity waiting, I heard my father's deep voice on the other end of the line. "Hallo, Bwian. What do you want?" he asked. I wasn't in front of him to give him the chubby cheek effect, so I tried another technique.

"Hello, DAD," I said softly into the phone...

CHAPTER 6

Child on Trial

As everyone returned back into the house from going outside to view my mother's brand-new hatchback Chevrolet, I sat there with a look of desperation on my face. I had just gotten off the phone with my father, asking if I could come live with him and his already-large-and-ever-growing family. I even called him Dad. Calling him Dad was very, very seldom. I was either in trouble or wanted something when I called him Dad. I didn't get the answer I wanted, but he also didn't say no either. He reminded me of the fact that he now had less room at his house after bringing more of my half-sisters and brothers up from Haiti. Maybe I didn't make it clear that LaDedra wouldn't be coming with me this time because he kept referring to the issues of having two more children there instead of just me. Should I call him back and tell him it was just me coming? Would that make him say yes? I was in a total state of confusion.

LaDedra had no problem with living in Hyenga Lake. I think she was more concerned about rumors going around that my mother was with child. I had heard the whispers about my mother potentially being pregnant, but all that was overshadowed by the grim thought of living in Hyenga Lake.

"I think Mommy is having a baby," LaDedra said as she gathered up more of her belongings getting ready for the big move.

"I ain't trying to live in no Hyenga Lake," I replied.

"What's so bad about Hyenga Lake?" she asked. LaDedra was a nerd. A straight-A student who had only one other nerd friend and didn't care about popularity. I, on the other hand, was a cool kid. I had a reputation to uphold and living in Hyenga Lake would've been a major loss of cool points for me. A major blow to my reputation. It was bad enough we already lived on Bethune Blvd, but at least Bethune had a reputation for being tough. Kids would be too scared to talk shit about you living on Bethune because they assumed you knew how to fight. Hyenga Lake was different. I thought about the kids I ranked on about living there and what they would say. I had to get out of this somehow.

"I think Carlos is the baby's father," LaDedra said as she continued to pack. Carlos was another Haitian guy who would come around to see my mother. Man, I didn't care about any of that, I cared about... Wait. That was it! *This can be my reasoning for me wanting to move with my father*, I thought. I had my OUT. Now all I needed was for the rumor to be true. I needed my mother to be pregnant with another child she couldn't take care of, so I could leave and not be a burden to her. Now I needed only to find out if the rumor buzzing around was true. I NEEDED it to be true. I didn't have the courage to just go up to my mother and say, "Hey Ma, I heard you got a bun in the oven." She would've probably smacked me. So, I figured I'd use Jamie to ask his mother and get some insight for me.

That night, while lying on the floor in the corner of the living room, I played out all the possible scenarios in my head. Was this the reason my father helped my mother get a new car, because she was having a baby? No, because LaDedra said she had heard Carlos was the father. My father hated Carlos; he wouldn't be helping that dude. No way, that wasn't it. Was this the reason my mom found an apartment, because she knew she needed room for the new baby? That wasn't it either. If anything, she would want my Aunt Lorraine's help. I just could NOT figure it out. Instead of driving myself crazy, I just closed my eyes and went to sleep. I'd find out the truth eventually.

A couple of days later, my aunt summoned us all into her tiny little living room. Jamie had failed at getting any information for me about my mother's status. LaDedra didn't seem to know anything other than what she heard, and my father had not given me a concrete answer yet. But here I am, two weeks away from moving into that hell hole and my aunt wants to call a family meeting. Was Benita smoking cigarettes again? Did one of Jamie's illegitimate dogs bite someone again? What was it now? Once we were all gathered, my aunt sits next to my mother with this big grin on her face. *Well, there goes the cigarette and dog theories*, I thought. She wouldn't be happy if that were the case. *What could it be?* I thought. What would my aunt have to tell us that she needed all of our attention?

"Guess what ya'll," she said with excitement. "Josephine is having a baby!" There it was. I had gotten my wish. There was my way out of moving to that nasty Lake. I tried to pretend to curb my enthusiasm, but I believe for the first few seconds, it was written all over my face. LaDedra was ecstatic with the confirmation of my mother expecting her third child. I was too, but for all the wrong reasons. All I could think about was using this as an excuse to go live with my father. Or to go live with Mama Sampson in that senior living facility. Maybe even back to Brooklyn where I was only one of two people who spoke English. Anything was better than Hyenga Lake. I would not be the laughing stock of recess. No way!

As I'm there envisioning NOT living in that nasty place, my sister said something that quickly drew me back to reality. "I can't believe I'm going to have a baby brother or sister!" she screamed.

Wait a minute, I thought to myself. *I'm the baby brother! I'm the baby of this family, period,* I said to myself. As fast as my excitement rose about this being my way out, it fell just as fast with the notion of me not being my mother's baby anymore. I swear something came over me that day. I was eleven years old and for those past eleven years, through all the ups and downs, I was still my mother's baby. Now I would not be the baby anymore. That was the day I decided that not only was I not HER baby anymore, I was not *a* baby anymore. Period!

We had about a week left before the move, and my father and I had come to the agreement we would do some sort of a tryout to see if it was cool to come live with him. I had lived with my father many times before, but it never quite worked out. He would either send me somewhere else to stay or send me back to my mother. But I was much younger then. The only difference this time was that now I smoked cigarettes and drank alcohol. I was good at hiding that from my mother so I could hide it from him.

The other issue was these new half-siblings that had come from Haiti who also lived with him. There were three at this point. Frank, Rolande and Jackson. I knew my stepbrother and sister, McGregor and Santia. They were his wife Luce's children from a previous marriage. I had a very close relationship with them already so that wouldn't be an issue. My half-sister Linda and I were like two peas in a pod so that definitely wasn't a problem at all. Although Linda and I had different mothers, we were very close. Now these new half-siblings who had come from Haiti, I didn't quite know them. They were all much older than I was, but I knew it would take some adapting to living with them. Though my father's house was huge, the numbers were adding up quickly.

When I went to do my test run at my father's house, I asked my sister to come with me. It always made me more comfortable being around my father's side of the family when my sister was with me. It kind of felt like I had an ally. I knew LaDedra didn't want to go live there, but I asked her to come stay there with me before they finally moved out of Aunt Lorraine's house and into that nasty place. She obliged and we were off to my father's house for my "tryout."

My father had moved all of the boys up into the attic area, while all the girls stayed downstairs. There were now five boys living in the house altogether. A far cry from the usual two. This could either be the most fun thing ever, or a complete disaster. Although both my stepbrother McGregor's parents were Haitian, he was born here in America and was raised like an American. My half-brothers Frank, Ronald and Jackson were fresh from Haiti and the culture difference was obvious immediately. It was like McGregor and I stayed on one side of the attic, while the other three boys occupied the other side. It would be very seldom we would integrate, or even speak to them at all for that matter. The only one who spoke a little English was Frank. Jackson and Ronald didn't speak English at all. Even when we would go outside to play, McGregor and I would play basketball while the three of them would find a soccer ball and bounce it off their knees and heads with extreme perfection. I had even nicknamed them The Pele Brothers on some joking shit. It was a weird dynamic, but it beat living in Hyenga Lake. *I can do this,* I thought. Life was good again.

It didn't take me long to notice that my stepbrother McGregor had a lot of the latest new Nike's that had just come out. I knew my father's wife Luce wasn't buying them for him because when she shopped for us, it was always Olympians or some other cheap brand from Fayva. Fayva was a cheap discount shoe store that has since closed. They sold the cheapest brand of sneakers you can imagine. Think of it as the Payless of today. I knew my father didn't get him these shoes because my father let his wife handle the clothes shopping. He didn't have a paper route or an after-school job, so how the hell was he affording all of these fly kicks?

I had one pair of Nike Court Force almost worn out at this point and it was time for me to get new sneakers. I asked my father and he told me he would give Luce money to go get me sneakers. I knew exactly what that meant: Olympians or Pro Champs. Nah, I needed sneakers like McGregor had. One thing I noticed is McGregor would never wear these sneakers around the house. Our sisters didn't even know he had them. I was the only person he would show his sneaker stash and he made me promise to keep it to myself.

"Bro, who be buying you all those sneakers?" I asked him while we played basketball in the driveway.

"I got my connections," he answered with a devilish smirk on his face. That smirk was flashed rather often when dealing with McGregor. He was always up to something.

"C'mon bro… I need come kicks," I said to him.

"Alright, I'm gonna put you on later, but you can't tell anyone." I immediately agreed to his terms and our game commenced.

My mother had made it clear to my father that I was Christian, not Catholic, whenever she sent me to live with him. She knew they all attended a church called St. Ann's, which was a Catholic church. I didn't understand the difference but I favored going to Catholic church over my mother's Pentecostal church. For one, the services were much shorter and were only one day a week. My mother's church was open Sundays, Tuesdays and Thursdays. Although we didn't have to go all the time, we went enough for it to be too much for me. St. Ann's was Sunday for two hours, and that's it. I remember Luce asking my father if it was okay if I joined McGregor in being an altar boy. I assume he had asked my mother because she respectfully declined. She would later tell me she had heard some things about Catholic priests and young boys and this was why I wasn't allowed to join. McGregor asked me time and time again to come with him on Sundays to do altar boy work, and each time I told him I wasn't allowed.

"Yo, Brian, you gotta come down to the church. How you think I be getting these sneakers?" he said to me one Sunday while he got dressed for church. I didn't care what my mother said. I would not be an altar boy, but I would definitely attend church this Sunday. I needed to figure this out.

On the way walking to church, McGregor said, "Make sure you wait for me after service. Don't walk home with Linda and them." I knew whatever reason he wanted me to wait for him had something to do with the sneakers so I happily obliged. After the quick service, I met up with McGregor still donning his long white altar boy robe. "We gotta wait until the church is empty," he said. I had no idea what was going on, but I knew I was willing to do whatever I had to do to get my hands on some sneakers like he had.

After about forty-five minutes, all the patrons had made their way to their cars and out of the building. McGregor said, "Follow me." We hurried to the side of the church and made our way to what looked like a side exit or something. We walked in and entered a part of the church I had never seen. This room was not visible from where the churchgoers sat. "Wait here," McGregor instructed as I stood nervously looking back every ten seconds to make sure nobody was behind me.

There was an eerily silence that made me extra nervous. What the hell was McGregor doing? After about two minutes, which seemed like two hours, McGregor appeared from behind a silk-looking curtain with a large box in his hands. "Help me," he said. *What the hell is going on?* I thought to myself. I grabbed the other side of the box and followed his lead as we turned the box over and shook it up and down.

As we shook the box, I noticed a bunch of loose coins along with $1, $5, $10, $20s and at least one $50 bill hit the floor. *Holy shit,* I thought, with absolutely no pun intended, we were robbing a church. With the loose change and dollar bills, checks and money orders were also falling out of the box, hitting the floor. We turned the box back upright and McGregor grabbed it and disappeared behind the curtain as I picked the money and checks up off the floor. "Give me all the checks, bro, we can't use the checks," he whispered loudly while sticking his hand from behind the curtain.

I didn't know the difference between a check and a money order, so I handed him anything that wasn't green.

No more than ten seconds later, he came from behind the curtain with a hand full of money orders and a very expensive Nikon camera dangling from his shoulder by the strap. "Go out the door we came in from and meet me at the house," he said as he handed me the money orders and the camera. I quickly darted out of the side entrance and made my way to the main sidewalk to walk home. I had more money in my pocket than I had ever probably seen in my life. It had to be at least $300, I guessed. And this camera was the nicest camera I had ever laid eyes on! As I walked home, I thought to myself, *Damn, I just helped rob a church...*

I thought about what Mama Sampson would say if she knew what I just did. She would be absolutely appalled. I would probably lose my rank on her Favorite Grandchild list. She was a very devout Christian. But this wasn't a Christian church, this was a Catholic church. This was the crazy logic I told myself to justify stealing from the house of God. It was okay because I wasn't Catholic. *McGregor is Catholic, and if anybody is going to hell for this, it will be him*, I thought as I quickly walked towards our house, thinking about which pair of sneakers I would be getting later on.

It was about 5 P.M. and McGregor had still not made it home yet. Usually, on most Sundays after his altar boy duties, he was home by 3 P.M. the latest. I got a little worried as I sat listening to my half-brothers speaking Creole in the next room. McGregor wasn't there to translate the shit they were saying and they were laughing as they spoke and it was burning me up. Where the hell was this dude? Did he get caught? Did somebody see us and rat him out? He should be home by now. I paced our side of the attic back and forth, completely annoyed by my half-brothers speaking their foreign language. I could not understand anything they said besides the curse words and it made me mad. I hadn't even counted the money; this was his lick. So out of respect, I would wait for him before I counted the take. I glanced at the digital clock on the dresser that now read 5:17. Damn... I was certain McGregor had gotten nabbed.

I went downstairs to talk to my sister Linda. I knew her and McGregor were close as well, so I figured I'd pick her brain about his tardiness. I wanted to know if this was a common thing or not. "Hey Lin, I wanna play some basketball with McGregor. Shouldn't he be home by now?" I asked as I dribbled the ball.

"Yeah, he is usually home already, and Luce is looking for him too." Damn. His mother was looking for him too? This had to be bad. We were fucked. And I was certainly gonna go down too because I was an accomplice. What is Mama Sampson gonna say when she finds out I robbed a church? I got scared. Hopefully, he wouldn't tell on me. I know I had a pact with Jamie, Chris and Caesar that if we did a crime and one of us got caught, there was absolutely NO ratting whatsoever. But I didn't have this pact with McGregor, and obviously, by the number of sneakers he had, his church robbing scheme had been working smoothly up until this point. Damn. He was most certainly caught and most certainly would implement me.

As I finished shooting the ball around by myself with the clock slowly ticking away, I decided I would go inside to watch some television and wait. As I walked inside and through the kitchen, I could hear a voice in the attic that wasn't one of my three half-brothers. The voice was speaking Creole, but it wasn't any of the three. It was McGregor. I quickly ran upstairs to greet my stepbrother. "Yo man, what took you so long?" I asked, excited as hell and now thinking about the loot we had to split.

"We gotta get rid of that fucking camera bro," he said immediately. "Where is it?" I walked to where I had stashed the camera along with the money and came back and handed him everything. "I was at the church all this fucking time helping them look for that camera. It belonged to one of the members of clergy," he said. "I figured if I stayed helping to find it, and they all saw me leave without it, none of this could come back to me," he explained, flashing that devilish grin again.

For fourteen years old, McGregor was wise beyond his years. "But we gotta get rid of that shit ASAP!" he continued. "You know anybody we can sell it to in Spring Valley?" he asked with a desperate look on his face.

"My man Caesar's mom got mad money," I said. "Maybe she would want it."

I knew I had no intentions of asking Mrs. Dow if she wanted to buy a hot camera stolen from a church. She was also a woman of God. But throwing her name in the mix did what I needed it to do. It got us past that subject and down to the nitty-gritty. "How much money was it?" he asked.

"I don't know, I didn't count it. I was waiting for you," I replied. He gave me a look between being surprised and proud. I mean, I had every right to count the money being I was in on it, but I wanted to show him he could trust me.

"Alright, let's see how much we got," he said as we walked to our section of the attic. "I seen these new Jordans that I wanna get, I can't wait!" We counted the loot and booked it to the first store of our choice.

As McGregor and I walked to the Army and Navy store that sold the newest, latest footwear, he was explaining the rules of the house when it came down to how to maneuver with our new items. Rule number 1: Luce was not supposed to see ANY of the sneakers or clothing she didn't purchase herself. Rule number 2: We were not to wear any of the fresh expensive items we bought with the stolen church money around the house, at all. Rule number 3: If our sisters see us in school wearing our fresh new items, we were to tell them they didn't belong to us and find a friend who would go along with our story. And the last and final rule, Rule number 4: If you hear Luce coming up the stairs, throw all the merchandise out the window.

I thought to myself, *if they don't know you're robbing the church, what's the big deal?* But instead of voicing this, I just walked along with excitement. I was ready to go on a shopping spree.

McGregor and I walked out of the Army and Navy store with two big bags in our hands. We each had two pairs of sneakers and new sweatsuits with matching headbands. Too bad it was a couple of weeks before school was scheduled to start or we would've crushed the first day. I wasn't even sure if I was going to last until the first day of school at my dad's house... But when I found out about this St. Ann's money grab, I sure as hell wanted to.

LaDedra was definitely not going to stay at my father's house. She had made up her mind she would stay with my mother and help with the new baby on the way. Every time I thought of the new baby, it drew me further and further away from the thought of living with my mother ever again. Here I was, jealous of a newborn baby that hadn't even been born yet. I was Josephine's baby, me, and just like that, I was being replaced.

As we approached the house, McGregor took our bags and threw them over a tall brown wooden fence adjacent to the neighbor's house. "Once everyone is asleep, I'll run back out and grab everything," he said. Damn, this was a pretty elaborate operation he had here. He had obviously done this many times before. As we climbed up the stairs that led to that attic, I could again hear my three half-brothers chatting away in Creole.

"What the fuck do these dudes be talking about all day?" I asked McGregor.

"Soccer and Haiti," he replied as we both burst out laughing.

The next day I woke up to find McGregor lacing his new pair of black and red Air Jordans. I looked around the room to see if I would spot my own new sneakers. "Yours are in the stash," he said. I didn't know where the stash was because as he had earlier explained, it switches up. The name of the game was simply 'keep the merchandise away from Luce.' He got up and summoned for me to follow him. We walked to the other side of the room, where he struggled to move a large dresser. Behind it was a small door. He opened the door and passed me a bag that contained the items

I had purchased with my share of the church money. While the door was open, I looked past him.

I peered inside that room and I had seen all types of cool things. Video game consoles, skateboards, basketball jerseys, the kind of stuff only a rich kid would have. *How long has this guy been robbing this church?* I thought to myself. Geesh. "Later on, when Luce goes to sleep, I'll break the Nintendo out," he said. This guy had the Nintendo game system when it had first come out.

I was in awe of McGregor at this point. I immediately asked him, "So how can I become an altar boy, bro?" He looked at me and said, "First, you gotta become Catholic, and you know Ms. Josephine ain't having that." I thought to myself, *Ms. Josephine has a new baby she has to worry about. She ain't thinking about me.* Why was this new baby bothering me so much?

***

One afternoon, while lying in my bed playing with a Rubik's Cube, I could hear music playing in the room next to mine. This was the room my three half-brothers from Haiti had shared.

Let us begin, what, where, why or when/Will all be explained like instructions to a game see I'm not insane...

"Oh shit," I said. "That's the new Boogie Down Productions!" I jumped up immediately to see where it was coming from. Did McGregor like BDP too? Now I knew my stepbrother was the man. As I followed the sound of the music, it led me to the room my three stepbrothers from Haiti slept in. *What in the hell did these guys know about Hip Hop*, I asked myself, BDP especially. When I knocked on the door, my half-brother Frank answered, "Who's that?" Oh shit, this guy could actually speak English.

"Yo what's up," I answered. "Yo is that the new Boogie Down Productions?"

"Hell yeah," he replied in his thick Haitian accent. "KRS-One is no Joke." I peered in to see if either of the other two brothers were in the room with him, but he was in there alone. I invited myself in and sat on his bed. He was playing the vinyl on a small turntable he had. I could see the blue Jive label spinning around and around as KRS's voice blasted out of the speakers.

"Where did you get this?" I asked him.

"From that Sam Goody yo," he replied. He had a heavy accent but spoke well enough for me to understand. This album had just dropped and this guy who hadn't even been in this country a good six months had it already. He reached and grabbed the album cover, which was so new it still had the plastic with the orange $9.99 sticker on it. He looked at it with admiration and handed it to me. I had seen KRS-One standing at the window like Malcolm X with a small Uzi or Mac-10 in his hand. I must've stared at that cover for ten minutes before I handed it back.

I had no idea anyone in this house listened to Hip Hop. McGregor clearly wasn't into it like I was because whenever I bought up rap music, he didn't seem to really care. I even told him about my friend Caesar from Spring Valley who could rap and he didn't seem to care about that either. He wanted to talk about skateboarding or back handsprings and shit like that. I was a Hip Hop fanatic at this point. I could quote the whole LL Cool J *Radio* album back to front. I knew all of U.T.F.O.'s songs. Well, the ones that played on the radio. I would stay up all night listening to Mr. Magic and Marley Marl on WBLS. Then I would go check out Red Alert on 98.7 Kiss F.M. I was tapped in and I was hooked.

Hip Hop was something I had fallen in love with the moment I heard my cousin Buttercup playing *Rock Box* by Run DMC in 1984. I was about six years old. I told myself that even though we couldn't ever afford them anyway, that I would NEVER wear Calvin Klein jeans because of that song. A few years later, while I was living with my Aunt Lorraine, a kid named Demetrius had gotten the Fat Boys' first album for his birthday. He promised me if I bought my own blank cassette, he would make me a dub of it. I saved up every penny I could get so I could buy one of the good TDK cassettes that cost a dollar. I could've gotten the cheap three-for-a-dollar tapes that came in a pack, but the quality of those weren't like a TDK or Maxwell. I gave him the blank cassette and never heard from him again. That would bother me for years and years to come.

Like most other little boys, I liked the WWF, I liked G.I. Joe, I liked most sports, I liked Karate movies, throwing rocks, but I LOVED Hip Hop. There was just something about the rawness of it. Since I was a child, I had been trying to convince my African American mother to buy me rap albums, and here I was sitting in front of my half-brother who was fresh from Haiti, and he is bumping the brand new BDP album, which he *owned*.

As I sat there listening to the album with him, I hear McGregor calling out for me. "Yo Brian! Yo Brian!" he yelled over and over.

"I'm in here!" I screamed back. He stuck his head in the door with the most surprised look on his face. He knew I really didn't particularly like my three half-brothers. I would complain to him about them all the time. But this was before I knew that one of them liked Hip Hop. "Yo, this guy got the new Boogie Down Productions album!" I said to McGregor."

"Yeah, he got all that shit," McGregor replied, not looking impressed. *Wait. There was more than this?* I thought. What other albums did he have? I began scanning around the room, looking for evidence of more Hip-Hop music. Low and behold, right next to his record player was a large stack of vinyl. If all of those records were Hip Hop records, there was NO WAY I was leaving this house. NO WAY.

The next morning, I could hear him again. "Brian! Yo, yo, Brian!" McGregor was yelling down the stairway, probably assuming I was downstairs with the girls.

"Yo," I replied as I poked my head out of my half-brothers' room where I had just discovered the day before this oasis of rap music he had. I'm talking Eric B & Rakim, Public Enemy, Run DMC; you name it, he had it.

"You wanna go play some basketball?" McGregor asked.

"Nah, I'm good," I replied. "You need to check out some of this music in here," I suggested. He gave me a look as if he were irritated that I had opted to listen to music with Frank over playing basketball with him. It wasn't about Frank at all. I hardly even liked the guy. But I loved that he had a plethora of Hip Hop tunes for me to listen to.

Back in these days, a lot of the rap albums came with the lyrics to each song typed on the inner sleeve placed inside the album cover. This would make it easier to follow with the lyrics of a song as you sang along. I noticed as I sang the lyrics to each song that blared through speakers, Frank would be smiling uncontrollably while nodding his head in agreement. I thought of the idea to have him try and read along to the lyric sheet. Although he couldn't read or write English I figured it would be a good way for him to practice on his learning of the language. I knew these songs would help me with my vocabulary in a major way and I was sure it could do the same for him.

I reached and grabbed L.L. Cool J's *BAD* album. I put the vinyl on the turntable and handed him the inner sleeve as the words from *The Breakthrough* came roaring out of the speakers. I began singing along as I pointed at the words on the sleeve he had in his hand, encouraging him to sing along.

CHAPTER 7

This Moment In Time
(Say His Name)

If you have read this book until this point, you probably can tell by now this is my first, and maybe last attempt at writing a book. As I sit and type the memories about my journey through life, I'm reminded at this very moment how much of a crazy journey it has actually been.

On every news outlet, I am watching all the major U.S. cities reporting fires, looting as protesters of all races mob together through the streets right now. New York has reported sixteen police vehicles having been burned by protesters while over one hundred seventy-five Target store locations across the country have closed their businesses due to the fear of being *targeted*, ironically. All of the uprising and protest results directly from a picture and video that's being circulated. This image is of a black man being murdered by a white police officer by way of him kneeling on his neck with his knee for almost nine minutes. The man's name is George Floyd.

I've been seeing various videos of George Floyd all over social media since his murder by the hand of Officer Derek Chauvin. In all of these videos, George Floyd always seemed to be offering encouraging words to both the younger and older generations alike. He always seemed to be in a good mood and spoke of doing the right things to create and see better days. Makes me sad I never got the chance to meet him. Seems like we were like-minded individuals. Most of the people on that side of my large family are pretty sharp.

I have known now for about four days now that George Floyd is a distant cousin of mine. George's father was a man named George Perry. If I'm not mistaken, George Perry's brother is my cousin Andrew and Sharon Floyd's father. Andrew Floyd is a guy I always looked up to growing up. Before ever even knowing we were related, I always thought he was super cool. He was always one of those guys who minded his business, stayed fly and carried himself in a respectful manner. His little sister Sharon was the same way. All the Floyd's were super cool and were a respected family amongst the community. It was my cousin Randolph Floyd who sat me down and gave me the rundown on how our families are related.

Mama Sampson is originally from North Carolina. She had come up to New York during the 60s with her husband Harvey Sampson, and then ten children, to escape the low work wages in the south. Randolph explained it was through our families in North Carolina, and another mutual cousin, how we were all related. From that point on, we treated and acknowledged each other as family.

Randolph, or "Coach Ran" (as he is affectionately referred to in the small town of Spring Valley N.Y.), is also like his brother Andrew for being beloved in that community. He coaches the neighborhood kids on a Pop Warner level, so he's seen a lot of these children go from their first day of ever playing organized football, to becoming top-ranked athletes who go on to use football to change their lives. He's also seen a lot of these guys squander opportunity and become criminals who ditch the game for street life. Regardless of which, anytime these kids get a chance to show their appreciation to Coach Randolph Floyd, they make sure they show it.

As I sat on Facebook yesterday connecting the dots with family members who are aware George Floyd is a relative, I realize these uprisings are the biggest ones we have seen. Not in damage, but in participation.

There has been protest in all fifty states in the country already. In over one hundred forty cities.

***

It's been six days since my distant cousin's death, and the protesting has not stopped yet. Not only are these the largest protests America has ever seen after a murder of an unarmed black man by hands of the police, it's also the most diverse, and most complex. Multiple races, including white, are joining forces with the Black Lives Matter movement in these protests. Ironically, it also actually seems this time around, the peaceful protests that turn violent seem mostly ignited by unruly white citizens, who I guess feel like they have had it up to here with racial injustice! Perhaps, but I also wonder if a lot of these white kids out here looting and burning up things ever cared about the plight of a black man in America even for a day before George was killed? Will they care about it a day after this thing dies down?

It is beginning to seem a lot of this "looting" and "uprising" isn't about the harsh treatment of George Floyd at all. His image dying under the weight of that clearly heartless officer's knee might've been what sparked a lot of the unrest, but it doesn't seem to be what's fueling it anymore. It has been said to be White Militia groups in masks actually sparking a lot of the unrest in a lot of these cities. This is something I've never witnessed before.

As I continue scrolling through Facebook pages reading condolences being sent to my cousins Sharon, Darlene, Andrew and Coach Ran, I see a picture with Coach, George and their uncle Isaac Floyd. This picture really made me realize how much more closely-related we are than I initially thought. I had recently shot a video for my song *2 for $5*, where I reenacted the barbecue scene from the movie *Boyz in the Hood*. The older gentleman in the scene who reminds me that "the ladies gotta eat first" is Isaac Floyd. George Floyd's uncle, who is also his father's brother. I have yet to go on social media and explain my relation to George Floyd because with all that's going on with his name attached to it, I don't wanna seem to be making an attempt to involve myself, or be exploiting his name for my benefit. I never had the chance to meet him, but seeing videos of him, and seeing we were like-minded human beings, makes me pretty sure we would've gotten along. I got along great with everyone on that side because the Floyds are good people overall. An amazing God-fearing family. Oh, I also heard that he rapped so who knows, we probably could've recorded a song or two together.

It really honors me to know it was someone from the same lineage as I am whose untimely, unjust, unfair and very unfortunate demise sparked the outcry heard around the world and change this society forever. Even as sitting President Donald Trump encourages governors around the country to be tougher while handling the protesters who get unruly; I get a feeling this is one moment in American history that changes the dynamic. A moment where the people realize the power they possess when they come together. I ask myself, should I be out there? Especially now knowing he is a relative. Should I use my voice to be out there speaking up against racial injustice? These questions run through my mind. I have, until today, dedicated my whole music career to using my voice to talk about the injustices with the lack of equalities here in America. But I haven't released music in a while so my voice is missing. Had what I done not been enough? I have this fight within myself a lot lately.

I most certainly don't see the point of looting or burning property. If the business is insured, they'll get most of that money back. If it's to let your voice be heard, there are various ways of accomplishing this outside of taking shit and burning property, right? I have this all-or-nothing mentality so if I'm going out there, I'm going to make an ultimate statement. If the point of it all is to show our displeasures with the way we've been treated in this country so far, that is going to take more than looting and burning shit.

Then I think about my children. Is becoming a martyr by sacrificing myself to make a point worth not being here to help guide and raise my children? Do I sacrifice my life and just hope I did enough to let them profit off of my name? Or do I just stay silent and play it safe and continue to be here for my children? I know if I were to go out there and be on the frontline, I would already be going out there with the notion of never coming back, so I would be thinking about the biggest statement I could possibly make in the biggest possible way. If I'm willing to suffer the ultimate sacrifice, which is my life, to make a point about how fed up we are with racial injustice here, my move would have to be so over the top, it would leave me in the history books.

The only thing I fear in life more than death, is not being there if my children need me. The thought of one of my children calling out to me and me being dead, incarcerated or where I couldn't help them, frightens me more than anything else. I honestly believe in my heart that if I didn't have my children when I did, I would've gotten assassinated by the United States government by now. I would've done so much more to get my message of black empowerment out. What slowed me down wasn't my fear of losing my life; it was fear of my children losing the guidance they may need.

I always wondered what the guys who lived long enough to have families yet were fighting for freedom felt about this. What did Malcolm X think would happen to his children if he suffered consequences for the speeches that went against the infrastructure of the U.S. government? Who did Martin Luther King think would be here to protect his children if he met his demise? It had to be something he thought about knowing the risk he was taking for his role in the civil rights movement. Whenever I look around at the conditions and the mindset of many people from my community, I ask myself, did these martyrs actually die in vain? Even Jesus. If Jesus died for our sins, why is sin still so prevalent now? If I went out and risked my life or my freedom to alter the lives of future generations for the better, who would be there to make sure MY children had everything they needed? These are the things that haunted me whenever I felt the urge to do something I felt would be an actionable item that bought awareness to how tired we are of the injustice.

The image of my distant relative George Floyd with a knee to his neck is burnt into my memory forever. It's an image that makes me question even my own reluctance. Although I know my calling isn't to be running around with a megaphone protesting, I wonder if I'm allowing parenthood to deter me from what I was born to do. Martin Luther King once said if a man hasn't discovered something he would die for, he isn't fit to live. I know there are many things I would die for, so what is this internal battle I can't seem to shake? I know it's more than just putting a message in the music. I can feel that it's more. Should I be out there allowing myself to be the example?

***

The City of New York has announced an 11:00 P.M. to 5:00 A.M. curfew today as an attempt to get a hold on the looting and uprising happening throughout the city. While the President is maintaining his threat of unleashing military force on his own citizens, the governors seem to be doing all they can to keep the peace and limit the outbursts of violence during the protest. It seems the more President Donald Trump speaks, the more he seems to be not even the slightest bit in tune about what the real issue is here. The brutal attacks on citizens by law enforcement is what got us to this point to begin with. What is he actually trying to say here by suggesting there be even more? This is the world we live in today, as unreal and unbelievable as it might sound.

Rest in Peace, George Floyd. My many condolences go out to Randolph, Lenny, Andrew, Sharon, Angela, Isaac and the rest of the family on this side, and on his mother's side. Your name will live on forever. Now, back to my story!

CHAPTER 8

Choke and Slide

As I think about the crazy times we are living in to start the decade of the 2020s, it makes it a lot easier to let my mind travel back to the 80s and 90s. Although there were the same injustices taking place, everything wasn't filmed or recorded, so it wasn't in your face as much. There were no timelines or newsfeeds constantly reminding you of whatever injustices were happening all over the country that week. Back then, you got the news only three times a day on television, along with a daily newspaper, and that was it. It gave you more time to think about the many other aspects of your life.

The year was 1988 and there I was at my father's house finishing up a tryout to get the green light to move in with him. Although I was initially worried about the dynamic with the other children he had moved into his house from Haiti, I felt good about it now. McGregor had shown me the St. Ann's Church altar boy money scheme, and I had now found out one of my Haitian half-brothers had a plethora of Hip Hop music to jam to. I was good to go. Not only was I not trying to move to Hyenga Lake, I had felt like I had some level of stability here for the first time in my life. For the next two or three days in a row, I would politely decline to play basketball with McGregor, to instead sit in the room with Frank and listen to his records. For some reason, this new routine quickly started some internal conflict within the boys' living quarters of the house. McGregor didn't want me in there with Frank, and neither did Jackson and Ronald, the other two half-brothers who had recently came from Haiti. Frank and I were the only boys there with this love and passion for Hip Hop music and culture, and this became the basis of our bond. Of course, I liked sneakers, video games and other things McGregor had to offer, but not like I loved this music. Jackson and Ronald didn't even speak English so it didn't even matter what they thought. My father thought it was good I was establishing a relationship with at least one of my older half-brothers, even if it was only because of some music he thought was a silly fad.

When I would finally leave Frank's room and would go back on my side with McGregor, all I would talk about is a new song I heard on Public Enemy's new album; or a new song that had premiered on Red Alert's radio show I dubbed while I fell asleep recording. I think he noticed my love for this music becoming an obsession.

"We need to get rid of that fucking camera this week," McGregor said, cutting me off while I yapped away about how dope Big Daddy Kane's verse on *The Symphony* was. I had totally forgotten about it being my responsibility to sell the hot camera we lifted from the St. Ann's church heist.

"Yeah, I told you my friend Caesar's mother has a lot of money, all I have to do is..." I began to explain as he cut me off.

"Yeah, well, you have until the end of the week," he snapped back angrily.

What was with this new attitude McGregor was displaying? I believe he was feeling slighted about me spending more time on the other side with the music. I made a mental note to make sure I made time to play at least one game of basketball a day with McGregor so I didn't mess up my chances of living there. This was one of the rare times I had actually wanted to live with my father and wasn't there because I didn't have a choice. I knew McGregor and I not getting along would definitely mess up my chances. I wouldn't let that be the deal-breaker.

"You wanna go shoot some hoops before dinner?" I asked McGregor in a somber tone.

"No, I'm good," he replied with the same attitude he had been displaying minutes earlier.

"Okay," I said as I went to grab my boombox to pump some of new tunes I had recorded the night before.

"And don't turn that shit up so loud!" he snapped again. I noticed McGregor was angry at me, and I could also feel myself getting angry at him for being angry at me. I got that all too familiar feeling again.

At my father's house, the rules at the dinner table were similar to the rules at my Aunt Lorraine's house. All the children sat at the dinner table and didn't leave the table until you were finished your food, or had the permission to dismiss yourself and go play or do other things. It was either Luce or my half-sister Rolande who usually cooked dinner for the family. On this night, Rolande had made the one dish I didn't enjoy. It is a popular Haitian dish made of cornmeal and beans. I hated when they would cook this and would ask for a peanut butter and jelly sandwich as an alternative. Usually, my request would be granted, but on this day, Luce suggested that I eat the cornmeal. It felt like everyone was turning on me. For the ten days I had been there so far, I had been sitting next to McGregor at dinner time while we would usually be in our own conversation. This night was a lot different. Tonight, I sat next to my sister LaDedra, my safe place whenever I felt overwhelmed, next to my big sister.

My Father Roland Carenard

McGregor sat with my Haitian half-brothers as they all four engaged in one of those huge Creole spoken conversations that LaDedra nor I understood. I concluded that dinner was halfway over with as I noticed everyone's half-eaten plate of this disgusting dish I hated. Mine was the only one that hadn't been touched. As bad as I wanted permission to get up and leave the dinner table, I knew it wouldn't look too good without me having not eaten even a bite of my dinner. I couldn't understand what was going on today. McGregor was mad at me, Luce had denied me my peanut butter and jelly sandwich, and now my three Haitian half-brothers were talking shit about me again; this time with McGregor's approval. I thought Frank and I had a bond through our listening sessions in his room, and now he was talking shit about me? I felt my temper boiling. LaDedra was the only one at the table aware of my violent outbursts. She was the only one at this table who had seen me in action. I can remember the entire room seeming to move in slow motion. That feeling had come over me. I could feel my eyes filling up with water as I bit my bottom lip. I knew what this meant.

I don't know what it was that made me focus my attention on my much older half-brother Jackson. As I stared at him, it seemed every word that came out of his mouth in Creole was directed at me. I don't know if it was because he was the loudest or because he was doing the most laughing. I can't really pinpoint what it was, but what I know is that in my mind, whatever he was saying in Creole was about me, and it was nothing good. Every time one of them would speak, the others would burst out laughing. I would look at LaDedra and she would look away. Before I knew it, I had gotten up as if I were walking toward the exit of the kitchen. I had to walk past Jackson and Ronald to get to the exit, but I hadn't planned to make it to the exit. I got up out of my seat with two eyes full of tears nobody seemed to notice and walked. When I was behind Jackson, who was still rambling on in Creole, I stopped and quickly wrapped my arm around his neck and applied the strongest chokehold my little eleven-year-old body could administer. I had learned to master this maneuver from practicing it with my cousin Jamie. He showed me how to get anybody to tap out with this chokehold.

As his body shook, and what looked to be foam protruded from his mouth, the looks on all the faces in the room went from surprised to concerned almost immediately. Jackson's body slumped down and fell to the floor. My sister Rolande let out a huge scream which prompted my father to run into the dining room area. "What the fuck happened here!?" my father yelled while kneeling down to assist his son now on the floor in convulsions. My sister Rolande said something to my father in Creole, and he looked up at me and cursed at me in his attempt to speak English. I was so out of it all I heard was "Fuck, fuck, muthafucker, muthafucker."

What snapped me back to reality was the smack my father had delivered to my face once he stood back up from making sure his son Jackson wasn't gonna die. "What the fuck Bwian, you almost killed him!" my father yelled at me. This was the first time my father had ever laid a finger on me, so I knew I had done something extremely bad. Every female besides Luce in the house was crying, including LaDedra. And now I'm crying because my father had slapped the shit out of me.

"I'm going to call Josephine and tell her to come get your ass and take you out of here!" he screamed. *Oh noooo*, I thought to myself. I had messed up during my trial period. How did I let this happen? Now I was almost certain I would have to move into Hynega Lake with my mother. There goes the sneaker connection. There goes the all the video games I would have bought with the fortune I would've amassed robbing St Ann's Church every Sunday. There goes the outdoor basketball hoop my father had in his driveway. There goes all those Hip-Hop records I had access to listen to at any time I pleased. I had messed up big time. I had once again allowed my temper to get the best of me and this time, I let it go too far.

After everything had died down, my sister Rolande had come to the foot of the staircase and yells out, "Bwian, your mother is on the telephone!" On my way down the steps, I prayed that my father and mom had spoken and my father forgave me and decided he would let me stay. This is what I was hoping for. I walked slowly to the phone, picked it up and spoke softly into the receiver. "Hey Ma," I said.

"What the hell is wrong with you, Brian!? Why would you choke the boy?" she screamed. Hadn't anyone told her this "boy" was almost nineteen years old?

"I don't know," I spoke into the phone. That was the absolute truth, though; I hadn't known exactly why I did it. All I knew was that my anger seemed able to control my actions.

"Well, your father doesn't want you staying there and when I come to pick up LaDedra, you gotta come back home too."

"Alright," I said.

"Are you okay?" she asked.

"Yeah, I'm fine," I replied.

But I wasn't fine. I knew in the back of my mind this upcoming school year would be my most challenging school year to date. I would be living in a place I was super embarrassed to be living in, I was being replaced as the baby of my mother's little bunch, and I had just had another outburst of anger I seemed to have absolutely no control over.

"Nobody was talking about you, man," McGregor attempted to explain as I slowly gathered my belongings to prepare to leave sooner than I had anticipated.

"If these dudes don't be talking shit about me, why are they always looking at me and laughing?" I asked.

"Maybe because they know you don't understand what they're saying. You ever see how uncomfortable they look while we're speaking English and they don't understand?" he replied. He had a point. They also seemed to hate not understanding the dialogue when we had been speaking about something. In my mind, I wasn't just blaming them, I was also blaming McGregor. He had been sitting with them today and feeding into something he knew bothered me. He had been treating me like shit the whole day. And then I get in trouble because he was playing two sides of the fence.

There I was again, looking to blame someone else for the reasoning of my own actions. Something I would come to do a lot during my life. Why did I just not want to face the fact I had anger issues? There was an underlying factor making *me* always lash out with violence whenever I felt even the least bit slighted? With me, it was always somebody else's fault. I needed to learn to take responsibility. This would be one of the hardest life lessons I've ever had to accept.

While McGregor and I were speaking, I could hear slow-paced, heavy footsteps on the wooden stairs that led to the attic.

"Luce is coming," he said as he jumped off the bed and sprang into action. He looked down at the pair of Michael Jordan sneakers sticking out from under the bed, then over at the Nintendo game system still hooked up to the TV, and then over at a new outfit he was sure Luce would spot immediately and identify as something she herself hadn't bought. It was too late to hide everything with her almost halfway up the stairs. We had been caught slipping. I ran over to try to unhook the Nintendo from the television as he yelled out, "Fuck that, hide that camera!" I had grabbed the expensive camera and wrapped it in a towel and threw it in a corner near the dirty clothes hamper. It blended in perfectly.

I had never experienced a Luce raid before that day, but in hindsight, it was eerily similar to being in a police drug raid. We scurried to find hiding places for sneakers, clothes and toys the same way drug dealers try to find places to hide drugs, weapons and other paraphernalia while the police are knocking down the door with a battering ram. We had managed to hide everything besides the Nintendo and a couple of other small items that were confiscated while McGregor was cursed out by Luce in Creole.

Everything was going bad I thought, and it was all my fault. I felt that usual feeling of being unloved, unwanted and unappreciated here just like I felt everywhere else I went. My own father didn't want me to live with him. My mother would let me go stay with anyone at any given time, so clearly, she didn't want me. The only place I felt loved was with Mama Sampson, and by then, her living arrangement had changed drastically. I felt something growing inside me, which would guide a lot of the decisions I would make over the next few years. I harbored a lot of pain at this stage of my life. I didn't know how to express it to anyone. I didn't even know what was going on. I just knew these would be probably the most important and formative years of my life. I would take my destiny into my own hands, by any means necessary.

"Brian and LaDedra, your aunt and mother are here," my little sister Linda yelled to us from outside as we sat, packed and ready to return to Spring Valley, N.Y. where my mother had found her new apartment. I guess my father was serious about me not staying with him because my mother was here and ready to take me with her wherever she was going. I automatically noticed my aunt in the driver's seat of my mother's new car. Just as I had predicted when she bought the car, she would never drive it and it would pretty much be Lorraine's car. This happened with every other car my mother had as well. After saying goodbye to Luce and the rest of my half- and stepsiblings I'd be leaving behind, I went over to McGregor to assure him I'd soon have his half of the money for the camera which was now stashed away in my luggage as soon as I made the sale. "Don't forget, that camera is worth a thousand," he said.

"I won't," I replied as LaDedra and I walked off to join my aunt and mother on our way to wherever.

We had about two days before we were officially scheduled to move into our new apartment in Hyenga Lake. My friend Chris Lowery couldn't contain his excitement about MY family moving to Hyenga Lake. What the hell was he so happy about? It wasn't him going to be teased every day. It wasn't him going to be fighting in school every day. All he knew was Chi and Gana lived there. At this time, I had no freaking clue who Chi and Gana were, and I didn't care. *HOW and WHY were they so important if they lived in Hyenga Lake?* I asked myself. Maybe our parents were right and something was wrong with Chris after all.

As Jamie, Caesar, Chris and I sat on the white wall in the front of the building we lived in on Bethune Blvd, Chris would attempt to explain who Chi Chi and Gana were. "Yo, they're mad fly and they got these two other cousins named Iris and Joanne, yo" he rambled. "I even heard they be fucking!" he said.

"Shut the fuck up, Chris" Jamie said. "I know Gana and she ain't fucking yet," he continued.

"I heard Chi Chi fucking though," Chris repeated. I didn't care about any of this shit. I was still thinking about all I had given up for choking out my older half-brother who hadn't even deserved it. Besides, I was still a virgin. It didn't matter who was or wasn't "fucking" to me at that time. "We gonna have mad fun in Hyenga Lake!" Chris repeated. What the fuck was he talking about? Hyenga Lake was hell in my eyes. I had a lot of figuring out to do because I wasn't going. I was NOT moving there, no matter what.

I had been calling around behind my mother's back trying to find potential suitors who would take in an eleven-year-old black boy with anger issues. This was one benefit of having a large family on your mother AND father's side. It left you with many more potential options to choose from when things like this would arise.

Just a few years earlier, I had been living with an estranged family member named Elka on East 58th Street in East Flatbush, Brooklyn. I was told this lady was my aunt and just dropped off there to live one day. This was another place where hardly anyone spoke any English. Elka hardly did, and her one son didn't at all. The only person who did was another older teenager who lived there as well, but he hardly ever spoke. While living here, my so-called aunt had become good friends with a lady named Florence who lived in Vanderveer Housing projects a couple of blocks away. Florence had a son named William who would become one of my best friends. William would introduce me to some things that would influence my life forever. Some good, and some bad; yet all valuable lessons. He would also introduce me to that one thing my mother hated more than anything in life: stealing and shoplifting. Don't get me wrong, I had shoplifted and stole little things with Jamie and my cousin Mister before, but with William, it was another level. William would also give me the nickname Catastrophe because of my ability to wrestle really well. Another thing I had learned from my cousin Jamie.

One day, before heading to the freight trains to steal boxes of cereal, William was explaining how we could join one out of two local gangs. We could join the Decepticons, a street gang which was one of the largest in Brooklyn, or we could be in a crew called V.I.P. that had started in his projects. I didn't like the idea of being in the Decepticons, because when I watched *Transformers*, I always liked the Autobots. The Autobots and the Decepticons were enemies on the cartoon, so me calling myself a Decepticon didn't appeal. When I decided I liked the second idea of being in the gang called V.I.P. better, I was told that I couldn't join because I didn't live in Vanerdveer Projects. He had just taken back an option he had given me only a few minutes before. This was William for you.

While we're walking around Brooklyn eating Frosted Flakes out of the box, I told him about the gang I had up in Spring Valley called the Black Sox. This was another name I had given to my little crew just a few years earlier. We went from The Prosecutors to the Black Sox. With my crew, the only thing that changed was the name. The name would change, but the members were always Jamie, Chris, Caesar, myself and sometimes Tyrone. We would alternate other guys in and out but these same members always remained.

As I'm ranting to my boy William about my old gang, he asked me who and what the leader of my gang's name was. Now at this time, to us, Jamie was the leader, but he didn't have a cool name or anything; it was just 'Jamie.' His one attempt at giving himself a cool name backfired horribly. He once decided he was going to call himself King Kool Silk. I told him that name was horrible, but he didn't believe me. He decided it was King Kool Silk and nobody would talk him out of it. He had written Kool Silk or just Silk on everything he owned. His bookbags, his Trapper Keepers, his lunchboxes and other school materials all had the name Silk tagged on them. One day, while Jamie rode the school bus to school with his bookbag blaring his new cool nickname 'SILK' tagged in big letters, he was approached by a small Chinese nerdy-looking kid. "You know this isn't real silk, right?" the kid said to Jamie.

"Excuse me?" Jamie replied.

"I notice you have SILK written on your bag, but it isn't silk. I don't even think it's rayon, probably polyester or cotton," the kid said while stroking the material of the bag.

"*I'm* Silk," Jamie uttered back with not even a speck of confidence in his voice.

From that point on, Jamie dumped the name Silk and opted to just use Jamie, or J, to be addressed. But while William was here asking me the name of the leader of my gang, I wasn't about to just say Jamie or J. I looked around at all the graffiti-riddled walls around us and looked for the coolest, toughest sounding name written on the walls. "His name is Kingsborn Ma Justice," I said.

"What?" he asked. I said it again as I read it off the wall, looking closer to make sure I was saying it right.

"Kingsborn Ma Justice," I repeated.

"What kinda name is that?" he asked. I had no idea what kinda name it was. Or even *whose* name it was for that matter. I just know it sounded cool. It sounded powerful. It sounded like somebody you didn't wanna mess with. "You gotta bring Kingsborn Justice or whatever his name is down here to Brooklyn one day," he added.

"I will."

Elka had picked up the phone on the third ring. The sound of her voice made the thought of wanting to live there go away as fast as it came. I would not go back there to live. I had hated it there. I hung up the phone immediately. I thought deeper. Would it be a long shot to call back and ask her for Florence's number so I could ask William if he could ask his mother if I could go stay with them in Vanderveer? I was really ready to try anything to get out of moving to Hyenga Lake. In my head, *anything* was better than Hyenga Lake. So, I dialed Elka's number again.

"Hallow?" the voice said. I waited for a couple seconds and hung the phone up again. I was still stuck with the same dilemma.

I went back outside to rejoin Jamie, Chris and Caesar sitting on the wall. "I'm telling you, I'm gonna get with Chi Chi when you move to Hyenga Lake!" Chris stated with confidence. In his mind, I was moving to Hyenga Lake and he knew it. This was the time I just decided I would have to accept it. I didn't want to, but it was time to. Damn.

CHAPTER 9

Watch Out For Your Friends

I could see the groups of kids gathering around as our large U-Haul truck pulled up to our small, little, broken-down dirty bungalow. This place looked worse than I had even pictured it. *Who could live here?* I thought as I stepped out of the truck, looking around the place. All the kids looked dirty and the place looked like it should just automatically smell bad. The one thing I remembered upon my initial observation of the place was there were so many kids there. I looked around, hoping not so to see a familiar face from school and I didn't, thank God. The school district we lived in prior to this didn't have a lot of kids from Hyenga Lake. I just remember the treatment of the ones who did attend, and it wasn't good, at all.

Another observation I had was these kids all gathered around didn't look as miserable as I assumed they would because of where they lived. These kids looked happy. They most certainly looked dirty, but they also looked happy. I wouldn't say this eased my mind altogether, but it was a step in the right direction. I was going to be living here and I would make the most of it. Or I would sleep on God knows whoever's couch again. Either way, my journey was continuing. I didn't speak to any of the kids gathered around watching us move in. I actually gave them the most mean and evil stares I could conjure up. Another thing I had quickly noticed was these kids, who were now blatantly staring at us, were all either white or Hispanic. I didn't see another black face in the crowd of kids now standing around. As I scoured the faces of the young Hispanic females watching us move in, I wondered if any of them were Chi Chi or Gana that my friend Chris Lowery always spoke about. We unloaded our belongings and got settled in our new place.

The next morning, I woke up earlier than usual. My first night of living in Hyenga Lake was officially in the can. It wasn't that bad, but it wasn't good either. The bungalow was rather small, and it definitely could use some maintenance. But this would be our home for

God knew however long, so we had might as well get used to it.

Me in Hyenga Lake circa 1989

I woke up immediately looking out the window to see if I would see the huge gathering of children who had been outside the day before. If anything, I was going to at least make some new friends here. Although I didn't see any black children out there, I was still eager to find some new friends.

I myself personally never had any kind of discrimination issues or qualms with someone because of their skin color; certainly not as a child. This isn't because I wasn't raised to be prejudice because my family weren't the fondest of Caucasian people. My mother's side of my family is from North Carolina and had still been living there during Jim Crow and segregation. They had also been living in the South during the height of the Civil Rights movement. My mother didn't actually dislike people for being white, she just didn't trust them if they were white. She would always tell us how we couldn't trust white people. She had it instilled in her they usually never meant well, and always referred to the Wolf in Sheep's Clothing ideology while describing them. Until that point, I had never experienced the blatant racism she had. Systematic racism, yes. I had attended the underfunded schools. I had been followed around a store by an employee pretending to be a shopper. I had dealt with that type of thing, but nothing really outright or blatant. Not until that point.

"You want to go outside?" I asked LaDedra as she left the small bathroom at the end of the bungalow.

"No, I'm not going outside," she replied. LaDedra hardly ever went outside regardless of where we lived. She was definitely an introvert who didn't care to socialize much. I actually asked the question knowing the answer already. Now that I was here, I really wanted to go see that nasty mystery lake I had heard so much about. I had heard many times that Hyenga Lake was named this because of a huge nasty dirty lake that resembled a swamp located directly in the middle of the property. Although I didn't want to be associated with this place when it came to living here, I could already tell that for a boy who loved the outdoors, this place would be extremely fun to explore.

As I walked outside on this early afternoon, I could now see up close why people didn't like to drive their cars into this place. The potholes were about three feet in diameter and up to a foot deep. I couldn't believe the size of these potholes. They were enormous! I noticed the red Chevrolet hatchback my father had helped my mother purchase driving up the shallow hill while dodging the potholes. My mother was inside our small bungalow so it was my Aunt Lorraine driving her car. This was my mother's second car, and if this was anything like her experience with her first, she wouldn't ever drive this car either. I don't know what my mother had against driving, but she hated it. She would basically buy cars and let Lorraine have them as long as she was available to drive her to run errands when she needed to. I guess even though my mother had moved out, the dynamic they had still remained. Maybe she even brought Jamie with her. We could explore this place together.

"Watch where you're going, you stupid bitch!" I heard a voice yell. I had heard it but didn't see from whom or where it had come from. I looked around for a source and still didn't see anyone. I noticed my mother's car had stopped. I walked toward the car to greet my aunt. *Maybe she had gotten stuck in one of those potholes*, I thought.

As I got closer to the car, I could hear my aunt's voice yelling loudly and screaming out expletives.

"You need to keep your little ass out the street!" she continued.

"Fuck you!" the voice shouted back. I could hear both voices from my standpoint, but I couldn't make out either of their faces yet. I walked faster toward the car to find out what was going on. Was that Jamie in the car with her? Where was this other voice coming from, I wondered. As I walked up on the driver's side of the car, I could see my aunt facing the passenger side, yelling out the window. For the first time, I could make out the face of a boy who must've been a couple of years older than me.

"What's going on?" I asked out loud as I walked toward him, sizing him up. I knew if he said the wrong thing, I was going to punch him immediately.

"This bitch almost hit me with her car," he said, still looking toward my aunt, not even seeing what was coming.

CRACK! Before he could even say another word, I had struck him with my fist across his jaw. The impact of the punch sent him stumbling to the ground. I immediately jumped on top of him and pummeled his face with multiple punches. It was my second day living here and I was already in a fight. As people noticed the melee, a crowd accumulated. Before you knew it, there were ten to fifteen people around either egging us on, or yelling for us to break it up.

"Get up, Jason! Get up, Jason!" I heard coming from the crowd. *So, this kid's name is Jason,* I thought as I continued to beat on him.

"Brian stop. That's enough, that's enough!" my aunt said as she pulled me off of Jason. "Get in the car!" she yelled.

I stood up and towered over Jason's body as I reminded him to 'never speak to my aunt like that again.' I gazed around the crowd with a grimacing look while making sure I caught eye contact with as many of the kids as I could. This was my way of letting them know the new kid on the block wasn't to be played with. Whoever Jason was, I had delivered my message through him. I knew this wasn't a good first impression overall, but I also knew if there were any tough kids out here, I had gotten their attention.

"What the hell are you doing out here fighting, Brian?" my mother asked as I held the ice on my swollen knuckles inside the bungalow. "You been here one fucking day and you're already out here starting fights!?" my mother yelled at me. She didn't seem to want to hear my reasoning for fighting. *I was protecting your sister,* I thought to myself. Before I could say anything to explain why I was fighting, my aunt interjected.

"That boy needed his ass whipped," she defended. "Brian was fighting the boy because he called me a bitch," she added to my mother. This made me feel proud. I was eleven years old, protecting my aunt, who was a full-fledged adult. I felt if I could protect my aunt, I could also protect my mother and sister. I was indeed the man of the house now.

"You better hope those boys don't get together and whoop your ass when you go back out there," she said. I hadn't thought of that. Who was this Jason guy? I did hear people telling him to get up while I was beating him up, so he had friends. I don't think

he had any siblings because nobody jumped in to save him. When my mother said this, I knew it was time to call The Black Sox. If the kids who lived here were going to plan to retaliate for Jason, they would have to take on me and my whole crew, including Tyrone. As I looked for the telephone to call Jamie and Chris, I heard a knock at the door.

"Who is it?" my mother yelled.

"It's Stanley Conklin," the voice replied. *Who the hell is Stanley Conklin?* Was this one of Jason's friends? Had they come back for revenge even before I could get any of my boys over here? My mother opens the door to find a short, dingy white kid at the door. "Can the new boy come outside?" he asked.

"The boy has a name," my mother snarled at the kid. I knew this kid showing up to my door wouldn't sit too well with my mother. As I stated earlier, she didn't quite trust white people. "What do you want with my son?" she asked.

"I just wanted to know if he wanted to come outside to play," he answered. I listened in on the dialogue between my mother and this young boy. I knew I wanted to go outside, but I also knew I had just had a fight. I thought about my mother telling me I couldn't trust white people, but my curiosity about that lake was stronger than my distrust.

Besides, Jason didn't look white. He looked either Hispanic or mixed. Why would a white boy knock on my door to avenge him? I moved closer to the door, so I could get close enough to see what Stanley looked like. I knew I would be able to look at him and tell if I could beat him up or not, and if I felt I could, I was going outside. I immediately lost any fear or worry of Stanley trying to set me up when I saw his small little white structure.

"Can I go back outside?" I asked my mother now standing between me and this boy.

"Get your ass outside and play, but if them white kids get you out there and beat your ass, don't tell me I didn't warn you," she replied. She stepped out of the way and I walked outside.

"So where are you from?" one of the white boys asked as we walked toward a broken-down basketball court that had rims made from BMX bicycle wheels.

"Brooklyn," I responded. Even though I had just moved from my aunt's house less than two miles away. I always referenced Brooklyn as my hometown whenever someone asked no matter where I was. Brooklyn had taught me most of what I know about street life until that point. Although I been raised in many other places, Brooklyn was home.

"But I have a lot family up here," I continued. By now, we had been joined by two other boys. Twelve-year-old Daniel Knowlton, and eleven-year-old Gregory Paul. As we walked toward the basketball court, I figured now would be the best time to ask what I had been wondering. "So, who is that kid, Jason?" I asked.

"Jason Enberg?" Daniel replied.

"The Jason I just had the fight with," I said in an aggressive tone. Stanley cut Daniel off before he could respond.

"Hold up, so you're the guy who beat up Jason today?" he asked, laughing out loud. Had he not known I was the same guy involved in the melee today? If not, why did he randomly show up at my door, asking if I could come outside? My mind wandered back onto the realm of this being a possible set up. Was this guy pretending to be uninformed to rock me to sleep? I had thought of what my mother said. She told me I couldn't trust these white kids and now I was feeling the same. I had been jumped before, so I knew with these kids, I could still win. I also had learned from William, Buttercup, Jamie and even Tyrone that a major part of winning any fight is having a mental edge. I decided if these guys were setting me up to jump me, I'd at least bluff them into believing it would be a bad idea on their part.

"Yeah, I'm the guy who beat him up, and my cousins are on the way up here from Brooklyn right now so they can finish him off." I bluffed with extreme confidence. "That was my aunt he cursed at, and her son is crazier than me," I added.

I knew my cousin was gonna come see me here eventually, and it wasn't any of my family from Brooklyn; it was my cousin Jamie who lived two miles away. Daniel and Greg looked a bit spooked, but Stanley maintained his courageous demeanor. "Jason is soft as baby shit," Stanley said in his hillbilly sounding vocal tone. "Cocksucker pops shit and can't ever back it up."

I had begun to feel as if I were in a movie or on a television program. Here I was about to play basketball with three white kids I had never met in my life; two hours after I had a fight with another kid I never seen in my life; one day after I moved into a place I had never been in my life. Things were certainly changing. As I continued walking with these kids attempting to establish my role as the Alpha of this group, the youngest of us, Gregory Paul, must've been reading my mind. We were probably only about one hundred feet from the broken-down basketball court when Greg asked, "Hey Stanley, you want to show Brian the lake?"

This is what I was waiting for. So, there WAS a lake after all. But did it look like a swamp? Was it as dirty as people had said it was? Were there really dead bodies in it? I was going to find out today.

"Hell yeah, let's go to lake!" Daniel chimed in.

"Say no more, follow me!" Stanley said as he about-faced and changed directions. Now I was excited. Long gone were the worries about these three little scrawny guys jumping me. Long gone was the thought of establishing my superiority. Honestly, I wanted Stanley to lead as we went into this terrain he seemed to know so much. I had become overcome with excitement and curiosity. Even too much to realize how far deep in the woods we were actually walking.

As Stanley led the way with Daniel following closely behind, I trailed Daniel and little Greg was behind me. I also knew from being in the streets that you're never supposed to be the last man lagging behind; especially when you have no clue where you are. Though I was past the paranoia stage altogether, I stayed well aware that little Greg was way too small to attack me and prevail. Even had he tried to sneak attack me, I knew I'd be too much for him.

"Do y'all come out here at night?" I asked almost certain they would say no.

"Hell yeah, that's when it's the best!" Stanley yelled back in his country drawl. Who the hell would come here at night? It was scary in the day. If the lake was anywhere near as spooky as these woods were, all the descriptions of this place were right. We walked about twenty more feet and there it was. A huge lake that resembled a swamp.

"I wonder if there's any fish in that bitch," I muttered.

"Hell, yeah, there is fish in that bitch," Stanley replied. "Bass, trout, stripe, catfish.... I wouldn't dare eat any of them fuckers though," he added while they chuckled and nodded in agreement.

The lake looked as if an oil spill or some shit had happened there. You could see old car rubbers floating along with other garbage. There was a beautiful silence about this ugly place. I thought about how it would be cool to bring a girl here once I knew my way around the place. "Let's show Brian the falls," Greg insisted.

"Follow me!" Stanley shouted back and off we were, back in single-file marching through the woods.

This huge dirty lake actually led to a waterfall that had a small dirty stream about thirty feet below. They called it 'the falls.' They each had their own story of a person they had heard of who had fell off the falls, only to land on the rocks and meet their demise. I could see how someone could get careless and easily get swallowed up by the current that lead to the waterfall. And down below was a stream where shallow water flowed through only being altered by the huge rocks that stood in its way.

SIDEBAR: Maybe 5 months after my first day in Hyenga Lake, while visiting from Newburgh, my cousin, Mister, would discover what appeared to be a human foot sticking out of the water. We reported it to Daniel's father who contacted the authorities and sure enough, they arrived and fished out the body of a naked white woman in her twenties. I guess some stories of the people who died there were true. But when they were telling me I thought they were just trying to spook me. Anyway, where was I?

As they went on with the stories and folklore of this lake, I was just thinking about how much fun I'm going to have living in this place. I thought about how Jamie, Chris and I would literally explore every inch of this place. Now Caesar, he would come with us most times we were out getting dirty, but this was a different kind of dirty. He was not leaving that mini-mansion to come down here. It was one thing to walk up the street and hang out; coming down to Hyenga Lake was a whole different ball game.

On our way walking out of the woods, I realized that my mother may have been wrong about these guys. Not only did they not try and harm me, but they were very cool, helpful and respectful. I could see myself hanging out with these guys again. Gregory even invited us all down to his little bungalow for some snacks and Capri Sun juice. My second day here was much better than I could've ever anticipated. I not only won a fight, I had finally seen the infamous lake and made a couple of new friends. The next step was getting Jamie and Chris here to show them our new jungle. I was surprised we had never come here before. Chris didn't even live that far away from here. That last thought led me to remember something.

"Any of you guys know a girl named Chi Chi or Gana?" I asked. Stanley immediately looked at Danny with a surprised look and they both burst out laughing. *So far, so good*, I thought. Hyenga Lake was something else. I liked it here already.

CHAPTER 10

Bulls vs Lakers

This must've been about the third or fourth time Jamie visited me in Hyenga Lake. I think he was liking the place more than I did. I hadn't lived there even a month yet and we had already swum in that dirty lake, played Run, Catch and Kiss with Chi Chi and Gana, built clubhouses in the woods and even started playing pickup basketball games there. Jamie and his guys would come down from Bethune Blvd and play against the team we had assembled at the lake. Jamie had dubbed the classic matchups, 'The Bethune Bulls VS The Hyenga Lakers.' Of course, his team was the Bulls and at this time, they had Michael Jordan, who Jamie emulated to the teeth.

He dropped about thirty points on us that day. We all decided after the game it would be a good idea to go across the street to McDonald's. We may have had

$2.00 amongst the eight or nine of us who went. While at McDonald's, Jamie had chatted it up with one of the managers. This manager was a tall, bald-headed black guy named Nate. After talking to Nate, he secured fresh warm apple pies for all of us with the $2.00 we had as a collective. He always was good at talking people out of shit, but this was a good play. As we all walked out, McApple pies in hand, Jamie walked over and spoke softly. "Yo, he told us to come back at 11 when they close and he gonna hook us up!" This was music to my ears. I had been staring at McDonald's every day since I moved to this place and never had enough for even a small fry.

"I don't think we should bring all these niggas though," I said in a tone as low as his.

"Definitely not," he confirmed.

Around 9:45 that night, we all sat around cracking jokes while the kids with earlier curfews fell off one by one. The only ones left were Jamie, Chris, Chris's cousin Daryl who had since moved from South Carolina, Stanley, and me. I noticed Stanley would be one of the last kids to go home every night. I didn't follow any curfew and Stanley would be out later than I was most nights. I had heard whispers about his father being abusive, but I had enough issues of my own at home to meddle in other people's personal issues. I was just trying to get people to go home, so there would be more of whatever Nate was going to give us. Nothing I tried seemed to work. No matter what I said or did to get guys to go home, or go do something else, it failed.

Chris's cousin Daryl was a smooth, laid back quiet type cat who didn't talk much. I thought it was because he was a Southerner new to being up here, but over the years, I would find out that was just his demeanor. Him and his cousin Chris were completely opposite. "What time is it, I'm tired as hell," I said, wishing a few of the guys would concur and decide it was time to turn in.

"I'm not," Stanley yelled in his strong redneck drawl. He was always the one who would emphasize his ability and willingness to stay up and stay out late.

"Yeah, I think I'm gonna go inside pretty soon," I said. It was only 9:56 P.M. and I was still figuring out a way to shake the other potential freeloaders. I knew Jamie could come inside my house; he was my first cousin. I knew Chris could come inside because even though my mother thought he was crazy, she liked him and was familiar with him. Daryl was his cousin and had also met my mother at this point, so him coming in would've been fine as well. The only two people who I knew couldn't come inside were Stanley and Daniel. Daniel couldn't come in because his cute, older sister Miranda would be calling him at any minute to come inside for the night. His curfew was 10 and if he wasn't in by 10, his dad would kick his ass. Stanley had no curfew, he just didn't have any melanin, and that was a bit of an issue with my mother. I wouldn't go as far as to call her a racist, but it seems like her trust issues started and ended with white people.

I stood up to walk toward our broken-down bungalow with my friends, including the white one in tow. How could I tell Stanley he wasn't welcomed inside my home? Never mind that; why wouldn't he just go home so I could kill this last hour and head over to McDonald's with my original crew and grab this food? All I could do was just imagine all the McDonald's fries we would have. *What if I even got a McDLT or something?* I thought. Back then, the McDLT sandwich at McDonald's was everything. It seemed like every second took a minute. The anxiety was killing me.

"So, what you gonna do," I said to Stanley as Daniel's sister began calling him out of their window. "What y'all doing?" he replied. I figured because Stanley didn't see Jamie, Chris and Daryl head towards Bethune Blvd, he assumed the night was still going on.

"I'm going in the house, I don't know what these guys are doing," I said. I could tell Stanley wasn't too thrilled about us separating. Either he knew about the McDonald's plot, or he, like any other night we had been hanging out, was reluctant to go home.

"Yo Brian, let me talk to you for a second," Jamie said. I guess he had also sensed that Stanley seemed kind of disturbed by us disbanding. We walked off to the side well out of earshot distance of the three others. "You think Aunt Jo will have a problem with Stanley coming in the crib?" he asked. Aunt Jo was a nickname many of my cousins called my mother. Her full name was Josephine, so Jo was just short for Josephine.

Jamie knew my mother's views and outlook on white people because his mother shared the same sentiments. They were raised together in North Carolina and had experienced the same injustices. My mother had been kind of standoffish with this kid just a few weeks earlier, but she also knew that every day since we had lived here, I had been hanging out with these same three white kids. She never said anything else negative about it.

"I don't know, honestly," I replied. "I really don't see why she be tripping on that kind of shit," I added.

"Well, I like the little nigga. I'll ask her if it's alright if you don't want to," Jamie said.

I had liked Stanley too. Although he looked and seemed like he could've been the son of the Grand Wizard of the KKK, I don't believe he had a racist bone in his body. It had become embarrassing that I knew any prejudices that existed, were coming from our side.

"Nah, I'll ask her," I told him. Now I was past the point of not wanting Stanley to partake in any of the food that would become sanitation if we weren't

there at 11:00 to retrieve it. Now I wanted my mother to see that not all white people were bad. Now it became a whole different agenda. "Yo Stan, come with us, we're going to my crib!"

"Who the hell is it?" my mother answered as all five of us stood outside the door. Our small bungalow was hardly big enough for the three of us who lived here and now here I was bringing four more people inside. Her tone let me know this might not have been the best of ideas. My mother was pissed about something.

"It's me, Ma," I answered loudly, trying to match her energy and also pretend her tone didn't worry me. It did. "Open the door!" I yelled as I knocked again. Before my mother could get to open the door, I asked the fellas to let me go in first to make sure she was okay with all of us being in there so late. I knew she wouldn't have an issue with Jamie or Chris even though it was 10:00 P.M. Besides, it was still summer and none of us had any school the next day. It wasn't the hour, it was Daryl and the white boy Stanley I was worried about. Daryl's quiet demeanor didn't win him any points with my mother. She had mentioned something prior to this night about him being "too damn quiet." But she tolerated him nonetheless because he was Chris's cousin. I could win her over on that one pretty easily. It was Stanley who would be the issue. Or at least that's what I thought.

My mother opened the door and I stepped inside. There was something I had learned from McGregor and how he dealt with his mother Luce that I had begun trying to incorporate with my own mother. Instead of asking for something and giving them the option to say no, you just pretty much laid out your plan and left it up in the air for them to let fly or shoot down. This was one of those moments I'd try it.

"Ma, me, Jamie, Chris and the fellas are going to hang out in the living room for a minute," I said. I purposely didn't mention Daryl or Stanley's name. I didn't want to volunteer any information that could've given her a reason to deny me. I could look at my mother and tell when she had been crying. Something was definitely wrong here. "Ma, are you okay, what's wrong?" I asked.

"Nothing," she replied. My mother was notorious for keeping her feelings bottled up. Sometimes I think LaDedra was the only person who my mother would share everything with. Although she was my mother's daughter, they were also like sisters. I knew exactly where I needed to go to get some insight on what was wrong with my mother.

"LaDedra!" I screamed out.

"I'm in here!" she responded. I walked toward the small bedroom we shared and stepped inside.

"What's wrong with Mommy? She looks like she has been crying," I said.

"I think it's something about the baby," she replied. "I don't think she thinks it's a good idea to keep it, but Lorraine told Mama Sampson, and you know Grandma don't believe in abortions so now Mommy has to keep..........."

As my sister rambled on, I totally zoned out. I had temporarily forgotten about my friends outside waiting for me. I forgot about the McDonald's plot. I tried to wrap my head around this new baby my mother was carrying. She had a hard enough time with just the two of us. She hadn't even gotten stable enough to where she could take care of us two without assistance; whether from the government or a family member. Although she kept a job, the wages were never enough to make ends meet. I agreed with my mother on this one.

As my sister rambled on, I finally snapped out of my spaced-out state. "So, I don't know what she should do. What do you think?" she asked.

"Huh?" I had missed most of whatever she had said.

"What do you think she should do?" my sister asked again.

"I think she should have it. I don't believe in abortion either," I said. This surprised my sister. I had been very vocal to her about me wanting to remain the baby of the family, but after the past few weeks, I guess I had a change of heart. I didn't want to be the "baby" of the family anymore. In fact, I didn't want to be a baby period. Although I was only just turning eleven, I was a grown man in my head. I drank, I smoked, I fought, I robbed. I did everything grown men did besides sex and pay bills. At that very moment, something shifted in me. That conversation changed my life. I was headed back towards my mother's room.

"I'm so excited to be a big brother!" I said to my mother. My mother had also known about my prior issue with this new baby coming. She had never ever heard me express not even an ounce of excitement about this baby. Now I felt the need to. Not only was I the man of the house now, I was the protector of these women. I gave my mother the biggest hug and headed back outside to meet my friends.

"She said no," I came out and said to these guys who had been outside waiting for me to return with an answer. "Fuck it, let's just go get some spray paint and tag up somewhere," I suggested. As we walked, I couldn't help but shake the thought of my mother being worried about her ability to raise another child. I reiterated to myself that if I could take care of myself, I wouldn't be a burden to her. This is something I would eventually become obsessed with. I began to obsess with not being a burden on my mother. I decided from this point, I would be an asset and not a liability to my mother. At only eleven years old.

As the five of us crossed the street at 10:53 P.M., heading toward McDonald's, my excitement for those fries and burgers returned. I was so hungry I could eat three of four cheeseburgers on my own. I looked around at how many of us there were and quickly knew the likeliness of me getting three or four cheeseburgers for myself was probably slim to none.

We entered to find the employees cleaning the machines looking eager to end their shifts. I could spot the tall, bald-headed manager Nate in the back, giving out orders. We walked in and sat at one of the tables waiting for Jamie to work his magic. We must've looked like the dirtiest kids in the world as we sat there with spray paint on our hands along with whatever other dirt we had accumulated throughout the day.

As I saw the last customer walk out, I wondered when Nate would come from the back to talk to Jamie now waiting at the counter. Nate walked up and gave Jamie a high five; I told myself this was a good sign. My excitement was steadily growing now. As Nate looked over to where we were sitting, I noticed him staring intensely. "Is that Stanley over there?" Nate asked. "Stanley, what is your little dirty ass doing in here, you know you don't got any money!" he shouted. Did he not realize that none of us actually had any money? How did he know Stanley... and why was he singling him out?

"Fuck you, Nate!" Stanley shouted back. "I'm with my boys," he said. Now I was confused as hell. Nate laughed and made his way toward the back.

"You know that dude?" I asked Stanley as he sat looking embarrassed.

"Yeah, man, that's punk-ass Nate, the McDonald's manager who thinks he's a tough guy," Stanley added. We all laughed quietly, trying not to ruin our chances of getting free food. As Nate walked back toward the counter, I noticed he had a hand full of sandwiches in Styrofoam boxes. He immediately handed one to Jamie and opened one for himself. He placed the other four or five sandwiches on the counter and returned towards the back. As Nate walked toward the back, Jamie looked at us and motioned for us to come over. We all got up and rushed towards the counter where the food was. I quickly grabbed a quarter pounder with cheese and munched. This was even better than I had anticipated! Nate returned with a tray full of small bags of French fries. *Awwww man, Hyenga Lake was doing me right so far*, I thought to myself.

Nate had now instructed one of the employees to lock the doors. McDonald's was officially closed and because of Jamie, we could hang out and eat free food in here after hours. I thought this was the best thing that had ever happened in my life. *Could we do this every day?* I thought. If so, I never wanted to leave Hyenga Lake. This was awesome.

We all laughed and joked while we ate. After a while, they unlocked the doors and we each headed to our respective homes to turn it in. As I walked toward my small bungalow, I could see Stanley walking slowly in the opposite direction of where he lived with his dad. I wondered where he could've been going and why he wasn't going home at this time of the night.

The next day I woke up to find my mother chatting with an attractive older Latina female. When I say older, that meant she was older than I was, yet younger than my mother. I walked up to see what was going on. "Hi, I'm China, I live a few houses down," she said. "I used to work with your mother," she added.

"Nice to meet you, China," I answered. I was just ready to go outside and play, but I was happy my mother didn't seem sad as she had the day before. I was also happy she found someone she knew who lived close by. We were both making friends and life seemed to be okay.

I headed over to pick up Daniel from his house. As soon as he came outside, I bragged to him about the free McDonald's we had gotten from Nate the night before. "Fuck that guy," Daniel said. I wondered how everyone knew Nate. Of course, McDonald's was right across the street, but why was everyone who lived here so familiar with this guy? And why didn't they seem to like him? The only commonalities they had besides them both living in Hyenga Lake, was that Daniel and Stanley were both white. Nate had said nothing remotely negative to either of the rest of us, but steadily took subtle little jabs at Stanley the whole time we had been in there. I first figured it was because they had a history. Now I was wondering if Nate also had a dislike or a distrust for white people.

"He seems like a cool guy to me," I stated.

"He's an asshole," Daniel replied. Stanley had called him a fake tough guy, Daniel had called him an asshole, yet he was nice to us. I chalked it up as Nate probably having similar ideologies as my mother with white people. Oh well. As long as he kept feeding us food we couldn't afford, he was alright with me. Whatever issue they had with him was their own.

***

'Keep on moving don't stop/Keep on moving don't stop no... Keep on moving...' I could hear Carol Wheeler's (of the group Soul 2 Soul) voice blaring from the two 12" speakers that sat in my cousin Dennis's back seat. I could also see the brand new white 1988 Nissan Sentra dodging potholes making its way towards our bungalow. "Yo Daniel, I'll see you later, I gotta go!" I said as I quickly made my way toward my house to greet Dennis.

Dennis was also my first cousin. He was the third oldest child of my Aunt Doshia Lee. Doshia Lee was the aunt who came with us to the hospital when I had stuck the bobby in the socket as a toddler trying to LIGHT UP. She was a bonafide church lady and had raised all of her kids heavily in the church. As soon as they were old enough, they all rebelled.

Dennis, at this time, was about eighteen- or nineteen-years-old. He had spent almost his whole life playing drums and other instruments in church, and now that he was of legal age, the only drums he blasted was Hip Hop music. I ran as fast as I could to meet Dennis. I wanted to see what new music he had and also show him the music I had accumulated from staying up late to record Red Alert and Mr. Magic on the radio.

Dennis was another one of the few who knew about my fascination with Hip Hop. One song, in particular, I wanted to show him was Special Ed's 'I Got It Made' remix. Special Ed was my favorite rapper. He had just edged out Big Daddy Kane as my top pick because I had walked past his video shoot in front of Erasmus Hall High School in Flatbush a few weeks earlier. My friend William from Vanderveer had brought me over there to see the video shoot. I didn't get to meet Special Ed that day, but I got to stare at him, wishing one day I would be in his position. That alone made him my favorite rapper, at least for the moment.

"What's up, lil cuz?" Dennis said as he stepped out of his new pearly-white Nissan Sentra.

"I'm chilling, man," I replied. Dennis and I had a very different kind of relationship. Because he was much older than I, he would sometimes get scolded for hanging out with me. It was not so much the age difference as much as it was the activity they suspected I was doing when I was with him.

My family knew since Dennis had stopped going to church, that he liked to drink 40 oz's of beer almost every day. And although he never got caught giving me beer, whenever he bought a 40 for himself, if I were with him, he bought one for me too. I had started drinking alcohol when I was around eight-years-old. Sad reality.

Although Dennis allowed me to drink in his presence, it wasn't him that got me into drinking. It was my Aunt Celestine's baby's father, Big Lance, who gave me my first sip of beer. I must've been around eight-years-old when my cousin Baby Lance Jr. and I were riding around N.Y. with his father in his sleek Black Corvette. He reached back and handed each of us one of the Budweiser mini cans they used to sell. Lance opened his and chugged as if he had done it before. I opened mine and as soon as I tasted it, thought it was the most disgusting thing I had ever tasted in my life. I finished it because I didn't wanna look weak, but I hated the taste.

I remember getting out of the car after drinking that can of beer and feeling a euphoria I was certain had come from that beer. It was the start of a very nasty habit. From that point on, if I went to visit my cousin Lance and found beer in their refrigerator, I would steal sips of it. It would be a couple of years later before drinking beer would become an everyday thing for me. It had gotten to a point where when I went to visit my cousin Lance Jr, I'd be showing up drunk already.

"Yo, I got two new tapes for you," I told Dennis. "Red Alert and Mr. Magic played some fresh new songs, and that 'I got it Made' remix is hot," I continued. Dennis didn't seem as interested as usual in the music today. Maybe he was just coming to smoke weed with my mother as they often did.

"Is there a girl in the house with your mother?" he asked. I was about to say, "Ugh, LaDedra" until I thought about the attractive Latina I had seen earlier on my way out.

"Oh yeah," I said. "There is some cute ass chic named China in there. Said they worked together before," I added.

"Yeah, that is her name, China," Dennis said. "I wanna bust her ass so bad." I had no clue what he meant by the term "bust her ass." Busting somebody's ass meant beating them up to my knowledge. I just shrugged my shoulders and kept on. "That new Queen Latifah joint is hot too."

We walked inside and I immediately knew what was going on. My mother was playing matchmaker. Dennis wasn't here for me or the music, he was here for this girl. This kinda pissed me off. I thought we would jump in that Sentra, grab some 40s and go to the park and bump some new Hip Hop. But he had other plans for this day.

"China, this is my nephew Dennis. Dennis, this is my friend China," my mother stated proudly. They looked at each other, greeted one another, and smiled. I realized I had run over there for nothing. I immediately headed back outside to look for Daniel.

On my way walking back towards where I had left Daniel, I thought about what Dennis could've meant when he said he wanted to bust China's ass. He couldn't have meant beat her up after the way he smiled at her. I was a bit confused. I made a mental note to ask Jamie about it later on. "Yo Daniel, I'm back," I said as I joined him to walk toward the broken-down basketball courts.

CHAPTER 11

Unhappy Meal

It was a week away from the first day of school and I still hadn't gotten any new school clothes yet. I wasn't even about to ask my mother for anything. I saw how she was struggling with the bills and could hardly put food on the table. Plus, she was still with child. Any extra money she had should go toward getting what she would need for the baby. I thought about the camera McGregor and I had stolen from St. Ann's church. I remember he said it was worth a thousand dollars. If I could even get half of that, I would be set for the whole school year. I was tempted to call him and ask if he needed me to come down and do another church heist. But then he would ask about the camera which I hadn't sold yet, so I decided against it.

I thought back to how William and my other friends in Brooklyn had gotten a lot of their school clothes. They would gather up about ten or eleven kids, head downtown or to midtown Manhattan, and just bum rush stores and take whatever they wanted. I had never joined in on any of their missions because I was afraid my mother would kill me if I got caught. I wasn't even living with her but her strong loathing for people who stole was strong enough to leave an impression on me. I had gotten many ass whippings in my life, but the one I got for stealing from someone was by far the worst.

I could remember this day like it was yesterday. I had walked over to LaDedra with supreme confidence trying to get her to notice the white-spiked belt I had been wearing. "Don't act like you don't see it," I said to her as she looked me up and down unimpressed.

"See what?" she replied. I pointed down at the white-spiked belt I had stolen from my friend Irving's house. Irving was a neighborhood kid we played with occasionally. His mother was a very sweet lady who would invite all the kids into her home and give us candy. On this day, I left with more than just candy. "Where did you get that?" My sister asked.

At this time, spiked belts were in style and every kid wanted one. They were a bit pricier than normal belts, so we certainly couldn't afford one. "I got it from a friend," I answered. Later that evening, we had gotten a knock on the door.

"Mommy, it's Irving's mother!" my sister shouted. *What the hell was Irving's mother doing at our door?* I thought. This couldn't be good.

My mother approached the door with a look of concern on her face. I could only make out small bits and pieces of the dialogue between these two ladies, but the little bit I heard let me know it could get messy very quickly. "Brian was the only one at my house," I heard the lady say. My mother vigorously defended me.

"My son doesn't steal, I ain't raising no damn thieves in here!" she screamed. I could hear my mother's anger growing and growing as this lady accused me of stealing from her house. "Brian, Brian!" my mother called out to me. "Get over here right now!" I walked to where the two ladies were now standing face to face with the door opened all the way. "Did you take a belt or something from this lady's house?" she asked.

"No, Ma," I said using my sad face, chubby cheek technique. My denial seemed to make my mother even more irate with the lady. "I told you my motherfucking kids don't steal. We may not have much, but I teach my kids not to take shit that doesn't belong to them," she added. At this point, my mother was furious and yelling loudly at the lady.

"What's going on?" LaDedra came in asking. All the yelling from my mother must've alarmed her and gotten her attention.

"This bitch is accusing Brian of stealing from her house," she said to my sister.

"What?" LaDedra replied.

"Yeah, you heard me. She said Brian stole a belt or some shit from her house." My mother didn't curse a lot unless she was really upset.

"Was it a white-spiked belt?" LaDedra asked.

"Yes, it was," the lady replied. "It is my son's belt." My mother immediately looked over at me. I knew my ass was in the hottest of hot waters now.

"Do you have that boy's belt?" she asked me. I didn't answer, I just stared at her like a deer in headlights. "Brian, I'm not going to ask you again. Do you have that boy's belt?" she repeated.

"Yes, he has it because he showed it to me today," LaDedra stated.

"Get your ass in there in there and get that belt and bring it to me," my mother said. As I slowly strolled toward the room to get the belt, all kind of shit went through my mind, but nothing more than the embarrassment I had just caused my mother.

As I walked back into the living room with the belt in my hand, I could hear my mother apologizing sincerely to the lady. "I'm so sorry, I teach my kids not to touch anything that doesn't belong to them," she said. At this point, the lady had a look of disgust on her face. My mother handed her the belt, apologized again and sent her on her way. When the door closed, she looked back at me and whispered in the softest tone, "I'm gonna beat your ass."

The beating I got that evening was so severe, it was one of the main reasons I had never joined William and the other guys on these shoplifting missions. But this was a desperate measure. I needed new clothes, and good ones at that. I was not only going to a new school but now I lived in Hyenga Lake. I couldn't actually be poor and *appear* to be poor. None of the kids who got teased at school for living in Hyenga Lake had nice clothes or shoes. Maybe that was it. Maybe if I showed up to school dressed in the latest fashion, I wouldn't get what I had seen other kids get. Maybe I could give Hyenga Lake a new image? I definitely was all for hitting these stores up this year. Besides, I lived back in Spring Valley now. We would be stealing from the stores in Brooklyn and Manhattan. Even if we got caught, my mother would probably never find out. I picked up the phone to call William. He answered and the play went into motion.

There were about fourteen or fifteen of us on the platform waiting for the A train. William had introduced me to a few of his friends and family from Brownsville who would be joining us on this shoplifting mission. I recognized one of them, a kid named Will G I had known from going to Yogi Bear. Yogi Bear was a bus trip that took all the kids from the ghetto to this place upstate for a fun day of activities. This guy Will G was a super troublemaker. As soon as I saw him, I knew this day would be one filled with a lot of mischief. I thought that trying to hock that camera might've been a better idea. I only cared about getting new clothes, so I was all in.

The look on the faces of the uncomfortable passengers who rode this train would be something I would remember for years to come. Women held on to their purses tightly. Other kids did everything to avoid eye contact with us. New York City in the late 80s was one of the most dangerous places on earth because of kids like us.

We jumped off the train at the Hoyt-Schermerhorn station and began to make our way toward the shops where we would all get new outfits for the upcoming school year. My friend William and Will G seemed to have had a lot of history as they spoke more than most of the others in this group of hoodlums we had assembled. "Tell ya boy the rules are to take whatever you touch," Will G said to my friend William, referring to me, I assumed.

We all quickly ran into what I believe was a Burlington Coat Factory and begin to ransack the place. William passed me a leather jacket that had to be three times my size, and I grabbed another one on the way out. This was like something out of a movie. Nobody was trying to be sneaky or take the traditional route of shoplifting. This was basically run in, grab shit, and run out. There were too many of us to chase, so security would be baffled. It was pretty much a foolproof strategy and way easier than I thought it would be. I was automatically hooked on this. We hit about five stores that day before we decided we had enough. This would become a very normal and frequent activity for a lot of us.

I jumped off the bus in Spring Valley with two large bags full of new clothes. I had traded the 3X leather jacket for a JV jacket with leather sleeves that actually fit me. Although the coat I made it out of there with was much more expensive than the one I traded it for, I felt it was a fair deal. I had about three or four hundred dollars' worth of new clothes in my hand, yet not a dollar in my pocket. I even had to borrow the four bucks from William to get from Manhattan back to Spring Valley. Here I was, an eleven-year-old child, walking on the highway with two huge bags filled with hundreds of dollars' worth of stolen clothes, yet not even $3 to take a cab.

I thought I was pretty set. I had all the clothes I needed to start the school year, and now all I needed was footwear. This could become a major issue if I didn't think fast. School was only two days away and I had no cool new sneakers to wear with the new clothes I had just stolen. Old sneakers with new clothes was always a reason for someone to go in with the jokes, so I had to avoid that. I still had that camera but hadn't found a buyer as of yet. If I could sell that thing, I most certainly would have enough to buy the sneakers I needed.

As much school as I would miss during a school year, the first day of school was a MUST to me. That day was like a fashion show. Some of the other kids would wait until the second week to bring out all of their new clothes, but not me. Their logic was they would wait for everyone to wear their new stuff the first week, and then come in and own the second week. I knew that I'd probably be already cutting school by the second week, so I was definitely one of the first-week guys. I had to figure this out fast. I had only two days left.

When I finally got to my house, I noticed the white Nissan Sentra parked out front. It wasn't unusual for Dennis to be at my house, kicking it with my mother. They were actually pretty close. This is also why Dennis felt comfortable drinking beer with me. If my mother didn't mind it, he didn't seem to care what any of our other aunts thought. Besides, there was no actual proof he was giving me beer anyway. It's not like I didn't know how to get it for myself, even at that age. It was nothing for me to stand in front of a store, wait for an older person who looked "cool" going inside, and ask them if they could buy a beer for me. For as many that would say no, there was always someone who would buy it. If that took too long, I would go down to The Parkers. The Parkers were a family who bootlegged alcohol out of their home. They would sell to anybody with the money, regardless of their age. I found ways to drink even without Dennis.

I took a page out of McGregor's book and left the two bags of clothes stashed outside. I was in no mood to make up a story of how I got all these new clothes. I most certainly didn't have any receipts for any of the items I had. A few even had the alarms still on them. William had showed me how to pop off the alarms, but I hadn't attempted to do it myself yet. As I walked in, I see Dennis and China sitting closely together on the couch. My mother was in the kitchen cooking and the house reeked of marijuana. I started to bother Dennis about those new tapes I had made, but then I remembered his disinterest that last time this girl was here. He just wanted to "bust her ass." I wondered if he ever had gotten the chance to bust her ass. They seemed a bit cozier than the last time I had seen them together.

As I begin to walk back toward my bedroom, I noticed a black and brown pair of brand-new Giorgio Brutini sneakers on the floor. Giorgio Brutini made some of the coolest shoes and sneakers of that era. If you had a pair of these, you were definitely showing out. I stared at the sneakers for at least forty-five seconds before the thought even came to my mind. I wouldn't say they matched perfectly with my new JV jacket, but I could most certainly pull it off. There were only a few obstacles in my way. For starters, the shoes were at least three or four sizes too big for me. That alone should have killed the thought right there, but it didn't. Second, as soon as Dennis was finished canoodling with this girl, he would get up, and put on his sneakers, and go home. Last, I had already asked Dennis if he wanted to buy the camera and he declined, so asking to trade for those sneakers would not only probably warrant another rejection, but it would put the fact that I wanted the sneakers on his radar. With the plan I now had in mind, I couldn't afford for him to know I wanted those sneakers. I'd be the main suspect if they were to ever come up missing.

No more than an hour later, there was a knock on the door. "Who is it?" Dennis answered.

"It's Jamie," a voice said from the other side of the door. The door opened and Jamie walked in with a huge smile on his face.

"What up, cuz?" Dennis said, offering his hand for a handshake.

"What's up, homie?" Jamie replied while shaking his hand. He then looked over to the lady now sitting alone on the couch. "Oh, I'm sorry, I didn't see you. I'm Jamie. How are you doing?" he asked with a smile.

"I'm China, nice to meet you," she replied. I could tell by the look on Jamie's face he was thinking about me asking him what Dennis meant by wanting to bust her ass. I could also see he saw why Dennis had even had those desires in the first place; China was sexy, but who cared? All I was thinking about was them damn sneakers.

"Yo, these Brutinis are fly as hell. Dennis, where did you cop these?" Jamie asked.

"I just got them today at the mall," he replied.

"Yeah, those are so hot," China chimed in. Now I was even more determined to get my hands on those sneakers. Not only had Jamie made himself the prime suspect if they came up missing, but this pretty Latina had said they were hot. That means the girls at school would think so too. I had to get these sneakers one way or another, and I only had two days to do it.

"Yo, Brian, let me holler at you," Jamie said as we walked away to leave Dennis to tend to his company. He got in whisper shot distance and asked softly, "You want to go back to McDonald's tonight?"

"Hell yeah," I replied. I immediately thought about the last time we were there and my excitement grew quickly. Now I had two things on my mind: free food and free sneakers.

"Alright, I'll be back around 10:30 to meet you," he added. "Don't bring Stanley this time, I don't think Nate likes him." We agreed, he left, and I immediately went outside to retrieve my stolen bag of clothes I had put next to the garbage for camouflage. This was another tactic I had learned from McGregor. He would say you could leave a bag of money near the garbage and nobody would touch it. Looking back, he was way too young to be so criminally advanced.

It was around 10:50 P.M. when Chris, Jamie and I started headed over towards McDonald's. The last time we had come for free food, we had all left with our bellies full. This time, there were even fewer of us, so we just knew we would all be going home satisfied again, maybe even more so than last time. We could see Nate in the back, giving orders the same as he had before. We headed over to the exact table we had sat at last time and decided to wait until 11:00 before Jamie went over to work his magic.

As an employee got up to lock the doors for the night, Jamie got up and headed towards the counter to talk to Nate. We could see them smiling and chatting and then Nate headed toward the back, just like last time. As he walked back with the five or six sandwiches in his hands, Chris and I immediately got up and walked toward the counter. It was almost as if we were dogs who walk toward their master when they see him/her filling up their bowl with dog food. "Where is the dirty cracker?" Nate yelled to us as Chris and I approached the counter. He was referring to Stanley. Now I was certain his dislike for Stanley had something to do with race.

As he lined up the sandwiches on the counter, he instructed us to wait before we touched any of them. I again felt like a dog being taught to be obedient. As bad as I wanted this food I couldn't afford, something about this whole thing felt wrong. We were practically begging for food that was going in the trash anyway. So technically, we were begging for trash. As we waited, I could see Nate putting on the same plastic gloves that the cooks wear. He then walked back over to the counter. "Which one do you want?" he asked, looking in my direction. I pointed at the McChicken sandwich in the Styrofoam container. "Take it," he said. I went to reach for it and before I could grab it, Nate quickly smashed the sandwich with his fist. He let out an evil laugh while he looked at me and disposed of the smashed sandwich.

"Three left, now which one you want?" he said, looking at Chris. Chris looked at me, probably only to see the embarrassment and humiliation I was feeling. He looked back at Nate and pointed at the Big Mac. "Take it," Nate said. Chris went to reach for it and WHAM, just like he had did to the McChicken I wanted, Nate had smashed the sandwich with his fist. He let out an even more loud, cynical laughter this time.

Obviously amused by his own mistreatment of us children, he continued on. "You little motherfuckers are going home hungry tonight!" he screamed out while looking at the two sandwiches left on the counter. "Only me and you left big man, which one do you want?" he said, looking in Jamie's direction.

"I want the...." before he could finish, Jamie grabbed the sandwich, ran to the door, quickly unlocked the lock and ran out of the restaurant. Nate jumped over the counter quickly in pursuit. Chris and whichever of the few employees watching us being humiliated stood behind laughing hysterically. Even though I felt belittled and embarrassed, I thought it was awesome that one of us decided we weren't going to be mistreated. That was one moment where my thought frame shifted permanently. I would never allow someone to belittle me again in my life. Especially not just because they had something I wanted. I would find another way to get it from here on out.

As I'm laughing to myself and coming to my epiphany, I hear the loudest scream I have ever heard from my cousin since I've known him. When Chris and I head outside to see what was going on, we walk past Nate walking back toward the restaurant smiling. "Ya'll better go check on ya boy, he fell somewhere back there," he said, pointing toward the back of the restaurant, which was pitch black. As we got closer, we could see Jamie laying in a small ditch with his leg bent like it was broken in four or five places.

"Call the ambulance, call the ambulance!" he cried out loud. Chris and I ran across the street to my house to do as such. Forty-five minutes later, the EMS was rushing him to the nearest hospital.

About 5 A.M., I left the Emergency Room that day. Jamie's knee was broken in multiple places and he was due to have surgery later that same day. They had to put all kinds of screws and pins in his knee to restructure it. Jamie's side of the story was that he didn't fall, but that Nate had pushed him. It was a pretty nasty injury, and all over a $2.00 fast-food sandwich. I really wanted to kill that guy Nate at that point. Now I could see why Daniel had said he was an asshole, and Stanley called him a fake tough guy. Nate had to be at least twenty-four or twenty-five years old. Who would get kicks out of treating some little kids this way? I wanted revenge. I also wanted to do something so I'd never be in these kind of positions again. I didn't wanna have to go beg for cheap food. I didn't want to have to steal clothes to go to school. I didn't wanna have to plot on stealing some sneakers three sizes too big for me from my own cousin. I hated being poor. I hated our living conditions and I knew I didn't want this for myself forever. I had to do something about it. I knew I did, and I would.

As I returned from the hospital and got closer to our bungalow, I see Dennis's Nissan still out front. This was very unusual for him to be here at this hour. Even if he had been drinking, he would always drive home.

It had to be that China was still over there. Had to be. As I walked up, I noticed the new rims Dennis had put on his car. In one day, this guy shows up with new rims, and those new Giorgio Brutini sneakers. I knew Dennis had gotten a little job to keep my Aunt Doshia Lee of his back, but I also knew what Dennis did to afford all of these nice expensive things he had. I had been with him when he dropped off the crack vials to the guys in the neighborhood who sold them for him. I had also been with him at times he had picked up wads of cash from these same guys. I had never spoken to him about the opportunity of selling crack for him. It wasn't my place as an eleven-year-old to be getting in a twenty-year-old's business ...or was it?

When I walked in the house, Dennis and China were sitting on the couch watching television and it smelled kinda musty. *Had he just bust her ass again?* I wondered. Before I could come to any conclusion, I again notice the Giorgi Brutini sneakers off to the side just calling my name. Maybe if I have this conversation with him about selling drugs for him now, I could have money in time to buy my own sneakers before school starts. On second thought, I realized that not only was school just a day away, but I couldn't sell crack without Jamie. I wouldn't have known where to even start. The Dr. said Jamie would be down for at least eight to twelve weeks minimum. What I didn't know was that the next eight to twelve weeks without him would also change my life forever.

***

I walked around my Aunt Doshia Lee's apartment complex twice. There was no sign of the white Nissan Sentra in sight. This meant Dennis wasn't home, so the only two people who could be there was her, my flamboyant cousin Tyrone, or both. Remember, Tyrone was my cousin who was on the feminine side but could fight like a UFC champion. I prayed he wasn't home because not only could I not stand the guy, but it would certainly make it more difficult to get the sneakers. He was nosey as hell and no way I could snoop around in Dennis's room without him noticing if he were there. If it were only my aunt there, she would more than likely be in her room reading the Bible.

I walked in their building and headed up the stairs to their apartment. I went to turn the door handle hoping the door was unlocked, but it wasn't. I knocked softly. "Who is it?" I heard my cousin Tyrone scream out in his deep yet feminine voice. I honestly wanted to turn and walk away right there.

"It's Brian," I yelled back.

"Dennis ain't here," Tyrone yelled from the other side of the door. He knew I didn't like him, so he would usually avoid me at any cost.

"I'm here to see my aunt, man, let me in," I said in a stern tone.

When I walked in, I seen Tyrone squeezing into a small-fitted velour jacket. This jacket was definitely not fashionable for men at this time, but him putting it on must've meant he was on his way out the door. This was great for me. "Hey, Auntie," I said as I pushed open the door to her bedroom. As always, she was in the bed reading her Bible.

"Hey, son, how are you?" she asked.

"I'm good, Auntie, how are you?" I replied.

"I'm good because I have Jesus in my life; you ever think about giving your heart to the Lord?" This had been a question I had heard growing up my whole life. Mama Sampson was the matriarch of this large family and she made sure that all her daughters knew about the church and God. "Come over here, son, let me read you some of this good word," she said while tapping a spot on the bed for me to sit.

Here I was about to let my aunt read the Bible to me before I steal something from her house. She read and the guilt inside of me grew. I pretended to be paying attention and then asked to be excused for the restroom. I made sure I stayed in there long enough for her to assume I was taking a dump. This way, she would forget she was reading to me, and I could sneak out of the bathroom and start searching for the sneakers before Dennis or Tyrone came home.

As soon as I walked in his room, I see nice expensive clothes sprawled out everywhere. Polo shirts on the bed, Guess jeans on the floor, even the most popular pants at the moment, a brand called Skidz that resembled pajamas. At this time, there was a rapper named Kwame, who was hot and had made wearing polka dots a trend. Dennis had polka-dotted gear everywhere! It looked like a department store in there so I decided to treat it like the last one I had been in a couple of days prior in Brooklyn. I grabbed a plastic bag I saw nearby and stuffed the bag with clothes. I didn't want to take too much, because it would be too noticeable, but I wanted to take enough and whatever would bring me the most praise in school. The good thing was back then, it was trendy to wear clothes that were four times too big so I didn't mind the big sizes. Clothes yeah, sneakers, eh?

Oh shit, I thought. That was it. That is what I had come for, the sneakers. I looked under the bed and there they were. The black and brown beauties China thought were "so hot," and now I had gotten my hands on them. I stuffed them in the bag, ran to the window, looked out, and when I noticed the coast was clear, I threw the bag three flights down onto the pavement outside. I walked out of the room and yelled to my aunt to ask if she needed anything from the store. It was very common for her to ask me to go to the store for her when I was at her house. "No baby, I'm okay," she yelled back.

"Okay, I'll be right back!"

I still felt the guilt while running downstairs to retrieve my stolen merchandise. I think it was at this point I learned that when the guilt comes in, one will start to foolishly rationalize with himself. I told myself it wasn't that bad I was stealing from him because eventually, I'd be selling crack for him, and I'd pay him back tenfold for stealing his shit without him even noticing I paid him back. This was my twisted logic. I ran to where I had dropped the clothes and went immediately into McGregor mode. *"You could put a bag of money next to the trash and nobody will touch it"* I heard echoing in my head. I grabbed the plastic bag of clothes, placed them next to three large barrels stuffed with trash and made my way back inside the building to my aunt's apartment. As I walked up the stairs, I could hear McGregor's voice again in my head. *"I stayed late at the church looking for the camera, that way I was empty-handed when I left and they couldn't blame me."* That was my gonna be my plan.

I stayed there and waited for Dennis to get home. Like McGregor had done at the church, I wanted to be there when he noticed his missing clothes, even *assist* him in looking for them if he wanted me to. This way, I'd never be suspected of taking anything. He arrived home about two hours later to find me sitting in the living room watching TV "Whaddup Cuz," he said as he walked in. I could tell Dennis had been drinking. This was a good thing for me I thought. When Dennis drank, he was always in a much happier mood. I was the opposite. I was a violent, angry drunk. But with Dennis, liquor and beer made him the coolest guy to be around.

"How long you been waiting?" he asked.

"I been here a couple of hours, bro," I replied. I watched out of the side of my eye as he made his way to the bedroom and turned on the light. I expected to hear him yell, but it didn't happen. The light turned out and he walked back out. I needed him to notice the shoes and clothes missing. He didn't. *Okay, I thought, all I needed to do now is make sure I leave with him and be back before the garbage man comes and I should be okay.*

"You wanna take a ride?" he asked.

"Let's go," I replied. We jump into the car and he immediately says, "I want you to hear something." He pushes play and a smooth R&B baseline comes on and a silky voice sings.

> *If you don't know, how I feel for you, it's time I let all feelings show......*

He was playing me a new single called "Closer Than Friends" by a brand-new group named Surface. I didn't want to hear this shit. *I want to hear some Hip Hop*, I thought as I bopped my head. Dennis was a music guy. He liked all kinds of music and had played instruments in church. I was 100% a Hip Hop guy. As we rode toward the store, going to buy some beer, I assumed, I figured now would be a good time to ask Dennis about that opportunity to make some money. He was in a good mood and about to drink more, so this was the time. Yeah, this was definitely the time.

As Dennis walked out of the store with two ice-cold English 800s in his hand, I decided I had conjured up enough courage to inquire about the position. As soon as he opened the driver's side door and sat down, I hit him with it. "Yo D, I was thinking, man, I'm ready to get some real money with you." It went silent for about ten seconds, which felt like a whole hour.

"What you mean, you wanna sell some crack?" he replied with a more serious demeanor.

"Yeah."

"Boy, Josephine would kick my ass if she knew I had you out here selling crack," he fired back.

"She ain't gonna find out, I ain't no fucking rat."

"Let me think about this one, Brian," Dennis said.

"I'm ready to start when you are," I concluded.

CHAPTER 12

Crack is Wack

I woke up bright and early, ready to face my first day at my new school since living in the fun hell hole called Hyenga Lake. I had found out a strategy so I didn't have to take the small little bus that the other Hyenga Lake kids rode to school. I would cut through a fence behind McDonald's, almost exactly where Jamie broke his knee, and cross over some train tracks that led to 2nd Avenue. 2nd Avenue was where Chris caught his school bus. Even though I would have to leave ten minutes early every day, this made it worth not having to be on that little yellow cheese bus for special kids.

I quickly grabbed the outfit I had laid out for my first day of school. I had some blue Guess jeans, a Ralph Lauren polo top, my JV jacket, and the oversized Giorgio Brutini sneakers I had stolen from Dennis. I literally put on five pairs of socks at one time to make my feet fill these shoes even a little more than they did. It would've been obvious to whoever had seen me in these sneakers that they didn't belong to me. It was even hard for me to walk without the sneakers coming off. I had not thought this through at all. I couldn't wear these big ass sneakers to school. But it was too late at this point. The only other sneakers I had were very, very ran down and would've ruined my whole outfit. I was in a super jam.

I called Chris and asked him if he had any sneakers I could borrow. He was in the same boat as I was. He had one new pair for the first day, and the rest were old and beat up. At least *his* new pair fit.

I left the house early enough to have extra time to walk over to catch the bus on 2nd Avenue. I couldn't walk fast or I would've possibly stepped right out of those sneakers. *This was a horrible, horrible idea,* I thought to myself. How would I get through the one day in school where everyone inspects what everyone else is wearing? Not only did these sneakers attract attention, they were clearly, clearly way too big for me. So, people would look down to see what sneakers I had on, notice how big they were, and start clowning me? Was this going to be my first day at a new school? It took everything in my power to convince myself not to play hooky on the first day of school.

As I slowly walked up 2nd Avenue, trying to keep my feet in these big ass shoes, I thought this day couldn't start any worse. I could see Chris walking down the block toward me. He had on a black Dickies suit with some fresh white Air Force One Nikes. Chris didn't come from money like Caesar, but his parents made sure he had the essentials. As soon as he got close enough, I noticed him looking down at my sneakers. "Damn, bro, what size is those shits?" Chris said laughing hysterically. "Them shits look like skis, bro!" he continued. I knew Chris always had jokes, and he was allowed to rank on me; he was my boy. I thought how mad I would be if this were just some random kid at school talking to me like this. Would my eyes tear and I bite my bottom lip? Would I get that mad? That would mean suspension on the first day because I would probably do something stupid.

As Chris laughed at the size of my sneakers, we traded jokes while waiting for the bus. Not even five minutes later, a little small yellow school bus pulls up and opens the door. "What the fuck is this?" I asked Chris. My whole purpose of agreeing to leave earlier and walk here every day was to avoid going to school in the little special ed bus! This defeated the purpose.

"Yeah, man, they played me, they got me in EH classes," he stated. EH stood for Emotionally Handicapped. In other words, Chris was in Special Ed classes and would be riding to school on a small little bus. Here he had been teasing me about my shoes being too big and he was in emotionally handicapped classes? *Some nerve*, I thought.

"We have to get moving!" the bus driver yelled out while clearly growing impatient. I would be the new kid, that lived in Hyenga Lake, getting off the special ed bus with the big clown sneakers. That vision didn't sit too well with me. "Yo, I'm out," I said as I made an about-face to head back toward my house.

"You ain't going to school?" he asked, looking surprised. "Nah, I gotta handle some business," I replied as I began to walk home.

On that walk home, with every step I took while those oversized sneakers almost slipped off my feet, I thought about how fucked up my life had been until that point. I wondered why God had made my life so hard. Why hadn't anybody wanted me growing up? Now, here I was, an eleven-year-old kid walking down the street alone in some shoes I had stolen that were way too big for me. On top of that, I had just played hooky on the first day of school and deep inside, I knew it would not be that big of a deal to anyone. Just like any other time, my mother would curse at me, tell me if I keep it up that the white man is gonna get me, then tell me 'go outside and get the hell out of my face.' That was her way of dealing with what was, in hindsight, me crying out for help.

There was a mindset developing inside of me I could feel and knew I couldn't contain. Especially if I had to keep living like this. I was caring less and less about my life. I knew I had a good heart. I knew I was a person who hated to see anybody going through anything bad. Whether I knew them or if they were a complete stranger. Mama Sampson had instilled all these good values, principles and morals in me, but my living conditions were forcing me to defy them. I knew how much my mother hated stealing, but here I was feeling like I had to steal. She couldn't take care of the children she had, and here she was pregnant with a new baby, and she was telling me not to steal? What else was I supposed to do?

When I did go to school, I was the kid who stood up for the Jamal Grants of the world. Jamal Grant was a fellow student in 5th grade. His family was obviously very poor. His clothes were always dirty and smelled of mildew. But this kid Jamal had the biggest heart, and was the nicest, sweetest kid you could ever meet. His shirt may have been dirty, but he would give you that dirty shirt off his back if you needed it. Straight A student and everything, but in the harsh world we live in, the bullies tortured Jamal. They relentlessly teased Jamal. The girls laughed at Jamal. Me, I was there to protect the Jamals, but I could never BE a Jamal and I knew this. I had to do something to change the way I was growing up. Nobody was going to do it but me.

I had made it home in time to go in the house, take off those big ass sneakers and put my raggedy ones back on. I had to be in and out of there before my mother woke up and noticed I wasn't in school. I figured I'd walk up to Dennis's house and see where we were at with the proposition I had made to sell crack for him. All I needed to do was avoid my aunt. As I was thinking of how I was gonna do that, I looked down at the Giorgi Brutini sneakers. I then emptied my bookbag and replaced the books with the sneakers. If I was going to go up there to talk to him, I might as well return his belongings. I would just have to find a way to sneak them back in. I wasn't about to just go in and confess. Even though I had stolen from stores a lot, stealing from a person didn't feel the same.

When I shoplifted a lot with my friends in Brooklyn, there was always some smart aleck who came along and reminded us that the things we're taking from these big corporations were minuscule to them. They would remind how the CEO's of these companies are multi-millionaires and billionaires and us stealing five or six hundred dollars' worth of shit from them is nothing. When I looked at it from that perspective, I didn't even feel like I was doing anything wrong. I was almost happy to be able to steal something from them. I knew it was against the law, but whose law? Man's Law or God's Law?

Stealing from people was different though. With this, you're taking from someone who might've needed whatever you took. Or may have spent their last dime acquiring whatever you took. It just never sat well with me. Honestly, I don't know if it just didn't sit well with me or if it was that ass whipping I got when I stole that white spiked belt from that lady's house. All I knew was I felt compelled to return those sneakers.

When I strolled up, Dennis was outside, putting some finishing touches on a wax job of his car. *Thank God I didn't have to knock on the door and explain to my aunt why I wasn't in school*, I thought. "Yoooooo!" I screamed out, startling him a bit.

"You scared the shit outta me, cuz. Whaddup, why you not in school?" he asked. I looked down at the beat-up old sneakers I had on my feet. His eyes followed mine as I spoke out.

"I can't wear these shits to school D, not on the first day." He laughed.

"Not on the first day, not on the second day, not on the last day," he joked. "Why didn't you tell me, man, I would've gotten you some sneakers," he added.

"I appreciate it, but I gotta get my own D, that's why I was asking about that other thing," I said.

"And that's why your here today?" he asked.

"Indeed." Dennis looked away as if he were contemplating something.

He continued, "Aight man, lemme finish this up and I'm gonna give you something." This was it. I was gonna be making mad money now. No more big dummy shoes, no more stealing clothes. Shit, I may even have one of these Nissans by the time I'm thirteen if I handled my business right. This is all the shit I began to tell myself when he agreed he would give me some crack to sell for him. I had just leveled up so much in my own head. *Watch when I come to school now,* I said to myself. All I had to figure out now was where I could catch a regular school bus.

"Yo, is Auntie upstairs?" I asked Dennis.

"Nah, she just went to work, but your favorite cousin Tyrone is in there," he said jokingly.

"You mean your brother from the same mother," I replied while laughing loudly. "I gotta go use the bathroom, D," I said.

"Go ahead, man, I told you he in there," he replied. As I walked toward the entrance, I wondered if Dennis would've still agreed to help me out if he had known I had his sneakers in my backpack. Hey, it didn't matter now because I was returning them, right? Besides, I would make it up to him by being the best worker he had. I was about to become the biggest crack dealer in NY. This is exactly what I told myself.

"Who is it?" the loud, deep feminine voice yelled after I knocked.

"It's Brian, Tyrone, open the door," I replied.

"Dennis ain't here and neither is my mother," he said with that flamboyant little funky attitude he had.

"I know, Dennis is outside, I just need to use the bathroom," I assured him. I could hear his teeth smack followed by the sounds of the locks unlocking.

"Your mother know you ain't in school?" he asked as I zipped past him making my way to the restroom.

"Mind ya business, Tyrone," I uttered back.

"My mind is my business," he snapped back. *Damn, I need to get these sneakers back in, get my work and get the hell outta here*, I thought to myself. I walked down the hallway toward the bathroom, opened a linen closet door, and tossed the sneakers in there. I felt redeemed.

Dennis had given me what he called a G bomb. It was $1000 worth of crack and I was to make $30 off of every $100. So, I would stand to make $300 if I sold the whole G Bomb. *"Depends on how hard you hustle"* was his answer when I asked him how long it usually took to sell one of these G bombs. I was starting brand new, I had no clientele. Jamie had dabbled in and out of selling it, but he was laid up healing from that broken knee. He couldn't help me. I decided I'd recruit Chris and Caesar to help me sell this and pay them out of my cut. However it was gonna work, I told myself this was the start of something big.

While I'm walking down the street with one hundred small bags of Dennis's crack in my pocket, an unmarked police car pulls up on the side of me and slows down to a crawl. "Hey, hey asshole!" the cop yelled out. "You hear me talking to you?" I could feel my heart sink to my stomach. I felt as if I was going to throw up. I had $1000 worth of crack on me in 1989. That's when those Rockefeller laws were depleting us, fast. Although this was during the George H.W. Bush administration, it was Nelson Rockefeller, a senator in NY who introduced these harsh laws back in 1973. They were handing out outlandishly long prison sentences for simple $40 to $80 dollar crack sales. In hindsight, can you see how truly unjust this was? $40 to $80 was worth eight or nine years of your life? How? That so-called "War on Drugs" was really a war on us. And here I was, walking down the street with a pocket of them. Not even twelve-years-old with a B felony in my pocket.

"Hey, what, are you deaf?" the officer screamed. I had just kept walking quietly because my voice was actually temporarily paralyzed by fear. I knew if they hopped out and stopped and frisked me like they usually did, I would be in some serious, serious trouble. I thought about running, but quickly thought against it. I would definitely run if they hopped out. I hadn't made a penny off of selling drugs and here I was about to go to jail for them. "Why aren't you in school, boy?" the officer in the driver's seat asked.

"My first day of school is tomorrow," I answered. Me responding seemed to put them at ease. They told me to be careful and sped off.

It took a couple of minutes for my nerves to settle. *I need to get these drugs off my possession*, I thought. I figured it would be safer to have the drugs in my shoe in case I did get stopped and frisked. I dipped into an alley and put fifty of the crack baggies in the bottom of one shoe and the rest in the other. It made it very uncomfortable to walk, but the comfort in my mind was worth it. I finally made it to my destination, which was my friend Caesar Dow's mini-mansion in the heart of the ghetto. I had called Chris and Caesar to meet up with me to go over our plan to take over the world via the drug trade. This first G Bomb would put us our feet, and we would never look back. My spew was convincing to say the least. I spoke with confidence about the perks and all the material items we would acquire by selling Dennis's crack. "So where are the drugs?" Chris asked.

"Oh, they're right here," I replied as I took off my shoes to retrieve the now separated G Bomb.

"What the fuck are we supposed to do with this?" Caesar said laughing uncontrollably. "We can't sell this bullshit!" he continued. Caesar had knew a little bit about the drug game because he had a big brother named Matthew Dow who had sold and used drugs over the course of his life. Matthew had exposed Caesar to a little more than he probably should've.

"What the hell are you talking about?" I asked while I examined the now-flattened little crack baggies which now looked like they had Elmer's Glue in them.

"You had them shits in your shoe!?" Chris asked also laughing. I felt myself getting upset.

"Either your cousin gave you that shit still wet, or the sweat from your feet fucked them up!" Caesar added. "That shit is gonna be hard to move, bro." I couldn't catch a break. I had finally mapped out my plan to make money and was already fucking up.

We had been standing on the corner of Fred Hecht Dr. and Bethune Blvd for at least three hours when Chris decided he wanted to leave. "We been out here for hours and ain't made shit," he complained.

"We made $30 actually, but that's Dennis's," Caesar said jokingly. "It's that bullshit ass work you got, man. We ain't never gonna sell that with all this competition out here," he added. There had been about five or six other guys on that corner selling drugs that day. Some chased the fiends while the others just waited for the fiends to seek them out. You could tell who had clientele and who didn't. It was my first day as a drug dealer and I hated it. I knew it wasn't for me. As I watched the other dealers out there pulling in loads of cash, it just suddenly dawned on me. I figured I could make twice the money in half the time if I just came and robbed these guys. I'd find a location to stake them out from, see who was making the most, and come and rob them once the sun went down. That seemed like the more logical thing to do. I wanted to share my sentiments with Caesar but decided against it. Chris had left so it was just us two out there now, not making a dime and looking foolish. "Yo, let me hear one of them raps you make," I asked him. He right away began rapping words to a song I had never heard before. I was in awe once again.

A couple of days had passed before I got the call from Dennis. "Yo, how we looking?" he asked into the phone.

"Good, good," I replied, knowing I was lying. I had had his drugs for four or five days and hadn't even made $100 yet. My plan wasn't to keep trying to sell them either way. They were obviously ruined anyway. Whether it was from being in my shoe, or him not letting it dry enough. Either way, I couldn't sell that bullshit. The ones we did sell was because the customer didn't have any other options. It didn't matter because I was going to rob a few of those guys anyway to pay Dennis back. Now all I needed was a gun.

I had gotten off the phone with my cousin Mister who was up in Newburgh wreaking havoc. I told him about my drug operation failure, and he immediately invited me to come back up there and work with him. His crack operation was a success. He was a thirteen-year-old kid making money hand-over-fist selling crack cocaine. I didn't call cause I wanted to sell crack, though. I called because I needed a gun.

Mister had advised me he had a newly-acquired arsenal of weapons stolen from Mr. Cole's house. Mr. Cole was an old man who would sit in his car all day on West Parmentar Street in Newburgh, NY drinking, singing and telling war stories. We loved Mr. Cole, that's why I was taken back when he said they had stolen the guns from him. But he advised me that Mr. Cole had actually passed away and they didn't go steal the guns until after he was buried. That made me feel a little better, I guess.

We must've reached Newburgh about 12:00 A.M. or something. I remember because everyone was outside enjoying the warm night autumn air, drinking liquor, smoking and chilling. I pulled up with Chris and a few other guys Mister didn't recognize. My cousin Mister didn't seem to like anybody he didn't know. As he grilled the other passengers in the car with me, I suggested they stay in the car while I got out and talked. "Who the fuck are those suckers?" Mister asked. "Where they from?" I knew my cousin well so him being inquisitive was expected. I wanted to get down to business.

"Where is the hammer, cuz? I wanna hit the road," I said flat out.

"In the crib, follow me." As we walked up the stairs to my Aunt Geraldine's beat down apartment, I noticed shit had looked a lot worse than when we were living up there. Newburgh was getting worse overall.

We reached his bedroom and he went into his closet and pulled out a big army bag. He opened it and there were a variety of shotguns and rifles inside. Some had scopes and some were pump action. He had some very nice hunting guns, but I was planning to do some stick-ups. I needed a handgun I could conceal, not a big ass shotgun or rifle. "You ain't got no handguns?" I asked.

"I got a .380," he replied. "But you ain't getting that because it's the only handgun I got." Damn, I had driven up here for nothing too? I just felt like nothing I did worked out. Nothing. I jumped in the car and we left. On the way back down to Spring Valley, I rethought things again. Maybe I should just try the school route or try to be more like LaDedra and just accept the fact we were poor and had nothing. Maybe I should just try the safe route: go to school, graduate and be an employee for the rest of my life. My life as a criminal didn't seem to be panning out. I couldn't even get a gun, for crying out loud.

As we pulled up to my house, I noticed my mother's red Chevrolet hatchback parked out front. Even though it was my mother's car, this meant my Aunt Lorraine was there. My mother still didn't drive the car. I was in no mood to see any family. I had had a long fucked up week that was about to get even longer. As soon as I walked in, my mother threw her shoe at me. "How dare you bring this shit in my house, are you fucking crazy?" she said. I had no idea what she was talking about. "You gotta get the fuck out of here tonight!" she screamed. "I don't want you here." I had no clue what she was talking about. "I will not be having this shit in my house! I'm pregnant and you're not gonna worry me to death, Brian!" she yelled as she began to cry. There was only one thing she could be referring to. The crack Dennis had given me that I couldn't sell.

I looked around to see if I could spot anything in sight and sure enough, I looked on the table and saw the plastic bag full of crack I thought I had stashed better. My mother hated drugs. My Aunt Lorraine had recently beaten drugs and hated them too. "Where the fuck did you get this shit from!?" my mother asked.

"That ain't mine," I replied. I then said the first thing that came to my mind. I don't know what compelled me to say this. It's almost like it wasn't even my own words. "Dennis gave me that to hold for him," I blurted out.

"What? Are you fucking kidding me?" she yelled. "LaDedra, bring me the phone!" she screamed out to my sister.

Damn. I had completely violated. Not only did Dennis not give me these drugs to hold, I had *asked* him for the drugs. He didn't even want to give me the drugs to begin with and I had persuaded him to, only to lie on him to my mother. I felt like a complete piece of shit. "That black motherfucker is lucky he didn't pick up the phone!" she shouted as she handed the phone back to my sister. I don't think my sister liked seeing me fuck up. She knew how smart I was. She knew how much potential I had. But she also knew there was that other side of me that made me my own worst enemy. A side that would come out more often than not.

I walked into my room to find all my clothes packed up. I don't know where she thought I would go, or if she even cared. But I knew it was time to go. I knew Dennis was also going to be upset with me. I knew my mother wouldn't try to get Dennis in any trouble with the police, but I knew this would probably cause a rift between my mother and her sister. Who wouldn't be mad if your sister's twenty-year-old son were giving your eleven-year-old son crack to hold for him? But this wasn't the case, and I should've come clean, but I didn't. I was just a certified fuck up.

I knew out of all my friends, the only one I could really count on for shelter was Caesar. His parents, the Dows, had loved me and were very, very comfortable with me. I told him I needed a place to stay for a few days and he said it was okay. I didn't tell him what I had done though. I didn't think I would ever be able to face Dennis again in life. We had moments before this where I thought he would stop dealing with me, but he never did. There was a time we had drank so much and I had gotten so drunk he couldn't bring me home so he snuck me into his house while my aunt slept. As soon as I got inside the house, I threw up all over my aunt's living room for about ten minutes straight. He cleaned up every bit of it and had me safely in bed before anybody noticed anything. Now look what I had done. How would this affect his and my mother's relationship? What would I say? "I got scared," he would've said.

"Well, then what would you do if it were the police questioning you?" And he would've been right. I don't know why I didn't admit to my mother that the drugs were mine.

At Caesar's house, things were a bit cooler. I had finally found a place where I could take a normal-sized school bus to school. This was refreshing, considering I had been missing a lot more school than usual because of my transport issues. Staying here was a whole different experience. Mrs. Dow cooked dinner every night. They had chores, a bedtime, and all kinds of normal shit I hadn't known much about. It was my second day going to school from Caesar's house and I felt okay for the first time in a long time. Other than the mess with Dennis, I had felt a brief sense of normalcy. As Caesar and I waited for the bus, we were singing this new rap he had written a few days earlier. Or so I thought he had written it.

'Never in a scandal and I'm never caught scheming, knew I was dope ever since I was semen/ Swimming in my Daddy's big nuts....' We collectively rapped as the bus pulled it up. *How did he come up with this shit?* I wondered. The school bus doors shut and we were off to school.

This had to be the second or third time I had seen this girl in my life. All I knew was it looked like she fell from heaven. I had never had a crush on a girl who wasn't from a television show prior to this. She was more beautiful than anything I had ever seen in my life. On television or otherwise. Her name was Nicolette Aiken, but everyone in school called her Nicky. I knew I didn't have the courage to say anything to Nicky, but whenever I would pass by her in the hallway, I would try to always do something for her to notice me. Whether I just blurted out some stupid words, shook the pair of dice I always carried around, or some other subtle thing. I would do anything to get some of her attention. I hadn't had a girlfriend until this point and was very shy with girls. My self-esteem was beyond low with those kinda things. I don't know if it were because I hardly liked myself that I thought no one else would like me or what; but with self-confidence or self-esteem, I had hardly any of it.

At one point, my self-esteem had gotten so low, Jamie, Caesar, Chris and I had made up a game to try boosting it. We would go to this packed mall with no money between the four of us. We would go solely to play what we named "The Self-Esteem Game." The premise of this game was simple. Whoever was up, could select another one of us to go and try to get the phone number of any female he chose within the whole entire mall; and whoever got the most phone numbers, wins the game. The catch was that the age, race, height, weight, etc., of the female didn't matter. It would usually start off serious, and end as a funny joke. Jamie would see a very heavy-set girl, or even an older woman and send Caesar or Chris over to try to get her number. To see some of the ways these women would reject us made it more fun than serious. I would always be the one to back out when I was picked upon. I don't know why I was so shy with girls, I just knew I was too shy to speak to them. Especially one as beautiful as Nicky.

On this day, Nicky would actually speak to me, and not just her standard hello she gave everyone. There would be some actual dialogue today. Every guy in the school was in love with Nicky Aiken, so I didn't feel too bad about my own crush.

She was like a celebrity in the school. Even the teachers admired her. I was walking down the hallway when I saw this beautiful specimen headed toward me. I was certain she was going to walk past me, but she started walking in my direction while making eye contact. As she smiled, I could see the deep dimples forming on her face. I was on a cloud. "Hey Brian, I heard you're going to fight Mike Boykin at recess today," she said, flashing that beautiful smile.

"Yeah, I am," I replied. She smiled even harder at me, winked, said "good luck" and walked off.

Mike Boykin was also new to this school. His family had just moved from Newburgh, so we had something in common. Other than that, I knew absolutely nothing about the guy. This was actually the first time I had even heard of any fight we were supposed to be having. I think I just said yes because that's what I thought Nicky wanted me to say.

Even though Mike was much, much bigger than I was, that didn't worry me one bit. Fighting was something I was very accustomed to doing. Hanging around Jamie, I had been fighting kids three or four years older than me regularly. I had already been on the child prizefighting circuit that my cousin Buttercup had put Mister and myself through since we were very young. I wasn't worried about Mike being bigger than me, I just wanted to know what we were supposed to be fighting over. *Did he even know about this fight?* I wondered to myself during the day. I didn't know and started not to care; I had told Nicky I was fighting at recess, and that was the plan. I hadn't thought about any consequences at all. What if got suspended? What if I got detention? What if I got my ass beat? None of that mattered. All that mattered was Nicky wanted to see me fight, and I was going to fight.

That day during recess, I stayed away from the basketball court where I'd usually be and played closer to the monkey bars. I was told that's where all the fights took place, so hopefully, they would be broken up before any teacher or staff got there. I looked toward the monkey bars and Mike and a few of his friends were already there. *Was this kid that confident?* I thought. Now I really wanted to fight. Now I had a reason. He thought he could beat me.

I get closer and see him standing silently. "So, what's up?" I asked.

"What's up?" he replied with a slight smirk on his face.

"Whaddup, what you wanna do?" I said. Before he could get out his rebuttal, I had cracked him over the face with an overhand right punch. I could tell by how bad my hand hurt I had done some damage. I had noticed Nicky standing around with the gathering crowd so I knew she was watching.

As I'm on top of Mike punching him repeatedly, I get grabbed up from behind by my collar. It was a male teacher who was much stronger than my attempted resistance was. "Break this up," he said as he restrained me. We were both brought to the principal's office and told we would be suspended. When the principal asked what we were fighting over, I had no answer whatsoever. Until this very day, I have no clue what we were fighting about. I wonder if Mike only wanted to fight me because Nicky had also asked him if he was going to fight me. This girl was *that* beautiful. She was my first official crush. Nicky would go on to feature in several popular Hip-Hop videos, even as a young teenager. She was a video vixen before there was even such a thing. She is one of the main girls in LL Cool J's video for *Doin It*. She is also the girl Frukwan of the Gravediggaz pushed in front of the train in their *Diary of a Madman* video. We remain friends until this very day.

The bus ride home from school was rough that day. Caesar and I were trying to come up with things we could tell his mother about why I would not be going to school for a week. She hadn't even known I got kicked out the house. He had suggested I tell the truth, but there was not a chance in hell. His mom thought I was the most-behaved child on the planet so how was I gonna tell her that not only did I get suspended from school, but I had also been staying there because I got kicked out of the house?

I'm sure my mother knew already because that's the number the school would've called. Luckily for me, my mother didn't know I was staying at Mrs. Dow's or she would've been called and told her about the crack she found in the house. My mother and Mrs. Dow weren't friends, but they knew each other, and knew their sons played together. That was the main basis of any relationship they had. Furthermore, if you lived on Bethune Blvd for even a day of your life, you knew who Mrs. Dow was. She was like royalty on that block.

"Why don't you just play sick for a week?" Caesar asked.

"You don't think she would wonder why I wouldn't go home if I were sick?" I replied. I wondered what my mother thought about me getting suspended. I was sure they had called her by now. In one week, she had found drugs in her house, and I had gotten suspended. I hadn't even hit my teen years yet and I was messing up to this magnitude. I'm pretty sure she knew she was losing any grip she had on me. I wondered if she even cared. I needed to call Dennis. I needed to apologize to him. If he would even accept it...

CHAPTER 13

Boy to a Man

My little sister Tyeshia Lorraine Sampson was born on March 31st, 1991. Even though I had been kicked out of the house by then, I stayed in contact with LaDedra. I would also call to talk to my mother occasionally to let her know that I was still alive. I tried to attend school as much I could so they didn't come after my mother like they had tried to before.

LaDedra was upset that my mother's new baby went from the hospital, pretty much directly to Aunt Lorraine's house. I think LaDedra thought this was the reason my aunt was so adamant about her not having an abortion; so, she can have the baby and give it to her. None of this shit made sense to me. My aunt had her own issues; she didn't need any more children herself. When LaDedra would rant about the problems going on at home, I would just listen, although I didn't want to hear about them too much. Did she not realize I had been couch-surfing between Brooklyn, Queens, Newburgh and Spring Valley for the past two years? The last time she had seen me in person, she cried all night and was afraid to go even go to sleep. Maybe she was worried for me, or even thought I would harm her or something. I had been out roaming and had nowhere to sleep, so I called my mother and begged to see if I could come home. My mother told me I could, but she didn't know I had been drinking Mad Dog 2020 from that morning, until I showed up at her front door that evening. I walked in the house stumbling and falling over everything. "Boy, are you drunk?" my mother asked. "Nah, I'm not drunk, I just had one beer," I said to my mother, slurring every word. LaDedra cried hysterically. All I remember was her asking my mother repeatedly if I was gonna die. This was the last time I had physically seen my sister, but we stayed in frequent contact.

I had lived everywhere besides back home since leaving Caesar's house. Mrs. Dow had never found out I had gotten kicked out of my own house, but after a few days of me not going school, she asked a lot more questions. Instead of me lying and possibly burning another bridge, I just decided I would leave on my own. Once I found out my new baby sister lived with Lorraine, I would try to go over there to see her.

Things had gotten a little different with my Aunt Lorraine after the whole blow-up I had with my mother. She wasn't exactly mean but she wasn't as nice and inviting as she once was. Once word got around that I had brought crack into my mother's house, a lot of my family members labeled me. There were about six or seven of the cousins who had that "bad apple" label in my family. And now, I had been added to that list. I guess the truth had eventually come out about why I had the drugs in the first place, because Dennis still hadn't been added to the list. I figured he told the truth about me asking for the crack, or maybe he just denied it. Either way, he wasn't on the list. Dennis had been in the church his whole life and had been on the street maybe, two years. Me, on the other hand, had seemingly been a fuck up in everyone's eyes since that blackout in July, 1977. The day I was born.

It took Jamie a while to get back to his normal, highly active self. The injury he sustained was much worse than anyone knew it was. It would be more than a year before he was fully active. His mother had sued McDonald's and the manager Nate on his behalf, so we all assumed Jamie would be entitled to millions of dollars. He used to assure me all the time that once he got his lawsuit money, that everything would be straight in our lives. "I know shit is hard for you lil cuz, but don't worry, I got you." Jamie would say to me. I believed if Jamie had any money, he would've helped me. I also believed if he hadn't gotten injured, our whole crack operation would've worked. Chris and Caesar were my friends, but they weren't the brightest bulbs on the tree.

Caesar was actually good for something, because by this time, I had learned from him how to put my own raps together. Once he showed me the format, I had it from there. I would write raps, and would recite them only for him. I called myself MC Precise and he assured me I was getting better and better with every verse. By my third verse, I thought I was a better MC than he was and he actually agreed. My rapper dreams were on the back burner for now, though. I was homeless, broke, and lonely, with no sense of direction. The only thing keeping me alive was shoplifting. Ironically, the same thing my mother hated the most.

I had joined a new crew out of Brooklyn called the Lo Lifes where what we did was steal, steal, steal, and then steal some more. The shit we didn't wanna keep to wear, we sold, and that's how we made money. It was normal for me to have on a $800.00 Polo sweater and not have $8.00 in my pocket. This seemed okay to all of us. We were the flyest broke dudes on the planet. As long as we had Polo on, nothing else mattered.

If you ask 100 Lo Lifes about the origin of the crew, you will get 100 answers. Some will tell you it started in Bed Stuy, some say Brownsville, Clinton Hills and so and so on. My understanding of the origin is that it was started by a guy named Ralph Lo and Curt Da Bu from Crown Heights. They then linked with a guy named Rack Lo and a bunch of other guys from Marcus Garvey Village in Brownsville. I came in on the Brownsville side. A guy I grew up with named Tasheem Lo knew I could steal really well and wanted me to join the crew. There was already a B Lo in the crew, so I became 2 B Lo. I hated that shit so I always went with B Lo anyway. He then introduced me to his cousin, who lived in Seth Low Houses in Brownsville, a young crazy mother fucker named Demell.

Me and Batman in Seth Low Houses circa 2004

I was very familiar with Seth Low Houses because during my couch hopping, I was living with a relative in an apartment on Osborne St, so I was practically in Seth Low Houses almost every day. Demell and I got super close, and once Demell and I got close, I pretty much moved into Seth Low and was staying there with our Uncle Don, Aunt Kathy and Demell's Dad, Woody, whenever he would pop up from running the streets.

Legend has it that the Lo Life movement was pretty peaceful until it made its way to Brownsville. It was more so just about the clothes and things at first. But once we got a hold of it, it became a much more aggressive thing. People would do anything to get their hands on some fresh Polo gear.

First, members were just boosting or geeing with nap sacks and booster bags. Then, us Brownsville guys started with the steaming. Steaming was the running in the store and just taking whatever you touch method. Will G had used the steaming method on our boosting trip in downtown Brooklyn years earlier. "Take whatever you touch." Those words would echo in my head for years and years after. First, it was just stealing, then it evolved into the robbing guys at knife and gunpoint for jewelry or Polo apparel. We just turned it into something totally different in Brownsville. I was there for every phase of that. It was how I was taking care of myself. I needed every dollar I could get, so if I had to act a little rogue to get it, so be it.

One tactic Demell had taught me to finesse a robbery was the playing victim method. He taught me this sweet tactic I would use repeatedly to rob people. First, you had to spot whatever valuable you wanted. (This tactic usually worked best with necklaces.) Next, you would size up your potential victim to gauge if you think you could beat him physically or not. This tactic didn't involve a weapon, so the potential of hand to hand combat was there. It hardly ever got to that, but it most certainly could've. Last, you had to be quick and convincing and that was it; this was your recipe for this type of robbery. After you complete the first two steps, you walk up to your victim with the most distressed face you can make, sometimes even with your hand by your waist. You'd walk up and ask, "Why'd you smack my little sister?" then punch them immediately and snatch whatever necklace they had on and continue, "If you touch her again, next time I'm going to kill you." If they don't fight back immediately, you will probably be walking away with a chain you took from a guy still asking who your little sister is, not realizing he's been had. I used this method around 8 or 9 times and only had to engage in combat once. These are just a couple of things I picked up on over the course of living in the streets. I had experienced all of this bullshit before I was even a teen.

"Hello," a deep voice said over the phone. "What's up, Cuz?" I spoke. "Oh shit, B! What's up, little cuz? Where are you?" Jamie answered. "I'm in Spring

Valley. I wanted to know if I could come up there and see my little sister," I asked. "Of course, man, I got some news for you anyway, hurry up," he said, sounding excited. I hung up the payphone and started walking toward Jamie's house.

My Aunt Lorraine had moved from Bethune Blvd. She had moved into a much bigger home in a much nicer neighborhood. It was also closer to where my mother had lived in Hyenga Lake. Maybe this is why they had agreed for her to take my little sister, Tyeshia. It was a much better environment for a child to grow up in.

I was super excited to see Jamie as I walked up. We greeted with a hug and tight handshake and just stood outside and talked. "Remember I said I had something to tell you?" he asked. "Yeah, what is it?" I replied. "Well, actually, I got good news and some bad news," he said. "Well, give me the good news first, I have been having enough bad news."

It had been a while since I had been around Jamie. I had been doing shit I knew he 100% wouldn't approve of. I had even lost my virginity to a girl ironically named Jezebel since I had last seen him. It was one of my worst sexual experiences to this day because I was freaked out that she had substantially more pubic hair than I did, so I assumed something was wrong with her. I still went through with it just so I could say I wasn't a virgin anymore, but it was horrific, and I wasn't about to share that with him.

"Nah, give me the bad news first," I said after thinking about my Jezebel ordeal. "The bad news is, I'm about to settle my lawsuit," he said. "How is that bad news?" I asked. Was this guy pulling my leg or what, I wondered. "Lemme finish, nigga," he said, smiling. "But, it's not as much as I thought it was and I can't get it until I'm 18." At this time, I was just turning 13, so he was 17. "That's only a year," I said. "I know, man, but now that I know it's there, it seems like time slowed up," he said in a more serious tone. "If that was the bad news, what is the good news?" I asked. "Oh shit," he said, seeming to forget there was some good news to share. "You remember Cosmo that owns the weed spot on White St.? Him and my mother are getting back together," he said with a smirk.

Cosmo was a guy who had owned the biggest weed spot in town and had also dated my Aunt Lorraine on and off since they were younger. I just didn't understand why Jamie thought this was good news, until he continued. "He wants me to run the weed spot," he said. Now this was a completely different story.

I immediately thought of all the opportunity that could come from Jamie being in that weed spot. Everybody in the whole town got their weed from this spot. "Word?" I said. "So, you're going to be there every day, all day?" I asked. "Yep, starting Friday," he said. I don't think Jamie realized I had been sleeping on trains, on couches, and anywhere I deemed safe. All the Polo gear I had on would throw people off. And because I always had a bookbag, people always assumed I was coming to or from school. In my mind, I was thinking, 'I will be there as long as Jamie is there; WE had a weed spot.' "Oh yeah," he said as I pondered all the opportunities. "There is some real bad news, Angela crashed your mother's car," he said. I didn't care about that, to me it was Aunt Lorraine's car anyway; she was the one who drove it. I shrugged my shoulders and went inside to see my little sister.

That Friday, I go over to White Street to see if Jamie had started his new position, and sure enough, he had. I knocked on the door only to see it crack the same way it would when I was coming to buy weed. When he noticed it was me, he removed the raid prevention bars and let me in. "Whaddup, Cuz?" he said with excitement. As I walked in, I seen two Jamaican, no-nonsense looking dudes sitting at the table bagging up pounds of marijuana. "Whaddup fellas?" I said only to get head nods in return. These guys didn't smile, talk or say much at all. Jamie must've felt the tension and spoke up. "This is my little cousin Brian, or B Lo," he said. They still hadn't uttered a word. I could feel the weirdness in the air, so I told Jamie I would be back later, hopefully when he was there alone.

That evening, I came back to White St. to find Jamie in there alone this time. "Yo, who were those dudes?" I asked. "That was Koola and R," he said. "Koola is Cosmo's son, and R is his partner," he continued. I had heard about Koola. He was supposedly a serious, no-nonsense type of guy. And from the way he carried himself, the rumors appeared to be true. "I don't think those guys liked me," I said. "Nah Cuz, that's just how they are, they hardly spoke to me," he said. I figured I wouldn't just intrude anymore and call before I showed up next time. At least to make sure these gangster looking dudes weren't here when I came.

I had been there for about an hour and noticed Jamie make about $300 at the door. "How much would you say this place makes a day?" I asked. "Yesterday we made about $2300," he said proudly. "And we could've made more, but we shut down at Midnight," he said. I noticed he was using the word "we" a lot. I wondered what his cut of all of this money was. "How much of that comes to you?" I asked. "Well, I'm just starting, so they pay me by the week," he answered. His response immediately made my wheels turn. "How much are they giving you a week?" I asked. "Like a G a week," he said. Now a G week for a 17-year-old wasn't bad at all. But when you considered what he made and the risk versus reward factor, I felt he was getting jerked around. "You ever think about selling you own shit out of here?" I asked. "Here you go with your bullshit, B Lo. I only been here a day man," he said. "I'm saying though, you said you could've made more money, but you shut down after 12 right, all you have to do is get your own weed to sell after 12," I said matter-of-factly. "Even if you stood outside to meet he customers," I added. Jamie didn't seem a bit interested in my idea. But I was. All I had to do was get comfortable enough around here, and if he didn't wanna sell his own weed, I would. I got up, gave Jamie a dap and then left.

A couple of days later, my friend William from Vanderveer and I were on the 7 train headed to a house party in East Elmhurst, Queens. I had another friend who had lived in East Elmhurst who would always tell me to be careful being over there at night. He claimed it was a racist neighborhood and they would do shit to Black people. We didn't care about that, there were girls there and the train was our only source of travel. So, here we were, 10 P.M. on the 7 train headed to Junction Blvd. When we got off the train, we noticed a couple of older white guys looking at us creepy. We were ready for any combat so we stared back. We began to approach them when one reached in his shirt and flashed a badge. "We're looking for Broadway," I said, thinking fast. "Beat it kids, we're on duty," he said. We walked away laughing and headed to the party.

As we were partying to the Jamaican songs, Super Cat's new hit, "Ghetto Red Hot" came on and people got rowdy. Just like with most house parties in the hood, a huge fight broke out almost immediately. I pushed the girl I was dancing with and put my back against the wall. If I got hit, it wouldn't be from behind. As I'm looking to make sure William is okay, I see something shiny on the floor. I couldn't tell what it was, but it was glaring every time some light hit it. I walked closer over to it and kicked it away. While people scurried to get out the door, threw chairs or just watch the action, I kicked the shiny item again over to where only I could get it, and quickly picked it up. When I looked at it, it was a beautiful gold and diamond-encrusted bracelet. I quickly threw it in my pocket and went looking for William.

On our way back to Brooklyn, I reached in my pocket and pulled out the bracelet. "Where the fuck did you get that?" William asked me. "I found that shit in that party, you think it's real?" I asked. "Hell no," he said. "You think anybody in there can afford some shit like that? That has to be at least a few thousand dollars," he said. I didn't know if he shot down the idea of it being real because he didn't find it himself and was hating, or if he really felt that way. He had a point about nobody in there looking like they could afford it. It was mostly full of kids around our age. I saw no one in there that looked over 18. "Let's take it to the scales tomorrow," he said. The scales were where we went to pawn the jewelry we had taken from people. "Indeed," I said.

The pawnshop guy had offered me $1,200 for the bracelet, so now, I indeed knew it was real. Instead of taking the money, I had opted to keep it. I hadn't been to school in about three days and now I had a reason to go. I jumped on the bus to Spring Valley, staring at my new shiny piece of jewelry. I wondered if Jamie would be okay with me sleeping over at the weed spot with him. He had told me Caesar and Chris were there all the time and Koola had no problem with them being there. He assured me it should be no problem. I couldn't wait to show them all my new bracelet.

As soon as I hopped off the bus in Spring Valley, I see a thousand dealers out there chasing crackheads getting their hustle on. This bus stop was like Crack Central. They had a small bar where crackheads would go dance after they got high and everything. On a good day, a dealer could stand out there for a couple of hours and sell everything he came out with. The only problem was if the Police saw you out there for more than an hour without catching a bus, they put two and two together and you were a target for an arrest.

As soon as I stepped off the bus, I saw a dealer I knew from the neighborhood. "What up, Brian?" he said. "It's B Lo," I snapped back. "I'm sorry. 'B Lo,'" he said sarcastically. "Where you coming from?" he asked. I knew this guy, but not well enough to be telling my whereabouts. "Near White Plains," I said, trying to avoid his small talk. I looked and noticed he had a nice bracelet on himself. "That's cute," I said, gesturing towards his jewelry. "But check this out." I showed him the bracelet I had on. "That is crazy. You hustling man. Where'd you get that?" he asked. "Don't worry about it, fam."

I said with a smirk. "How much you want for it?" he asked. "I ain't selling it." I replied. "I'll give you $1000 for it right now, just walk me to the crib," he said. I had just turned down $1200 for it. I honestly knew I was going to sell it eventually, but first I wanted to show off with it a few times. "No thanks, homie," I said confidently. $1000 was a lot of money back then. He didn't back down at all. "Aight $1500," he said. As hard as it was to walk away from $1500 when I was dead broke, I declined again. "I gotta go homie," I said, trying to act important. "I'll give you a .25 automatic for it." That stopped me in my tracks. "What's up? I got a brand new .25, I'll give you that and $300," he said anxiously. "Where is it?" I asked, smoothly trying to conceal my excitement. "At the crib up the block" he said. "Let's go," I replied as I followed him up the street.

The whole bus ride back, I had been anticipating showing Jamie, Chris and Caesar my new bracelet, but now I had something better to show them. The only issue I had was this gun had no clip, nor any ammunition with it. For this, I asked for the gun plus $500 and he obliged.

As soon as I got to White St., I walked up to the door only to hear a bunch of females laughing and joking while loud music played. This shit sounded more like a party house than a weed spot. I knocked and Caesar opened the door for me with a big smile. "Whaddup my Nigga?" he said with a huge grin on his face. "Why you didn't tell these niggas you can rap?" he said out loud. This pissed me off. My rapping was supposed to be our little secret. The only person who had heard any of my raps was him and my sister LaDedra. I gave him a look, and he knew to shut the rap talk down. "Who are these females?" I asked. "This is Shaconda and this is Celeste," Jamie said. "How ya'll doing?" I said. For some reason, even with no clip or ammo in this gun, I already felt like a whole new man. I felt more powerful than anyone in the room. I flirted with Shaconda for a while before I called Jamie and Caesar to the back room.

"Check this out," I said while I pulled the chrome .25 automatic out of my pocket. "I'm gonna go down to the sporting goods store and buy some shells for it tomorrow," I said. "Oh shit," Caesar said. "Where the hell did you get that, Lo?" he asked. "I just copped it." I continued as I then pulled out the big wad of money I also had in my pocket. They both looked at me like I was a whole new person. I was only 13, but I definitely had just become a whole new person. "Now let's go fuck with these broads. Whose is Shaconda? She kinda cute," I said with my newfound confidence. "That's all, you big dog," Caesar said. Damn I was a BIG dog now. Yeah.

Jamie had the weekends off, so this would be our new time to chill. The only difference was now, we weren't as broke as we used to be. Especially not on this day. I had the $500 from the bracelet sale and Jamie had his money from working the weed spot. It was time to chill. "Yo, let's go to the mall," Jamie said. I immediately got excited because that usually meant I was going to steal. But I remembered, I wasn't little Brian anymore. I was B Lo now. I had even changed my rap name from "MC Precise" to "Catastrophe." Who needed to steal with $500 in their pocket? Scratch that. Who needed to steal with a gun in their pocket? I thought to myself as Jamie hailed down a cab. "Take us to the mall," he told the driver as we all jumped in.

Jamie and I jumped in the backseat while Chris hopped in the front next to the driver. As we began our 15-minute trek to the mall, something just came over me. I had been sitting behind the driver and something inside me just said, *"Rob him"* and without hesitation, I put the gun to the back of his head. "Pull this fucking car over and give us the money," I said with my unloaded .25 to the back of his head. He spoke very loudly in Creole, which reminded me of my half-brothers. This pissed me off even more. "Give me the money or I'll blow ya head off!" I screamed.

Almost seeming like it was planned, Chris punches the driver in the face and rambles around in his cab looking for money. After he was struck, the driver jumps out the car and we all followed. I jumped out now pointing the gun directly at him. "I know ya muddah, why you do dis?" he shouted at me. I had a *Menace to Society* moment when he mentioned my mother. "My Mother?" I said. "Your Muddah," he repeated. "Give me the fucking money or I'll kill you." I screamed again. I guess, at this point, he figured I was bluffing because he walked over to the trunk and tried to open it. Did he have his own gun? I was ready to run until I seen him grab a baseball bat. He ran to the driver's side window and began swinging the bat through the window at Chris now rummaging through his cab looking for money. "Chill, Chill Yo Chill," Jamie kept yelling at this point. All I kept telling myself was, if I had even one bullet in this gun, I would shoot this guy. I didn't know why, but it kind of felt like I wasn't even myself doing this. We all disbursed and ran until we were out of breath.

When we stopped, Jamie looked at me like he wanted to kill me. "What the fuck is wrong with you?" he asked. "Do you know who that was?" he continued. "That was Renee, he used to live downstairs from us on Bethune," he said. I didn't recognize him from the back of his head or I probably wouldn't have done it. Who knows? But now I understood why he kept mentioning my mother. He knew both of our mothers.

Oh well, I thought, my mother had given me to the streets years ago. I had nothing to worry about, maybe Jamie felt he did. As long as Renee didn't go to the cops, I was good. That night I gained a whole new respect for Chris. He was READY without even a word being said.

I called Chris the next day and asked him to come with me to the Sporting Goods store to get some .25 rounds. I also needed a clip. Chris was about 15, but he had a full beard and looked much older. After getting rejected twice, we struck pay dirt and bought a box of 50 .25 rounds. They didn't have the clip that fit the gun, so I just bought the ammo. At least I would have one shot until I got a clip. I vowed to Chris that what had happened with that cab driver would never happen again. Even if I only had one shot.

The next day, I call Jamie to ask if that guy Renee had contacted his mother. He said he didn't think so. In my mind, we were all good either way, but this also gave me the idea to call my mother, too. I always made it my business to let my mother know that even if she didn't see me, that I was okay. I also sent her my report cards to let her know I was still going to school, and passing. That put her at ease. I liked putting my mother at ease. As I said, my mother loved me very much, she just was never good at expressing her love. "Let's meet up," I asked Jamie. "Aight, bro, but you gotta leave that gun in the house," he added jokingly. "No doubt," I replied. It sounded like a joke when he asked me not to bring the gun so I took it as one. "Meet me at Mini Mart," he said. I hung up the phone and began walking and thinking what Jamie had said: *"Leave that gun in the house."* Didn't he realize that I didn't *have* a house?

Mini Mart was another hangout spot where all the drug dealers, gangsters and hood rats gathered. On any given weekend, there would about 50-100 people in front of this small strip mall. Although people would get shot and killed in front of that place all the time, the business they got made it worth it to the Indian owners to keep it running. As long as we were killing ourselves, it was all good to them. They would shut down for a day while police investigated, and then it was right back to business. Our money was what they were after. Black Money Mattered to them. "You ready to go?" Jamie asked as the crowd gathered. "Nah. Let's chill," I said. I had the gun on me and Jamie didn't know. I also made Chris swear he wouldn't tell I had gotten these rounds for the gun.

Something always happened in front of Mini Mart, and this time I wanted to be there so I could make my own movie with my .25 automatic with one bullet. "This shit about to get hectic man, let's just go chill at White St.," Jamie said. *'Is this guy getting soft on me?'* I asked myself. When we were younger, Jamie was down for anything. I chalked it up to him getting soft. This wasn't a good thing.

As we walked back to White St. from Mini Mart, we spotted this crackhead walking from out of the shadows. "Look at this motherfucker," Jamie said. And that's all he needed to say. I quickly backed out my small .25 automatic and pointed it at the crack head who ran while I chased him. I got as close as I could and fired my only round into his back as he screamed and ran faster. Jamie and I ran the other way towards the weed spot on White St.

When we got in front of the spot, Jamie demanded I give him the gun. I declined and tried to walk past him to go upstairs. "I'm not playing, Brian, give me the gun." Once, I would listen to anything Jamie told me. But something had changed in me. I was becoming a fucking monster. "You shot that man for nothing," he said. "I didn't shoot him," I said, knowing I was lying. "I just wanted to scare him, Jamie, chill," I said. He bought my lie and we went upstairs.

"I'm starting to worry about you Cuz," Jamie said. "You been a little out of control lately." If only he knew some of the shit he didn't see me do, he would've definitely KNEW I was losing it. I admit, I honestly believed I was losing my mind. I didn't care if I lived or died, or if anyone else lived or died. Only people I wanted to live was Mama Sampson, my mother and LaDedra. Nobody else mattered to me. Not even him. I gave Jamie my word I would chill out to ease some of the tension he was creating, but I knew I had no plans to stop.

It had been about three days since I had been to school and I knew it was time to show my face. I contemplated whether I should bring the gun to school or not and decided against it. At least not today. While I'm in the cafeteria, I notice this light-skinned girl with braces and dimples I had seen a few times when I would show up. When I did go to school, I usually would hang out with Daryl, that was Chris's cousin. Daryl and I were cool, but all Daryl wanted to do was chase skirts every day. Since he had been up here from South Carolina, he had made quite a name for himself with the ladies. I didn't hang with Chris in school because he was stuck in the EH special class all day.

His class had more teachers than students. It was literally Chris, our friend Caesar and a guy named Todd Stephens in that class with about five teachers.

"Who is that?" I asked Daryl as she walked by. "Oh, that's Dawn Richardson," he said. "She's in 7th grade," he continued. "She thick as hell for a 7th grader," he said. Daryl was in the 8th grade at 15 because he had obviously gotten left back a bunch of times. He claimed it was because of his move from South Carolina. I also was in the 8th grade, but I belonged there. "I want that," I said to Daryl. "Actually, I need that," I reiterated. "She may be out of your league, B Lo," Daryl said, laughing. Did he not know I had just shot someone a couple of days ago? Did he not know the man I was becoming? No female was out of my league anymore, I thought to myself.

Chris Lowery, his cousin Daryl and me circa 1990

Not since Nicky Aiken a few years back, did I have a crush on a girl like this. I had had my little crushes, but nothing like what this was. I decided the best thing to do was write her a letter and take it from there. That day, while I was supposed to be paying attention in Social Studies class, I began my letter.

Dear Ms. Richardson, I hope this letter reaches you in the best of health....

This was the greeting I had seen on a bunch of letters I had received from my incarcerated friends and family. It always made me want to read the rest so I used it for my own letter. At the end of class, I waited to see her in the hallway and passed it to her.

In my letter to her, I had let her know that I had been seeing her around and if she was single, I'd like to get to know her. When I gave it to her, she smiled, showing me her braces and dimples as she took the letter from me. That was a really good sign. I was happy, yet anxious throughout that entire day in school.

At the end of that school day, while we were going to board the normal size school buses to go home, Dawn Richardson walked up to me and passes me a return letter she had written to me. I could see her pretty handwriting on the outside reading, To: Brian, with a smiley face next to it. Even though this was very 7th grade-ish of her, it made me ecstatic. I couldn't wait to read the letter. I got on the bus and yelled for Daryl. "Yo Daryl, Yo Daryl!" I yelled. "She wrote me back." And this is what sparked our teenage love.

Dawn and I would date for the next six months. We would do corny shit like take walks in the parks. We would go to the library together. She honestly was the only sense of normalcy I had in my life. She knew and understood my family issues, and she totally accepted them. I really thought she was good for me. I had missed the least amount of school days while I was with Dawn than I ever had before. And if we had done a survey of the baddest girls at our school, it was Nicky Aiken, and then Dawn Richardson at a close second. I definitely was a sucker for beauty, and Dawn was very beautiful. Everybody who knew me would say there were two Brians; The Brian when Dawn was around, and then the Brian when she wasn't around. It was literally like night and day. If there was a real definition of puppy love, this was it.

One thing that Daryl had said that was very true, was that Dawn was out of my league. She was so sophisticated for a person her age. I never let her see the violent side of me because I wanted to hide it from her to keep her. She knew how to speak so eloquently that I would sometimes avoid getting into deep conversation with her because I knew this 7th grader was probably smarter than I was. Honestly, my only issue with Dawn was she was a virgin, and she was intending on staying a virgin. It didn't even bother me until we hit that six-month mark.

Don't get me wrong, she wasn't a total prude. We would make out all the time at Margetts playground when there was nobody around. Margetts was an elementary school near her house. We would go as far as third base, but she would always stop me there and say she wasn't ready to go any further yet. Most kids in our school had had sex at least once. There were only a couple female virgins left, and Dawn was one of them.

One spring day in school, I notice an unfamiliar kid in the lunchroom with a big curly afro. He had about three or four girls at his table, laughing at every joke he told. I tapped Daryl on the shoulder. "Uh oh Playboy, looks like somebody is taking your spot," I said. "That's some new kid from Brooklyn named Jamal Barrow," he replied. "He is in Lakeside." Lakeside was a residential home for juveniles who had been in trouble and were too young to go to Rikers Island. Once I heard he was from Brooklyn, my curiosity piqued. Who was this kid? Daryl seemed a little jealous that all the ladies were on this Jamal Barrow guy. I had Dawn Richardson, the second cutest girl in the school, so I didn't mind it at all.

CHAPTER 14

What the Lovers Do

I don't know what it was that made her change her mind, but one night while we were on the phone, Dawn had told me she thought she was ready to go to the next level. She had been my girlfriend for a while, so the next level was her losing her virginity. I had also only had sex one time with that hairy Jezebel chic, and that was a horrifying experience so I was pretty much a virgin myself. I never told Dawn this because I wanted to pretend to be experienced. For guys, it wasn't cool to be a virgin or to have had limited sexual experience.

Her parents had been away along with her two older brothers, so she invited me over. We would laugh and joke and play board games for most of the night, and as it got later, we started to make out. We got to our usual third base, and I asked her if she was sure she was ready. She shook her head yes and we made our way to the floor. Jodeci's song 'Forever my Lady' was blasting through the speakers as we slowly kissed. I won't get into any details about how that night went because we were both minors and it wouldn't feel right as a man right now. Briefly, we made love that night. She didn't realize it was also the night I officially lost my virginity; the correct way that is.

After I got back to White St. that night, I was beaming from ear to ear.

"Damn homie, you cheesing like you just got some pussy," Jamie said. *Damn, is it that obvious?* I thought.

"I'm going to tell Dawn," he said jokingly.

Jamie knew how much I liked Dawn. He had also known her big brother and they were over protective of her. Jamie knew to keep what he knew of the "Brian who wasn't with Dawn Brian," far away from her brothers.

That night I had made one of the first major mistakes a man can make in a relationship, I shared some of the details of my time with Dawn with my friend Daryl. And he would go and do the dumbest shit in the world the next day.

That next day in school, Dawn came up to me crying hysterically.

"I fucking hate you," she said. It wasn't even like her to ever curse, so I knew something was wrong.

"How could you do this to me?" she said, crying. "The whole school, Brian? I thought you loved me." I had no idea what she was talking about at first. But it could obviously only be one thing. "I didn't tell anybody anything," I said. "Then how does the whole school know my business?" she said. Dawn had come from a very upper-class family, so any stain on her name would be a stain on the family name. "I hate you and I hope to never see you again," she said. *Wow*, I thought to myself. Those were some pretty harsh words. People finding out we had sex was enough to make her hate me? That bothered me, and then the other me came out. As much as I liked this girl, I wasn't gonna allow her to belittle me. I wasn't going to do it in front of anyone, but the same way I got her, was the same way I was going to officially lose her.

Dear Ms. Richardson, I hope this letter reaches you in the worst of health and your day gets worse as you read this...

I explained how if we were real, it shouldn't matter if it got out that we were intimate. And being she made that scene about it, I agreed we should split up. Let's be clear, I didn't want to break up. I was simply saving face and that was that.

Not long after Dawn and I broke up, I was back to not going to school, and honestly, the darker side of who I was becoming was enhanced by this experience. Because of this whole ordeal, now I didn't trust females. She had no reason to break up with me. I had told ONE person, my close friend Daryl and he ran his mouth. That was something I was going to deal with. Just had to make up another reason to want to fight him. It wasn't cool to be fighting over a girl or even anything that had to do with a girl. Especially with one of your homies.

A few weeks had passed since Dawn and I had split up, and I go to school only to find her walking in the hallway holding hands with the kid Jamal Barrow with the curly afro. By this point, she had learned the knowledge of who I really was. While we were together, I had done everything to hide my lifestyle from her, mainly to protect her reputation. I didn't want her to have the stigma of dealing with a "Bad Boy" who probably wasn't going anywhere in life. I had even started to come to school and everything for this girl. I had hidden the real me from her and she starts dealing with this guy who everyone knew was in a juvenile detention center? The nerve of this girl. I would just smile when I would walk past them because now it was more of an ego thing to me. 'I hit it already' was my attitude. Although I played it well on the surface, I still cared deeply for her.

One day, on a day I had cut school, of course, Daryl comes running up the street to meet us all hanging out outside of White St. "Yo, that nigga Jamal knocked

Dawn's teeth out in school today," he yelled. I thought I heard this wrong. "What did you say?" I asked. "Yeah, she ran up to him and said, 'You telling people you fucked me, Jamal,' and then smacked him," he said. "And then, Boom, he just tee'd off and punched her in the mouth." I almost couldn't believe my ears. I felt so bad about this shit. This girl hadn't been in any kind of shit like this until she started dealing with me, I thought. I had messed this girl's whole life up, I thought. "The craziest shit is they both got suspended," he added. Because everyone had seen her smack him first, they both got in trouble.

That night, I conjured up the nerve to call her to see if she was okay, she wouldn't talk to me so I chalked it up as a loss. I returned to school the next day only to get a letter from Dawn. She didn't deliver it herself, which I thought was weird. But when I read it, the letter said, 'If you really cared about me, you would beat up Jamal for me.' Did she mean the guy she was walking down the hallway with a few weeks after she had broken up with me? This offended me. I vowed to never speak to her again, and I never would.

The next time I would see Jamal outside of that school was in the XXL magazine while I was in solitary confinement. He was actually on the cover of the magazine. By now, he was going by the name "Shyne" and had been P Diddy's replacement for the loss of the late great Notorious B.I.G. I thought to myself as I laid there, 'Good for him. At least one of us turned out okay.'

As the school year was coming to a close, I was very excited about the summer coming up. I had started hanging out with a guy named Lesley Pierre who, like me, was very ambitious, but had the worst case of Attention Deficit Disorder I had ever seen. The one thing about him though, he was a hustler. He was actually a super hustler. This guy worked at Shop Rite, worked at an Exxon Gas Station, sold cocaine and turned on illegal cell phones, all at 15. He wasn't violent like me, but he wasn't a pushover either. Lesley Pierre and I hung out even more than Daryl and I, at least in school. After the whole Dawn ordeal, I fell back from him a lot. All of that mess was his fault, even what happened with Jamal I reasoned. Lesley was a lot smoother. He would come to school in truck Jewelry that made everyone else in school look like children. I had the rep of being wild, he had the rep of being rich and when people seen us together, they hated it. One day Lesley told me, "Before the school year is over, I'm getting the Ac." What he meant by the Ac was the Acura Legend. This was the car to have in the early 90s. When he said he was gonna get something, I believed him.

Although my trust for women was dwindling, I still was a sucker for a pretty face. One afternoon, while I was hanging out in this apartment complex called 244 in Spring Valley NY, I see a beautiful girl in a car with one of the guys I knew from being in the street. I noticed her looking at me, but she was with him so I wasn't gonna stare. The guy was my dude Amarr. Amarr was also a Lo Life. We had a decent relationship, it was cordial, nothing more, but that girl he had in that car was gorgeous. *"How this nigga get that girl?"* I said to myself. But Amarr, or Shapone Lo as they called him, was a fly dude. He had a main girl at the time named Melissa, so I wondered what he was doing with this pretty girl in the front seat. I wasn't about to hate though. I just spoke to him and kept it moving.

I don't know if it was by chance, fate or whatever. But two days later, while walking, I spotted this same girl who had been with Amarr sitting in the passenger seat of another car. We caught eye contact and she smiled. I smiled back and she motioned for me to come over to her. "You're Amarr's girl," I said as I stuck my head in the driver's seat of the car she sat in. "No, I'm Amarr's friend," she said. "Amarr has a girl." Now that this part was clear, I asked for her number. "What's your name?" I asked. "It's Lesly," she replied. I immediately thought about my friend Lesley Pierre and that reminded me he had given me a Motorola Startac cell phone earlier that day. I pulled it out and asked for her number again. It was a very big deal to have a cell phone back then. If someone had one, they were rich or a drug dealer; but not a 13-year-old child. "You got a boyfriend?" I asked. I knew myself and had made it my business to stay clear of girls who were involved. "It's kind of complicated," she said. As her friend came back to get in the driver's seat, I said my goodbyes and parted ways.

Lesly and I would speak from time to time, but after seeing her with Amarr, and then her telling me she had a boyfriend; I automatically thought this was a girl that couldn't be trusted, so I just went ahead with my life.

"Three more weeks of school and we're out of here," I thought as I sat in class. Part of my passing strategy was to make a strong finish at the end of the school year. I still wasn't doing any homework, but anything less than a 90% on a test was unacceptable. The work came so easy.

On this day, Lesley Pierre didn't come to school so I was hanging out with Daryl. As the school day was coming to a close, Daryl says, "I'm gonna fuck Jermaine Paul up after school." Jermaine Paul was a neighborhood kid from Fred Hecht Houses. Fred Hecht Houses was a small two-level apartment complex in the heart of the hood. This is where most of the action went down. But Jermaine had come from a very large family that was heavily into church. He wasn't a bad kid at all. Nobody in his family was. You could automatically tell his parents were raising them right.

I shared a chorus class with Jermaine Paul, and when I say this kid could sing, he could really, really sing. He made me realize how much nobody else in the class could sing at all. Not one of us. One day, the chorus teacher had everyone try out for the lead part of Tevin Campbell's song, "Tomorrow." Even though I was a certified active gangster in the street, I wanted this lead part. The teacher must've known what Jermaine could do, because she had him go last. Not only last, but directly after me. After he finished and got the standing ovation, I knew that was my last day attempting to sing ever again. I liked Jermaine. I liked him a lot. He was a very genuine guy. This is also where dumb loyalty comes into play.

"Why do you want to fight Jermaine, he's a cool guy?" I asked. I can't remember what his excuse was, but I remember it was senseless. Probably just trying to impress a girl. "I ain't gonna do it in school, but I'm going to take his school bus home, and when he get off, I'm gonna kick his ass," he said. Now I knew Jermaine had brothers and a bunch of cousins that lived right there in that apartment complex. No way they would just let some kid just fight their family and win, I thought. I knew he was only telling me because he wanted me to go with him. "You want me to go with you?" I asked. "Yeah man, just to make sure I get a fair one." I had zero issues with Jermaine Paul. I was cool with him and his brother Charles. But here I was going to make sure this kid, whose ass I wanted to kick because of the Dawn ordeal, got a fair fight. At the end of the school day, I kept my word and got on the school bus that went to Fred Hecht Houses and rode next to Daryl.

Jermaine had a look on his face as if he didn't understand why I was on his school bus. I think he knew he had a problem with Daryl, but why was I there? I had been hanging out with Lesley Pierre in school almost every day, not Daryl. I don't think anyone thought Daryl and I were close enough that I would make his problems my own. Deep down inside, I was hoping Jermaine kicked his ass for what he had done.

The bus stopped, Daryl followed Jermaine off the bus and they got right to it. Daryl swung and missed and Jermaine grabbed him and they fell to the floor. People started to quickly crowd around so I started to be a little aggressive telling everyone to back up and that it would remain a fair fight. Not even a half-second later, Jermaine's sister Crystal had jumped on top of Daryl and began to punch him in his face. Without even thinking, I kicked her off of him with all of my might. When I heard the scream that had come out of Crystal, I knew I had fucked up, badly. "What the fuck did I just do?" I thought as I picked up Daryl so we could run away. At this point, everyone was tending to Crystal, and we ran away.

I knew I was in deep shit, so I did something I hadn't done in a few months. I went home to my mother's house. She was surprised to see me, but I needed to tell her what I had done. I knew it was only a matter of time before the police came to her house; and I didn't want her to be worried. As I'm explaining to my mother all that happened, I get that Police knock on the door. "Who is it?" My mother asked as if she didn't know. "It's the Police," a deep voice answered. "Let me get my coat." My mother said to me before even answering the door. She knew she was about to take that ride with me.

After fingerprinting me and giving me my assault charge, they released me to my mother's custody because they knew I had school the next day. The school couldn't punish anybody because the fight had taken place after everyone was off the bus. We had learned that trick early on.

After the silent cab ride home with my mother, I jumped out, kissed her on the cheek and headed to White St to meet Jamie and the crew. Everyone had known what happened by the time I got there. Daryl hadn't even been arrested. I just got a charge over a dude who made me lose my first girlfriend. I really wanted to kick his ass now. Today, Koola was there and this was the first time we had any actual dialogue. He said, "I respect you for what you did, you should've kicked that bitch's eye out." Wait. *What*? This was a female. I had only did it because it was a reflex. I wasn't proud I hurt a girl. I knew Jamie had a decent relationship with the family and I had actually come there to ask him to accompany me to go apologize. "No doubt," I said to Koola. A ton of potential respect I could've had for him, went right out the window.

"Yo, Jamie, you think you could walk with me up to Fred Hecht to try to apologize to that girl?" I asked. "I don't know them like that, but I'll go with you," he replied. "What the fuck is wrong with you Lo, you been chilling lately," he added. "I know," I uttered, "I feel like shit."

As Jamie and I were walking toward Fred Hecht, I noticed a guy who I heard had been talking shit about me. A guy named Jerime Ikner. Right away, I had totally forgot about the mission I was on to hopefully try and fix the mess I made, and I was right back in me mode. "Yo, isn't that the nigga Jerime right there?" I asked Jamie. "C'mon man, now ain't the time for that shit B," he said. "Fuck that," I said. "I'm fucking him up." I blurted out and dashed across the street like a dog off a leash to attack him. Jerime tried to fight back, but I was too much for him. I had punched him several times before I threw him to the floor. When he tried to get up, I kicked him in his face as hard as I could. This was like deja vu on the same day. He had let out a scream reminiscent of the one Crystal had let out earlier. At that point, Jamie and I quickly ran down the street.

When we got to the weed spot, Jamie grabbed me by my collar and hemmed me up against the wall.

"What the fuck is your problem, nigga?" he asked. "You wanna go to jail?" he continued. "Yo, you better get the fuck off me," I said, trying to sound intimidating, but Jamie wasn't scared of me. "What you gonna do?" he said. "You gonna shoot me, you gonna fuck me up, you gonna kick me in the face like you did that girl?" he said.

That let me know Jamie was really mad. He hit below the belt. The person I had kicked last was a guy who was older than me, but here he was making me feel guiltier for something I already felt guilty for. "Give me my gun, I'm out of here," I said after he let go of me. "You can go, but you ain't leaving with that gun," he said. I went to take a piss, opened the door and slammed it on the way out.

When I got outside, there were two plainclothes cops and three uniformed cops on their way into the building. "Brian Carenard, turn around and put your hands behind your back," one officer demanded. I could see Jamie looking out the window, I knew he wasn't going to come out of the weed spot. They put me in the car and drove me back to the same exact precinct I had just left hours earlier.

After they processed me, I could hear them on the phone with my mother explaining this wasn't a mistake and I had a whole brand-new charge from that same day. This time when my mother came to get me, she had tears in her eyes. The only thing that made me cry, unless they were tears of rage, was seeing my mother cry. I started crying as we took another silent cab ride home from the precinct.

I stayed home that night instead of going back out. I knew my mother liked it better when I was home, especially now. Also, I couldn't afford to run into another problem and get arrested for a third time that day. I would also make sure I went to school from her house the next day, even if I had to ride that small little bus. I needed to make my mother happy somehow and I would do whatever.

After I stepped off the little, small bus from Hyenga Lake, I walked into the school feeling bad about the whole Crystal ordeal. I wondered if she was okay enough to come to school. I wondered would Jermaine be in school. Would I have to fight him today? My life was out of control and I hadn't even made 14 yet.

As soon as I stepped inside the school, I felt a whole different energy. People were staring at me; guys were giving me approval nods. I had done some terrible shit, why was everyone acting like I was a hero? I found Lesley Pierre and he says, "Bro, you got arrested twice yesterday?" and starts with his funny laugh. "Yeah, how'd you know?" I asked. "Everybody knows, that's the talk of the whole school," he said. So that's why everyone was treating me like this. This wasn't good for me. I expected to be shamed and ridiculed. I had kicked a female. I expected to be hung, and rightfully deserving. But it was the opposite. It seemed even the teachers were treating me differently. I even think Nicky Aiken smiled at me. This kind of admiration for getting in trouble was not what I needed. Not with a mind like mine. Fast forward two decades later and I'm smiling ear to ear watching Jermaine Paul being crowned the winner of NBC's hit TV show "The Voice" after doing a near perfect rendition of R Kelly's hit song "I Believe I Can Fly." As I'm watching, I reflect back to our competition in chorus class and the day I had the incident with him and his sister. I reached out and we reconciled and became great friends all over again, even recorded a couple of great songs together. Now let me get back to my story.

    I ran off the school bus and up the stairs to the door at White St. I had to use the bathroom bad and was holding it all day. I had a rule about not taking a shit at school. If you did, and someone recognized your sneakers under the stall, the whole school knew about it. Jamie opened the door and I darted past him to the bathroom. While I was in there doing my business, I could hear Koola come in the spot. He had been more loud and vivid than I ever heard him before. "I don't want that little nigga in here no more," he said. Was he talking about me? Isn't this the same dude who tried to give me props for kicking a female? "That little nigga had the police here. He can't come here no more," he continued. I waited for Jamie to defend me.

He didn't. He could've at least told him I was in the bathroom. *Does he know I'm in here?* I wondered.

He stayed about ten minutes and left. I came out the bathroom to find my cousin with a somber look on his face. "He don't want me here. I'm out," I said. "He's a sucker anyway," I added. I went to the closet to get my gun. This time Jamie had let me take it. Inside I was hurt that Jamie hadn't defended me, but I would not let him see it. I grabbed my gun along with the little belongings I had there and walked toward the door. "Yo I'm gonna talk to Koola," Jamie said. "Fuck him," I uttered on my way out the door.

I had no idea where I was going to go. Maybe I should just go back to my mother's and see how long I could last there. I needed to be there more often anyway because I had those court cases coming up. I had been to youth court prior to this, but this was the real deal. These were both serious charges.

My first court date had come and as I stood beside my public defender facing the judge, I would periodically look back at my mother sitting in the front row of the courtroom. He ran down my list of charges and scolded me for being in the same police station twice on the same day. That whole thing seemed to be an ongoing joke I couldn't shake. I was pretty sure they were going to place me in Spofford or Tryon or one of those places, but because the judge liked my mother, he sentenced me to a year probation. I had two serious assault charges and was sentenced to a year probation. I didn't seem to understand. First, I'm treated like John Gotti in school for getting arrested twice in the same day, and now I'm at court getting probation for causing serious injuries to two people. I was lucky, I guess. It was pure luck. How long would this last? I was the unluckiest guy in the world until that point. This had to be a fluke.

Months went by and I had only reported to my probation officer once. They had been calling my mother's house, but I hadn't been there in months. School was out and I was back in Seth Low Houses with Demell. This would be the summer that would alter my life forever.

As me, Demell and Black Chris walked over to the Chocolate Thai weed spot on Mother Gaston Blvd, I asked Demell if he knew anything about selling crack. "Why? You got some? Let's sell it," he joked. I had asked because I had seen my friend Lesley Pierre making a lot of money selling it, and he hardly even left his house. "I don't know about up there where you at Lo, nigga start getting it like that over here, we gonna tie him up," he said. "Unless you're Ap or Ike Livingston or one of them type of niggas." Chris added.

The Livingston family was very strong Family in Brownsville. It was nothing to see Mike Tyson pull up in a Rolls Royce to come check them in the projects.

Their sister Pam was always very nice, too. I thought about Demell's gesture of tying up drug dealers. This had been my initial thought when I tried to sell crack for Dennis years earlier. I wasn't a drug dealer, I concluded. I was becoming a stone-cold gangster, and my life of crime had only just begun.

"There is a warrant for your arrest," my mother assured me over the phone. I hadn't planned on going back upstate anyway. Aunt Kathy and Uncle Don seemed okay with me being there for the time being, I was straight right there in Brownsville.

"I know," I said. "I'll figure something out." I added. I knew I was definitely getting locked up whenever they caught me. So, my motto was just live it up until I got caught. I hadn't even turned 14 yet, and I was a fugitive from the law.

At this stage, I'm walking around with a gun on me every day. I still didn't trust women, so I wouldn't let any girl get close to my heart. If I had a girlfriend during these times, I probably would've made much better choices.

I was empty and actually planning to die any day, at 13 years old. I didn't plan for a future or a family. I didn't plan to graduate High School or go to college. I didn't see that far. I didn't even plan for a long prison sentence. I was prepared for one thing, and that was death.

One afternoon, I get a call from a 495 number and immediately knew it was Black Chris. Black Chris was a smooth cat from either Tilden or Van Dyke. Maybe even Brownsville Houses. I forget. In Brownsville, you can be in one project and walk directly into another without even noticing. You sometimes didn't realize where you are until you were getting chased out. I answered my Motorola. "Who this?" I said. "Yo, the homie Demell was doing a robbery and got hit up son," Chris said over the phone. "We gotta help this nigga," he said. Demell had been attempting to rob someone when shells rang out, and he got grazed in the foot. He wasn't hurt too bad, but he was bleeding a lot. And the problem now was, neither of us could go in Aunt Kathy crib. Not like this. Not with bullet wounds. My only option was to have us jump on that bus and go to my mother's house. I knew I was running from the law, but I hadn't been there for months. I'm sure they wasn't staking her place out over no damn probation violation.

We wrapped up his foot, jumped on the bus and headed north. When we got to my mother's house, she was mad at me, but happy to see Demell. My mother loved Demell. Almost like how Caesar's mother thought I was such a sweet kid, my mother had thought the same about Demell. "Boy, what happened to your foot?" my mother asked him. "Oh, Ms. Josephine, I was fooling around on the train and I hurt myself," he replied. My mother knew he was lying after she inspected his wound. She gave him peroxide, made us some oodles of noodles, and we went to bed not for one second expecting what tomorrow had in store.

Demell and I left my mother's house around noon the next day and decided we would go check our boy James ZiZi out. James ZiZi was another young trouble maker who lived across town from where my mother stayed. He too had since joined the Lo Life crew and was very, very aggressive with the shoplifting. The last time we had seen James ZiZi, we had to yell down to him from the fifth floor to stop walking through Seth Low Houses with his jewelry on the outside of his shirt.

"You better tuck that shit in," Demell yelled to him as he walked through the courtyard totally oblivious to what could happen if the wrong person noticed him. This guy James ZiZi was one of the most fearless people I've ever met. My first high-speed chase was with him behind the wheel of his Pathfinder outrunning the police through a residential district. Long story.

By the time Demell and I got on James ZiZi's block, summer school was letting out and there was a large group of young kids walking down the block. Black Chris had slept at James' house the night before, so the two were still in the house asleep.

Demell, hole in his foot and all, was scheming on these summer school kids. As soon as I saw the set up, I knew exactly what was about to happen. I saw him walk up to one of the kids with a tiny little chain on and run the play. Demell punches the kid, takes his chain and then berates him. "The next time you smack my little brother, I'm gonna kill you," he said. "Who is your brother?" the kid stood there asking as we walked away. It took these kids a good 45 seconds before they realized what was going on.

As Demell and I were walking towards James ZiZi's house, we see a group of about 20 kids walking fast behind us. Mind you, Demell had recently been shot in his foot. We couldn't run or anything like that. If anything, we were going to have to stand there and fight all of these kids. As they got closer, Demell advises me to get James ZiZi and Black Chris from inside. I get to the window of the room where they were sleeping and hollered inside. "Yo, we got a little problem outside." Almost seeming as if he had been waiting for me, Black Chris jumps up and springs into action. He runs out the house with me now in tow, and Demell limping, and starts literally chasing these 20 kids by himself. One of them picks up a stick and Black Chris charges toward him and says, "What you going to do with that?" and the kid hauled ass running from him. I was laughing so hard, I couldn't even help him. Next thing you know, we hear sirens and see three or four blue and white police cars speed up. These same kids running, were now loud and boisterous again with the Police present.

As Police jumped out to sort things out, the kids were taking turns telling what happened. It's funny when you're dealing with civilians and expect them to follow street code and they don't. Who is to blame? The kids had told the cops it was Black Chris who punched the kid and took his chain; when it was actually Demell. They handcuffed him and put him in the car. They then came back over to Demell and I. I told them my name was Lance Fraser and that I was 13 years old and coming from summer school. When they asked Demell his name, they must've didn't buy his answer because they put the cuffs on him and put him in a separate car. We had only come up here for this guy to heal, and in less than 24 hrs., we had gotten Black Chris a robbery charge for nothing, and gotten Demell jammed up. I was on probation with a warrant and was praying they didn't take me in. Me using my cousin's name had worked once again.

Demell got out the same day, but they slapped Black Chris with a $50,000 dollar bail; for absolutely nothing at all. He was gonna have to sit up for a minute. When Demell left the precinct, we headed back to my mother's house and she sat me down to speak to me to in private while he watched TV

"I spoke to your probation officer and they said, if you turn yourself in, you can get a few months in DFY, and/or a year in a residential place," she said. I think my mother had noticed that Demell's injury was from a gun, not the train and that scared her. Why did she suddenly, want me to turn myself in? My mother had known more than I did about juvenile detention centers. She had been in and out of them throughout her teenage years. DFY stood for Division For Youth. That's jail for kids who get sentenced as adults, but are under the age of 16. In NY State, they cannot house a minor with adults until he is 16 or older.

My mother knew when I wasn't at her house, I was more than likely somewhere I probably wasn't supposed to be. "You know if they put you in one of those residential places, if you behave, you can come home on the weekends," she said. It was something to think about. Maybe it would be good for me. I needed a break from this life. But now wasn't the time to think about that. I needed Demell to get better because we had a few more things we needed to do before I was turning myself into anybody. Unfortunately, we wouldn't be doing anything because when we got back to Brownsville, he had got snatched up for some other wild shit he had done, and I was headed back to Spring Valley to figure my life out. Turning myself in was sounding like the most rational thing to do. I needed a break because I was mentally and emotionally falling apart.

CHAPTER 15

King Cabrini

It was about an hour and a half drive to Hyde Park, N.Y. from my mother's house in Spring Valley, N.Y. For some strange reason, I had an extreme sense of calmness for someone about to be incarcerated for the next 12 months. By now, I had written a ton of my own raps and I told myself that I would just practice on rapping for the next year and come home and make a demo tape. I vowed to my mother I would stay out of trouble so I'd be able to get those home visits she told me about. This was a juvenile facility so I wasn't really too worried about not surviving. Boys my own age were like little kids. I had been hanging around older people my entire life.

When I finally got to the facility, they bought me to the infirmary to get a physical to test the state of my health. And unbeknownst to me, this place was co-ed.

I actually thought my eyes were deceiving me when I first seen her. She was a very pretty girl I would later find out was named Veronica. Once I realized this facility had females in it, I knew it was gonna be hard to stay out of trouble. Especially if the guys and girls interacted. The two assaults I had been in here for, both had a female as an underlying factor. Crystal Paul had attacked Daryl, and Jerime Ikner had been talking shit about me over a girl he dated, who had a crush on me. I didn't start either of those issues, yet here I was. Once I saw it was co-ed, I was excited, yet worried at the same time.

They gave me bed linen and showed me to my living quarters. Each dorm had about fifteen beds with not even a divider separating one bed from the other. The facility housed 45 boys in the boys' cottage, and 45 girls in the girls' cottage across the street. While I was making my bed, a very dark-skinned man named Howard Wilson came in and yelled like a drill sergeant. "Welcome to Alpha, Mr. Carenard, and let me lay some of the ground rules down for you," he yelled. "There are three dorms here, Alpha, Omega and Beta. This facility is run on points and levels. You want recreation, you need points. You want to go on trips, you need points, you want to go on home visits, you need points," He continued. "You get points by your school grades and your behavior, and if you want co-ed recreation, you gotta be on at least level 2," he said. So, they let the boys and girls interact. Interesting

I thought. "If you can make Level 3, you get a two-man dorm and you go home every weekend." I wondered how many boys were on level 3. Home every weekend? Was I hearing that right. "Welcome to St. Cabrini," he concluded and walked out. As soon as he walked out, the dorm got extremely noisy. It went from everyone being very quiet and listening while he was there, to almost like a party in seconds. What caught my attention the most was somebody playing "Ill Street Blues," a song just released by one of my favorite rappers, Kool G Rap.

"Yo, where you from?" a voice asked out of nowhere. "Brooklyn," I responded. "Oh, somebody said you were from Spring Valley," he said "I am" I replied. "I actually am from both, I bounce around a lot ya know," I added. "Do you know a kid named Dave Jones from Spring Valley?" he asked. "Yeah, I know Dave Jones, that's my homie," I said now getting a little irritated. "He told us you were coming here and told us who you were, I'm Erik Parker," he said. "I told him I would hold you down in here."

Dave Jones was a kid I had known since I was about 10 or 11. When I say this kid was a trouble maker, he got in just about the same amount of shit as I did. He had just recently got in trouble for putting a kid's head through a window, and was sent to a much worse facility. It didn't take me long to realize that while he was here, he ran the place.

Random guy and Me at ST. Cabrini Juvenile Detention Center

That evening in the day room, Erik got up and turned off the TV to the disapproval of a lot of the boys watching. "I got an announcement to make, my boy Dave is gone, but his man is here to take his spot so things will still be as they were. We run the TV, we run the rec room, and we gonna run Alpha," he said in a stern and confident voice. I was waiting for a rebuttal, and when there wasn't any, he turned the TV back on. Now I was definitely anticipating having some enemies here. This guy just volunteered me to run some shit I knew nothing about. I was wishing I could've spoken to Dave and gotten some insight on who was who and how this shit ran, but here I was. I honestly didn't want any trouble. I was going to do my time and get back to the streets.

"Mr. Carenard, can I see you upstairs," he asked. I didn't know who this man was but since he was an adult, I assumed he was part of the staff. I followed him into the main office. "My name is Lorenzo and I'm the head of security here," he said. "Now it's been bought to my attention that you're close with Dave Jones." He added. "Yeah, I know him from the neighborhood." I stated. "I'm gonna be very clear with you, if you carry on like he did in here, you're not going to last long," he said, looking directly in my eye. "That guy was in some shit every day, and it made my job a lot more difficult than it needed to be. I don't like people who make my job difficult. You understand me? Now carry on," he concluded. What the hell was Dave doing up in here? As soon as I walked out, I noticed a kid with his head bandaged. Later on, I would find out that was the same kid whose head Dave had put through a window a few weeks prior.

After a couple weeks, I had got settled in and was enjoying my position as the top dog. Although I didn't work for it, I had to do enough to maintain it without also having to put anybody's head through a window. Erik was scheduled to get discharged in a few weeks, so I'd be pretty much running the place by myself after that. There was only one kid out of the 45 boys here who wasn't as accepting of my leadership role. He was a kid from the Bronx named Rich Hines. Rich must've been 6' 4" 250 lbs. at only 12 years old. I had never seen a kid so young that size in my life. You could tell he was a very immature 12-year-old, as all he wanted to do was crack jokes, sleep and fight. And from the word going around, Rich could fight. As Erik had put it, he had "grown man" strength and that's why it was hard to win a fight against him even if you had more technique.

They had had a fight months earlier, and supposedly Rich knocked him out, but apparently, Rich was terrified of Dave and that's why Erik still maintained his position even after his loss. I guess now that I was involuntarily taking Dave's role, Rich and I had a silent issue. In my mind, I was thinking, if he was afraid of Dave, he certainly didn't want to get me upset.

It didn't take me long at all to differentiate the trouble makers from good kids. If you had been there for more than a month or so, and you were still in the Alpha dorm, that meant you weren't getting any points because your behavior wasn't up to par. Rich had been in Alpha dorm for 6 months. I wondered why these kids wouldn't just behave to at least get home visits, and then I realized, a lot of them like Rich, didn't have a home to go home to. My home wasn't the best, but I did have a place I could go.

The day Erik had gotten discharged, I kind of noticed this was what everyone was waiting for to try to knock me out of the top position. We were in the gym playing a pick-up game of basketball. I went for a lay-up and Rich fouled me really hard. "Don't do that shit again," I said to this enormous 12-year-old. "What the fuck you going to do about it?" he said. "You heard what the fuck I said."

As soon as I said that, he went from 0 to 100. He stopped playing and walked towards me. When I saw that, I walked towards him. See size never mattered with a fight. Win or lose, I would get down. Two staff members, Dwight and Don, ran over to get between us before any punches were thrown. Dwight, the bigger of the two, grabbed Rich while Don grabbed me. Rich flung Dwight off of him with so little effort that Don let me go and went to help Dwight restrain Rich. These two big grown men were having a very hard time restraining this child. I see what Erik had meant by "grown man" strength.

At this point, a few of the other residents are holding me, calming me down. In a way, I was happy Dwight and Don had got to this kid. He probably would've won that fight. As they were pulling him out of the gym, I knew even though he was stronger than me, that I was smarter than him so I needed to do something to get a mental edge over him. We were going back to the same boys' cottage after all. I knew Rich could still see me while they were pulling him away, so I got loose from the residents who were holding me and punched the thick glass in the gym door shattering it. Blood quickly began running down my arm as I started screaming loudly like a lunatic. "Let that motherfucker go! I'll kill that motherfucker!" I shouted. I could see his face go from looking angry and fearless, to confused and concerned.

I had been in Omega dorm working to get my points up when this incident happened. I was doing everything I could to get a home visit. I was getting so much better at rapping and couldn't wait to go home and show Caesar my new material. Plus, I heard Jamie had even started rapping. My mother had moved out of Hyenga Lake, found a better place and my little sister Tyeshia was even back living with her. Things seemed to be getting better at home. I missed LaDedra, too. I had been trying to go home and had just let Rich make me mess it all up. I had lost all my points and had to go back to zero. Everything in the place was based on points. Losing all my points also meant I had to go back to Alpha, but that's where Rich had lived for the past 6 months. Alpha was his domain. They knew they couldn't put us together, so for whatever reason, instead of just leaving me in Omega, they put me in

Beta. And that was the worst move they could've ever made.

Beta was the complete opposite of Alpha. Alpha was loud and boisterous, while Beta was as quiet as a library. My new bed was next to a window. This was the bed most kids preferred because it made it easier to go AWOL at night. Sometimes a group of guys and/or girls would go AWOL on campus to meet up and smoke, fight, fuck or whatever they did. If you could make it back to your bed before you got caught, you could keep your points. If you got caught going AWOL, on or off campus, you would lose all your points. For this reason alone, most kids wanted a bed near a window, and it usually came with seniority.

"I made sure you got that window bed homie," a voice said from behind me. I turned to see Marquis Hooks talking to me. Marquis was a kid from Rochester N.Y. who was 14, but carried himself like an adult. Him and his cousin Joseph Mitchell, also from Rochester N.Y., were in there as well. Joseph also carried himself like a person wise beyond his 14 years. "Thanks a lot," I said to Marquis. "I notice all you wear is Polo man, what is that about?" he asked. I sat with Marquis and Joseph for the next 3 hours breaking down the history of the Lo Life crew. They had never heard of the Lo Lifes and were intrigued.

That evening was when I knew I was gonna be really cool with these guys. Around 11:00 PM, after the night staff had done their last head count, Marquis and Joseph had come over to my bed. "Yo, you smoke weed?" Joseph asked, "Hell Yeah."

I replied. "Go in the bathroom," Marquis added. I went into the bathroom to find all three showers running hot water to create steam. There was so much steam you could hardly see anything. Marquis came in behind me and lit up a fat joint and we got so high in that bathroom that night. Beta was the place to be.

I knew I still had to deal with this Rich situation. I didn't know if my intimidation tactic had worked or not until the next day in school. Rich had come up to me and even with my hand bandaged up, I stepped back and got in a fighting position. I quickly noticed that his demeanor was totally different than before. "Nah, bro, I just wanted to apologize to you, I was wrong," he said. My tactic had worked and now I had the upper hand. "It ain't nothing man, just don't let that shit happen again," I said with a stern tone. I had beat him without even throwing a single jab. Now I just had to find out how Marquis and Joseph were getting that weed. And that would be my mission for the next few days.

I had started talking to a female in the girls' cottage named Kelly Dickerson. She was kinda cute, but she was the rudest, meanest female I had ever known at this point. I don't even know what I liked about her come to think of it. She was one of the girls who would go AWOL to come down to the boys' cottage to fool around. One night, her and a group of girls had gone AWOL and came down to the outside of the Beta dorm where we stayed. She and I had kissed and made out a few times, but nothing much more than that. Dawn Richardson had been my only real sexual experience, and that was a one-time thing because of Daryl. And here I was, in this place because of Daryl. In hindsight, *it had been this guy Daryl ruining my life, not even me.* Ha. Jokes!

On this evening, Kelly was trying to get me, Joe and Marquis to AWOL and join them. When I declined, she tried another method and used the promise of us having sex if I came out. When I declined again, she berated me and called me names. "You scared of pussy you bitch ass nigga?" she said as her friends laughed along. "No, I'm just trying to get a home visit," I said. "You need points to get a home visit dummy," she replied. Everything had to be an insult with this girl. "Marquis, you come out, you ain't scared of pussy, are you?" she said. Kelly was also from Rochester, N.Y. so that insult kind of stung a little more. In there, it was like a civil war between the kids from New York City, and the kids from upstate N.Y. I had grown up in both places so I played whatever side I chose. Besides, I was tough so I did what I wanted. "Bitch, I ain't going out there," Marquis said to Kelly. I was certain Kelly was going to have a fierce rebuttal after him calling her a bitch. I hadn't ever called her a bitch and she always had nasty things to say to me. "Whatever," was all she said. I thought that was super strange. Maybe it was because they were from the same hometown, I thought. But that whole dynamic always stayed in my head. Many years later, again while in solitary confinement, I wondered if Marquis and Kelly ever hooked up after that, or even before that? Either way, now I knew you could call a girl a bitch and get away with it.

It took a minute, but Marquis and Joseph had explained to me how they kept a steady supply of weed in there. They hadn't had the points or levels to go on many home visits, so they kept this young guy named Pudgy around and made sure he always had enough points and levels to go home. They would fight his battles and even convince staff to not deduct points from him if he did anything wrong. They made it seem like they were looking out for him like a big brother would. But he was like the mule. Pudgy was also from Rochester. One thing I admired about those Rochester kids was, they stuck together no matter what.

I decided it was time for me to build my own little team in there. I had been in there four months and hadn't went home yet. I needed a mule of my own. I also knew I needed to enforce my role as top dog, even over Marquis and Joseph, who you can arguably say was running shit in their own way. People respected all three of us. But I needed fear, that's what would be what would set me apart.

One day on the basketball court, this kid named Etoyi Booker from Albany, NY just couldn't miss a shot, and he reminded everyone that whole day of how hot he had been. Etoyi was cool with everyone. All he cared about was the girls up at the girls' cottage, and going home on the weekends. Etoyi had the points he needed to go home so we would usually only see him during the week. As we're getting ready for the last head count, Etoyi, in a playful manner, keeps reminding everyone about how he was unstoppable on the court that day. He said the one wrong thing that sealed his fate that night. "Then, this nigga B Lo tried to guard me, I told that nigga he better stick to rapping or whatever he be doing," he said while giggling. I know he didn't mean it in a malicious way, and I hated that it had to be Etoyi; but at this point, this was a chess move. "Very funny," I said while we all laid on our bunks, getting ready to go to sleep.

About 45 minutes later, while the majority of the room was asleep. I got up and turned on the light. Marquis was still awake reading a book and this is what I needed.

I needed Marquis to see what I was about to do. While Etoyi slept with his bare feet exposed, I took a sharp number 2 pencil, and with all my might, jammed it about an inch and a half into his foot. He let out a blood-curdling scream and before we knew it, all the night staff had rushed into the Beta dorm to tend to his injury. I had made my point that even though I was calm and collected, I was also very, very violent. This is the message I wanted to convey, and I did.

This didn't help me as far as getting home visits because some little pipsqueak from Harlem who was awake when this happened had implicated me as the one who stabbed Etoyi. It was his word against mine, so I didn't get the punishment anyone else would've gotten for that, but I lost all my points and had to start from zero simply for being implicated. Anyone else probably would've ended up where they sent Dave Jones for putting that kid's head through the window. Etoyi maintained his position of not knowing who stabbed him and was adamant about never having an issue with me. I felt kinda bad afterward because although I had stabbed him for my own personal reasons, he had remained honorable knowing I was indeed truly the culprit.

It would be another two months before I would get my first home visit and boy, was I looking forward to it. I got off the bus at the bus station and seen the same drug dealers and addicts I had left there months earlier. I should've went straight to my mother's house, but I really needed for Caesar and Jamie to hear my new raps. I know Koola didn't want me in the weed spot, but I had been gone for months. Maybe he forgot about it. I was going to go there anyway. If anything, Jamie would have to tell me to leave.

When I got there, Caesar, Jamie and Koola were all in the spot drinking, smoking and playing loud music. I had never seen this place so alive while Koola was there. Koola seemed happy to see me that day, which shocked me. The last time I heard his voice, he was telling Jamie how he didn't want me there because I was a liability. As I was sharing stories with them about my life in a residential juvenile detention center, Koola interjects and asked for Caesar and Jamie to do the routine they had been doing earlier. They immediately start rapping back and forth, trading bars over a fresh beat in the background. As they rapped, I was so proud to hear they had been still been creating new material. It seemed at one point, I was the only one who cared about being a rapper. I realized that my raps were a lot more intricate than theirs were, but this was my cousin and my childhood friend so the idea hit me right then.

"We should start a group," I said. "I'm with it," Caesar said with no hesitation. "I just be doing this shit for fun, I ain't trying to be no rapper," Jamie said. "Nah, you bugging, ya'll niggas sound good," Koola responded. This was the first time I seen a nice side of Koola. He usually always had a very serious demeanor. "We should call ourselves the He-Menz," I said. This was a name I came up with on the spot. I had been doing 300 push-ups a day up at St Cabrini and it showed. Caesar had the football player stocky frame, and Jamie had muscles ever since I could remember.

We were all pretty jacked so the name was fitting. Plus, He-Man was my favorite cartoon growing up. "We're all strong like He-Man, so together we are the He-Menz," I said, nodding confidently. "I like that shit," Caesar said. "Me too," Koola added before insisting we play a game of spades.

The spades game was Caesar & I versus Jamie & Koola, and they were kicking our asses something awful. I was blaming Caesar, and he was blaming me about why we kept losing. Caesar knew I was extremely violent when I got mad, but I guess something must've made him forget. "Act like you know how to play," he screamed at me after we got set for a second time in a row. Jamie and Koola would laugh at us arguing with each other because the more we fought, the more they won and rubbed it in. Koola had never seen an episode when I went overboard, but he was about to witness it on this night. "This nigga plays like he's stupid," Caesar said, shaking his head. I felt a tear coming to my eye and bit my bottom lip. I don't know what my mother knew about her son, but she was right. When that happened, something would go wrong.

I got up without saying a word and walked to the kitchen and grabbed the first knife I saw. It must've been a five-inch steak knife. I walked out the kitchen with the knife and instead of heading to my seat, I walked to his side of the table. He stood up looking confused on why I was walking towards him, before he could do anything, I plunged the knife into his stomach. As he screamed and grimaced in pain, I grabbed my bag, gave Jamie and Koola a menacing stare and left the house.

I felt like shit walking to my mother's house with my friend's blood all over me. *Over a spades game, Brian?* I thought to myself. I had some serious issues with my anger and it seemed to be getting worse. I didn't want to tell my mother what had happened, so when I got there, I found the bathroom and quickly changed my clothes before she could notice any blood.

She didn't notice the blood on me, but I noticed her belly. It was much, much bigger than its normal size. My mother was pregnant again. This time with a set of twins. If I thought I would never live with my mother again before, this confirmed it. I gave her a big hug and a kiss and went looking for LaDedra.

The next day I called Jamie to get an update on Caesar's condition. I really wanted to apologize to my friend. He said Caesar's injury wasn't as bad as it initially looked, "I guess the nigga is just a bleeder," he said in those exact words. He told me Koola wanted to talk to me and I should come over there. When I got there, Koola was telling me how he seen I was a real nigga and how when I got discharged from St Cabrini, I could make some real money with them. I was a 14-year-old kid, and here was this grown ass man telling me I was a stand-up man. If only he knew how much this fed my ego in the worst way. I had heard many stories about this dude being a gangster, and here he was saluting me. After we spoke, he left and I immediately walked over to Jamie. "Yo, is my gun still here?" I asked. "Of course it is," he responded.

CHAPTER 16

Same Ol' Me

Over the next few months at St. Cabrini, I had learned to rule this place with an iron fist. I was not only controlling the other residents, I had the staff bringing me cigarettes, weed, fast food or whatever I wanted. The only staff I couldn't break were Lorenzo, Dwight and the creep Howard Wilson. By now, I had dismissed mean ass Kelly and talked to this cute light-skinned girl from Long Island named Iela. Iela was more my type personality-wise. I had made it to level three and got a two-man dorm I used as the headquarters of my young, criminal enterprise.

I shared the room with a kid named Kenny Smith from Mount Vernon. I had learned from Joseph and Marquis how to build my own team in there. The same way they had pudgy, I recruited a bucktoothed skinny kid from Crown Heights, Brooklyn, named Phil Harris.

Phil didn't get many home visits, but when he did, I could be certain he would bring me back at least three or four dime bags of weed. I liked Phil a lot because he was super loyal. I could count on him for anything. When I was going home on the weekends, he would tell me everything Iela was doing, and if she was getting out of pocket or not. I can't lie when I say it hurt me to have to physically assault him one day.

On this day Phil and I were slap boxing, which we all did often. Something in my head told me he was throwing real punches, so I threw real punches and it didn't end well for Phil. I hit him with a barrage of hard fast punches to the head and face. When the staff had seen him, they knew he had been assaulted, but he maintained his story of falling in the shower. None bought it, and I believed they all knew it was me because nobody else in there would have the courage to lay a finger on Phil because they knew he was my guy. To his defense, Phil was rather skinny and couldn't do much with me physically. This is also the reason, to complete my team, I needed some muscle.

My muscle would come in the form of a kid named Allah "AJ" Murphy from the South Bronx. We were on the basketball court when I saw him walking to the Boys' Cottage with his bed linen. I had remembered taking that same walk and watching the other boys scoping me out the day I got there. I knew he had to start in Alpha dorm where Rich Hines reigned and that could mean trouble for him.

He was very tall with a lot of size for a 13-year-old. He wasn't as big as Rich, but not far behind. I expected him to sit in that dorm and feel everything out before he had come outside to join the other boys as I had done, but this wasn't the case. He must've walked in the dorm, threw his linen on his bed and headed out to join us on the Basketball Court.

He not only came to join us, he made jokes on random people out of the blue. I was gonna love this kid, or hate him, and I was about to find out right then. My little homie Phil was wearing a "PHILLIES" T shirt, which was a popular cigar brand back then. AJ, not knowing Phil from a can of paint, walked over and said to him, "Phillies? Phillies Nuts," as to say feel deez nuts, and everyone broke out laughing, except Phil. "Fuck You, you don't know me," Phil replied ready to fight. He knew he would have to do or say something with me standing there. "Chill, Chill fellas," I said. "Yo, what's ya name man?" I asked. "Call me AJ," he said and the basketball playing commenced.

AJ was one of the funniest guys I had ever met until that point. This kid's sense of humor was unparalleled. I liked to laugh and make jokes a lot too so we got along great. Within a week, I used my power to get him transferred to Beta and my reign in that place only got stronger. Joseph, Marquis and I were all really cool, but I needed dominance. They had all the Upstate kids on deck and I had all the NYC kids on deck so the only way there would be any issues was if us three weren't cool.

The staff loved me for keeping the violence to a minimum. They knew about the weed, the cigarettes, even us sneaking the girls into Beta and didn't care. When word got around that I was bringing guns in there, they buckled down on us and began doing random shake downs. They never found not even a shell though.

One of the staff members, Don, who I became extremely cool with had pulled me to the side one day. "Yo you think you can get me a piece?" he asked. The gun I had brought there was the same .25 I had traded for with that drug dealer that had no clip and only shot one shell at a time. "I don't fuck with guns man," I replied. We were cool, but he was still the authority and though I liked him, I didn't trust him enough for all that.

When it neared time for me to be discharged from that place, I kind of didn't want to leave. I had made some new solid relationships, and had learned how to run a criminal empire. All at 14 years old. I didn't realize this place was preparing me for a life of crime that would span for the next 2 decades.

In 2019, I was invited to join a Facebook group called "SC" or "St Cabrini" which is where I got a lot of updates on the kids I was in that place with almost 25 years earlier. Joseph Mitchell, Marquis Hooks, Allah

"AJ" Murphy and I had all kept in touch occasionally after we left that place. We're all still actually friends until this day. In 2011, Joseph Mitchell had got arrested for running a huge drug empire that spanned from Rochester to Elmira NY. When they arrested him, they found $520K cash hidden in a bottom compartment of a fish tank. While awaiting trial, he did the impossible and escaped from Monroe County Jail. He was captured a week later in a shed in somebody's back yard. In 2013, they sentenced him to 25 years in Federal Prison and labeled him a Kingpin for his dealings. AJ is still like my muscle to this very day. He's younger than I am, but much bigger and very protective of me as he's always been. The oldest of all the staff, Howard Wilson, the guy who gave me my initial scolding on how the point system worked, was sentenced in 2011 to probation for raping one of the young girls there. The reports wouldn't say if the sex was consensual or not, just that he was a 59-year-old man having sex with a 16-year-old resident. How he only lost his job and got probation is beyond me. I would see the staff member named Dwight Hunt again, but we'll get into that later.

It was my last bus ride leaving this place and I was going to miss it. On the ride down to my mother's house in Spring Valley, I just looked at the scenic mountain ranges I would never see again. In my mind, I was never going back Upstate again in my life. Not against my own will, at least. My mother thought it was a good idea for me to come stay with her in her new place. It was still the ghetto, but it "wasn't Hyenga Lake" she would say. She had been fighting the East Ramapo school district to allow me to come back and enter a normal public school. The only real issue they had was my poor attendance history, but she had promised them I would do better because I had promised her that. It was already June and there were only a few more days of school left, so I couldn't miss that many days anyway. I was really eager to come home and go to real high school, even if only for a couple of days.

By now, my mother had given birth to paternal twins. My younger brother and sister, Stephen and Stephanie. She had gotten my other little sister Tyeshia back from my Aunt Lorraine, had a new place, and had even started to drive her own car as I stated before. Now that she had all of her five children at home, she felt complete.

The East Ramapo School district had agreed to let me come back and attend a normal High School under a few conditions. The one that bothered me was, I would have to be in one of those E.H. classes Chris and Caesar were in. They said this was because I was coming from a juvenile detention center. They agreed that if I went a semester or two with no incidents, they would consider putting me back in mainstream classes. My family life seemed good, I had my freedom back and now it was time to put my rap group, He-Menz on the map.

Every day at the weed spot on White St, we would rehearse our little routines when I wasn't running the streets. Lesley Pierre was a full-time drug dealer by now. At 16 years old, he would drive to school in a 65k dollar brand new Acura Legend with Gold BBS rims. He had a better car than 95% of the teachers. We would link up almost every day after school and take a ride to 145th St in Harlem to a weed spot called Shaka Zulu. The weed at White St. was cool, and even free for me, but there was nothing in NYC at the time like Shaka Zulu weed. I was still only 14, but I felt like I had been through enough that I was ready for anything.

Lesley Pierre had sold me the latest Motorola flip phone with the illegal service. I was the best local rapper around in my opinion, and I felt like the man.

One day, Lesley Pierre had dropped me off at Fred Hecht Houses where Caesar's brother Matthew had a drug spot. I was fresh out and didn't want to be hanging in a drug spot too long, so I decided I would go show my face and be on my way.

When I got there, the place was full of people. There had been like a party going on. Caesar, Matthew, a cute neighborhood girl named LaToya, my cousin Adonis and some other people had all been gathered there enjoying weed, alcohol and music.

My cousin Adonis was a couple years older than me, but this guy was the epitome of a trouble maker. He was a guy that only cared about three things in life:

getting girls, basketball and fighting, and he did all three pretty well. Adonis and I had a very weird relationship. Although we were distant cousins, we had met later on in life during our very early pre-teenage years. We would be best of friends one day, and fighting each other the next. He was not the easiest guy to get along with.

On this day, I noticed everyone was a little bit drunk so I left early and walked the few blocks over to White St to kick it with Jamie. When I got to White St, I noticed I had left my brand-new Motorola flip phone up at Caesar's brother's drug spot. I quickly turned around to go back and get it. When I got there, I looked in all the places I had been and couldn't find the phone anywhere. I turned off the music and asked if anyone had seen the phone and nobody seemed to have seen anything. I looked again and again. I got irate. I told everyone I will ask one more time before I cause issues, and they laughed it off.

I jogged back down to White St, grabbed my pistol with the one bullet in it and headed back toward the party. When I opened the door this time, I had a whole different demeanor. I had started to tear up, and bite my bottom lip; and this only meant trouble.

I walked in and pulled out the gun, "Nobody leaving until I find my phone." I yelled. Immediately people looked under couch cushions and began looking behind appliances etc. This gun had changed the dynamic. After about 20 minutes of looking, some kid I didn't recognize attempted to leave. I grabbed him by his collar and struck him with the butt of the pistol. He winced in pain and ran to the back of the room crying. "I'm not playing with none of you motherfuckers." Caesar gave me the *what's wrong with this guy* look as I went from person to person hitting them each with the butt of the gun.

When I got to Adonis, he looked at me as if I would be sympathetic because of our relationship. And I probably would've, until he attempted to grab my arms. When he did, I struck him in the head with the pistol. Adonis was very street smart and had seen that while I was pistol-whipping the others, that the gun didn't have a clip inside of it. "I should shoot you right now," I said to Adonis as he had tried to wrestle the gun out of my hand. While we were tussling over the gun, someone else ran out the door and I let go of Adonis and gave chase. I assumed that person may have been running away with my phone. I didn't catch him. And I never found my phone.

When you're in a small town, word travels very, very fast. By the time I had got back to White St., Jamie had already known what happened. "What the fuck is wrong with you man? Now you're about to go back to jail over a stupid ass phone?" he said. "You just got out, man." I had become so accustomed to Jamie asking me what was wrong with me. I almost had come to expect it. I also didn't know if it was because St. Cabrini didn't feel like jail or what, but it quickly became obvious that I hadn't learned my lesson. Not at all.

A couple of days later, while I was walking to the corner bodega, I spot the girl Lesly I had met over a year earlier, and she was even more beautiful than I remembered. She had a creamy, smooth, "Butter Pecan Rican" complexion, with long brown hair that went past her shoulders. She was about 5' 4," super-thick with the prettiest brown eyes. "Oh shit, It's Amarr's girl," I said playfully. "You mean Amarr's friend," she replied with a smile. "How have you been, Brian? It's Brian, right?" she asked. "It's B Lo, only my friends can call me Brian," I said with a smirk. "So, I guess that makes us friends then, huh, Brian?" she replied. "Oh, you mean friends like you and Amarr?" I said, trying to match her wit. "Very funny," she said.

We must've talked for three hours before she told me she had to go home. She was very smart for her age, and could engage in conversation on a variety of topics. We talked about family life, school, both our past relationships, etc. She even admitted to kind of dating Amarr. She said they attempted to date but then she found out he played football with her ex-boyfriend and that made it kinda "weird," so they discontinued it.

Her ex-boyfriend was a guy named Mark Scott known for being a super good athlete. I had heard of his older brother Donavan, who was supposedly a street dude, but never of Mark. She told me she and Mark had been on and off since she was very young, and he had been her first of everything. Usually when a girl tells you that, there is always a part of that girl that is going to love whoever that person is. I explained about my relationship with Dawn and what had happened. I even told her about Kelly and Iela, I was still very inexperienced when it came to females. I literally knew nothing besides females can get you in a shitload of trouble.

The whole rest of the night, I did nothing but write raps, play black jack with Jamie and Koola, (who, at this point, was leery of me being around) and think about this beautiful girl Lesly who I couldn't seem to get off of my mind.

It got back to me that Adonis had wanted to fight over what had taken place with my missing cell phone. I knew Adonis was a better fighter than I was. We had had many altercations prior to that. Jamie and I had even jumped him once over him running off with $10 I had given him to buy some beer. Adonis was my cousin, and I loved hanging out with him, but he was the definition of super grimy. He was just one of those Bronx niggas who you had to watch at all times.

I sent word back to Adonis that I don't fight anymore. My name was B Lo, and I'm busting my gun from here on out. Once I got the feel of the power that gun gave me, I was hooked. I knew we were going to bump into each other eventually. I didn't want to shoot Adonis, but I wasn't about to let him slam me on my head as I seen him do to many, many people.

I don't know what kind of classes Lesley Pierre was in, but he was allowed to leave school every day at 12 PM while all the other kids had to stay until 2:20. I wondered if this guy was paying off the teachers or something. He would leave every day at noon, and although I was on some sort of probationary period to get back into mainstream classes, guess who would leave with him? Me.

It was a hot summer day in June and Lesley Pierre and I had left school to head to Harlem to get some Shaka Zulu & Knotty head. Knotty head was a slang term for Seagram's Gin. Snoop Doggy Dogg was a new artist blazing the airwaves, and had made drinking Gin and Juice the popular thing amongst kids in the ghetto. We had been hanging out on 125th St. for hours getting drunk, high and flirting with any pretty girl who would walk up to the Acura Legend asking whose car it was.

Lesley Pierre had also used his connections to get his hands on the unreleased debut LP *Illmatic* from an artist named Nas who had been tearing up the underground and college radio stations. When I heard that CD, I made up my mind that no matter what, I was going to be a rapper someday. The way he put words together was like a poet who had no limits. It was almost as if this kid had been here before, died and came back as a ghetto prophet. He had a raspy vocal tone with a lot of pain and clarity in it. We listened to that tape over and over and over and over until we memorized every word. It would've usually been Gangstarr, or A Tribe Called Quest, but for that time being, it was all *Illmatic* by Nas.

At around 10 PM, we left Harlem to take the 20-minute drive back up to Spring Valley, N.Y. The last thing I remember was closing my eyes on the George Washington Bridge for a nap while Lesley Pierre drove the car.

I opened my eyes to find my Mother and Father standing over me, looking down. At this point, it was very rare to see them in the same room together so my initial thought was that I had died and went to heaven. Don't ask me why that's what I assumed, but that was it. I then tried to get up, only to realize, I couldn't move the bottom half of my body. I immediately got very scared by my lack of ability to move. "What the fuck is happening, what the fuck is going on, Mommy, Mommy." I cried before I was again heavily sedated.

I woke up the next morning in a two-bed hospital room with Lesley Pierre in the bed next to me. "Yo, man, I'm so sorry, yo, I'm sorry," Lesley began to plead to me. "What the fuck happened?" I asked. "Yo man, I fell asleep on the Palisades Parkway, and we flipped the car and fell into a ditch," he said "I thought you were dead, man. The car caught on fire and I was trying to pull you out, but I couldn't..." he continued while his voice shook. "I'm just glad you're alive B, you wouldn't talk or say anything, I thought you were gone," he said. While he was talking, he sat up and hung his legs off the bed. When I looked down at my own legs, I had all kinds of machines attached to myself. I had a catheter in my penis, IV tubes in my arms, and a device attached my leg that held it in place. While I'm looking at all this machinery attached to my lower half, he gets up and walks toward the restroom. I'm thinking to myself, *this guy goes to sleep behind the wheel, flips a car and I'm the one all fucked up while he's up walking*. Although I knew it was beyond his control, I was kinda mad about it.

"Good to see you're up," a tall white doctor said to me as he checked my vitals. "Had a pretty good night I see," he said sarcastically. I wasn't up for the jokes, I just wanted to know exactly what was wrong. "Excuse me, Doc, what exactly is wrong with my legs?" I asked. "Well, we're still running some tests and X-Rays, but what I can tell you so far is that you shattered and dislocated your right hip, you broke all the toes on your left foot, you broke your left ankle and your right fibula," he said. "And, we're waiting for some test results." "How long before you think I can go home?" I asked. "Well, that big weight on your leg, that keeps your leg in traction so your dislocated hip will heal correctly," he said. "We will look at that again in a few days, and if it looks good, you'll get a couple of casts, and you can be on your way," he said with a smile. "But if it doesn't look good, you can be here for as long as it takes to get you right." I didn't want to hear this, especially knowing the guy who had done this to me was up and walking already.

Lesley Pierre left the hospital the next day. I stayed there, not only not moving my legs, but having to shit and piss in pans and through tubes. The doctor said once I had my cast and was discharged, if everything went well, I should be walking with crutches in 6 to 8 weeks.

While I was laid up in there, my cousin Jamie told me he had gotten his lawsuit money from the incident that happened at McDonald's and was looking to expand and open more weed spots. They found a new spot on a street coincidentally named West St, so now there was White St, and West St, I didn't care about that; I just wanted to get back to my old self again.

I went home from the hospital about a week later. Well, I should've went home, but I figured it would be more fun to rest up at the new weed spot on West St. Adonis knew there would be no fighting, especially while I was in the condition I was in, so we squashed our little issue. He would be there with me often because while Jamie ran the spot on White St, he thought it would be a good idea to let Caesar and

Adonis run West St. I thought it was a horrible idea, but it was his money.

It had been about three to four weeks before I was getting around on my crutches. When I would go to the doctor for check-ups, they were astounded about how fast I was healing. One day, I got a call from Lesley Pierre's dad and he had summoned me to their house for a chat.

Lesley Pierre's dad was a slick-talking old school Haitian car salesman. He immediately told me I should be compensated for my injuries and gave me a card with an attorney's name on it to call. "No disrespect Mr. Pierre, but it's not Lesley's fault, we were both tired," I told him. Back then, in my mind, suing was the same as snitching. People would tell me I should sue Lesley Pierre's insurance, and I would fire back with "Hell no, that's my boy." I had no idea of how the insurance thing worked, and obviously neither did my mother. She had not once mentioned that we were entitled to compensation for my injuries, and that Lesley Pierre was insured and wouldn't be in any trouble. Why was it his dad telling me these things and not my own family? I took the card and left their house more confused than anything. I threw it away as soon as I was out of his sight.

While it had been Lesley Pierre who almost killed me, it was Lesly, the beautiful half Puerto Rican girl who was giving me life. We would sit up all night on the phone talking until we fell asleep. I had really begun to like this girl a lot. She would always call to check up to see if I ate or if I needed anything. This was something nobody besides my mother had ever done for me. She would try to convince me to leave the weed spot and go stay at my mother's house to heal. "What could you do if the cops raided there?" she asked. "You couldn't even run," she said jokingly. I was falling for Lesly; hard and fast. It kind of bothered me she said her and Amarr had whatever they had. Amarr and I were cool, but how cool? I decided I would need to talk to him before I continued to pursue this girl. And I would do it as soon as possible, because I wanted her, bad.

Amarr pulled up on his brand-new motorcycle while Caesar and I kicked it in Caesar's front yard. He offered me a ride on his bike, but I was on crutches, had a cast on my leg, and was terrified of motorcycles anyway so I declined. I needed to get him alone so I could ask him about Lesly and the extent of their relationship. What I really wanted to know was if he fucked her or not. Who was I kidding? I knew if he had fucked her, there wasn't but so far her and I could go. As shallow as that sounds, this was the reality of it.

Before I could pull Amarr to the side to chat, Jamie had pulled up in his new Pre-Owned Volkswagen Quantum. Damn, was I the only one out here not doing big things? Amarr had a Bike, Jamie had a new car, and

I had crutches. "Yo, I want ya'll to meet Quanie, my new wheels," Jamie stated excitedly.

Jamie had gotten that lawsuit money and was running through it fast. I was about to mention to him about spending so much until he said what he said next. "Yo B Lo, in a little bit, Buttercup is coming down from Newburgh and we're going to head into the city to get some work, and some jewelry," he said. "Remember that chain Rakim had on in "The Ghetto" video, I'm getting one for both of us." Now, I was excited. I don't know how much money Jamie had gotten in that settlement, but he was looking and acting like whole a new man.

As Amarr jumped off the bike and put the kickstand down, Caesar jumped on as if he were about to start it and take off. "Be careful man, that shit ain't your 10 speed," he said while walking towards me. "You wanted to talk to me?" Before I could answer, Caesar asked Amarr to give him a ride up Bethune Blvd and back.

Amarr reached in the small of his back and handed me a black 9mm. "Yo, hold this for me real quick, lemme give this nigga a ride." They both jumped on the bike and sped off.

While they were gone, I marveled over this beautiful black semi-automatic weapon I had in my hand. This was so much better than my little .25, and it had a clip. I couldn't help but stare at this gun intensely. Jamie was fiddling around in his new car and hadn't even noticed I had it. I threw my crutches down and limped over to where he was and put the gun in his face "Give it up Motherfucker." I yelled out playfully. "Yo, where the fuck did you get that?" he asked. "This is Amarr shit, he asked me to hold it while he gave Caesar a ride on his motorcycle," I said. "That shit is beautiful," he said while also marveling at the weapon. "I'm going to ask him if I could hold it when he gets back." This made Jamie's attitude change. "What you need another gun for? You don't need that shit man." If only he knew. I had seen him with a new car, Amarr with a new motorcycle, and I decided as soon as my legs were fully healed, I was about to get my money up as well.

Amarr and Caesar returned within the matter of five minutes. I was hoping it would be longer so I could play with this gun a little longer. "That shit was crazy," Caesar said while hopping off the bike. Amarr walked over to me and motioned his hand as to tell me to give the gun back. "You said you needed to talk to be about something?" I had wanted to ask him about Lesly, but now that I had seen this gun he had, I had a different plan. "You know Jamie and Koola got that new weed spot over there on West St., right?" I said in my most somber tone. "Well, I be up in there every day with no kind of protection and I'm on these crutches ya know, I need to get my hands on something like this," I said while attempting to hand him the gun back. "Damn,

Jamie got you up in there with no piece?" he looked over in Jamie's direction as he continued to speak. "Well, I'll tell you what, you hold on to that for now, and I'll get it from you later," he concluded. That would be the last time Amarr would ever see that gun again. And that also might've been the worse decision of my life at the time. I was mastering the art of making fucked up decisions.

If I thought my little .25 with no clip gave me a sense of power and superiority, this big black .9mm with 16 rounds in it made me feel like I was the king of the world. Even while on two bad legs, wearing a cast and on crutches, I had the power of life or death in my hands, and that sense of power would eventually lead to my downfall.

After Amarr pulled off on his motorcycle, I ran into Caesar's house and stashed the gun where I knew nobody would be searching. I ran back out, jumped in my cousin's new Volkswagen Quantum, and we headed to meet our cousin Buttercup. I made a mental note not to mention to Jamie that Amarr had given me the gun. He already thought me having that little .25 was corrupting me. I wouldn't quite call it corrupting, but I was most certainly a different person when I was carrying it around.

We met up with Buttercup and headed out to go on this McDonald's lawsuit sponsored shopping spree in Harlem. There was a shop on 125th St. called Mart 125 that sold everything from jewelry to bootleg C.D.'s, to you name it. There was something about Harlem I loved. The culture there was like nowhere else in the world. Sadly enough, it's been gentrified to where you'd be hard-pressed to find someone selling Muslim oils and incense on the streets today, but back then, it was an oasis for anything pertaining to black culture.

While looking at the jewelry, Jamie picked out one of those big gold hollow Gucci links that Big Daddy Kane and Rakim wore in their videos. "How does it look?" he asked as he stood in front of a mirror. I couldn't stop staring at my cousin, he looked like a real rapper. "Man, you look like a millionaire," I said. He immediately told the jeweler he wanted to purchase the chain. He also purchased the same chain a few sizes smaller for me, and had even offered to buy Buttercup one. "I don't want no fucking chain," Buttercup said, sounding rather convincing. "You know what I want, Cuz. I want to go get some crack."

Jamie had mentioned picking up some work earlier, so I guess it was for Buttercup. I hoped Jamie hadn't went back to selling crack. He had a pretty good thing going with the weed. We left 125th St and shot over to 141st and Amsterdam where they made a quick transaction with a couple of Spanish cats and we hit the highway to home. Everyone had gotten what they had come for so the ride home was full of laughs and jokes.

CHAPTER 17

Drive Slow

Instead of Jamie and I going back to Spring Valley that night, we decided we would stay in Newburgh since we had to drop Buttercup off anyway. Plus, we wanted to go up there and show off our new car. In my mind, I believed what was Jamie's, was also mine. This is how close we had become.

We had another cousin up in Newburgh named Arron. Arron was the son of one of Mama Sampson's two boys. He and Jamie were at the same age of 18, but Arron had been steadily selling drugs for well over six years. He had all the toys and trinkets to show it as well: Cars, bikes, homes, jewelry, you name it, Arron had it.

As we pull up in Quanie, our new Volkswagen, Mister, Onta, Beatrice and a few other people ran over to check out the vehicle. "This shit is nice," Onta said.

Onta was a distant cousin we had grown up with since we were babies. He and his brother had reputations in Newburgh of being extremely skilled fighters.

Mister, forever the instigator, had drilled Jamie about how his car was nice, but Arron's new Acura Legend was way better. Mister was notorious for stirring shit up. We couldn't wait for the day to become night so we could jump in the cars, go park on Broadway and show them both off.

As we were waiting, Buttercup pops up with a big gallon of Seagram's Gin. He immediately passes out cups and starts encouraging everyone around to partake. He didn't have to encourage me, I loved to drink Knotty Head so I was all in. We sat around drinking, laughing and shooting dice until it was time for us to hit the strip.

Nights like this in Newburgh, Broadway would be full of girls, guys and violence by the night's end. We would usually try to be out of there before the shooting started, but most times, we weren't. We actually seemed to NOT be able to leave until the shooting started.

As we headed to the car, me limping but keeping up, Jamie throws me the keys and says, "Hey B Lo, you want to drive?" Jamie knew that I couldn't drive. He also knew the one time I attempted to drive, I almost ran him over in the middle of the street. "Hell Yeah," I said while jumping in the driver's seat. Onta and

Mister quickly jumped in the backseat while Jamie hopped in the passenger. I could hardly see the gas pedal because of my cast, but I was excited and anxious that Jamie was letting me attempt to drive his new car.

As soon as I cranked the engine, he laughs and says, "You know I'm just playing man. Get up and exchange seats with me." Before I could say anything, he had opened his door and got out to come over to get in the driver's seat, and that's when I had put the car in drive and took off.

I must've been doing about 45 MPH going down West Parmenter St. I noticed I was quickly approaching a stop sign at an intersection at the end of the street, but was going too fast to stop in time. Mister and Onta were now in the backseat screaming with fear and excitement because they by now can tell I don't know what I'm doing. I ran the stop sign and almost fish tailed a Police car driving down the crossing street. I quickly hear a siren blare.

At the bottom of West Parmenter St was a dead end where you can either make a left turn, or crash through a large gate surrounding a cemetery. Still doing about 45 to 50 miles per hour, I make a super sharp left turn and the car hops the sidewalk and smack dead into a large oak tree. I felt the impact of the hit, and knew I was badly injured, but all I could immediately think about was Jamie.

I quickly jumped out of the car followed by Onta while Mister stayed in the back- seat, pretending to be in more pain than he was. In less than a minute, the same cop I'm assuming was the one I almost hit, was behind Jamie's now totaled vehicle with his siren still blaring.

He jumped out with his hand on his gun looking to be aggressive, until he looked and seen and noticed how young we were. The oldest kid in the car was only 15 years old. "What the hell happened here and who was the driver of this vehicle?" the officer asked. My adrenaline had been rushing so much, I hadn't yet realized the impact of my face hitting the steering wheel had split my whole bottom lip in half. "The driver ran," I said, trying to think on my toes. "Well, you're bleeding pretty badly, so Im going to call an ambulance for you; do either of you need an ambulance as well?" He asked. "No, I'm okay." Onta said "How about you in there?" the officer asked Mister, who still hadn't exited the back seat. "Yeah, my leg, I think it's broken," Mister screamed from inside the car. The officer got on his radio and called for an ambulance.

The cop believed my story about the driver having had ran off. That was until Jamie came around the corner huffing and puffing and out of breath. "Brian, why the fuck did you take the car man, why man?" he said, looking like he was about to cry. "Damn, Brian, damn man, damn..." he continued. "So, you were the driver?" the cop asked me.

By now, two ambulance emergency vehicles had come to get Mister and I. As I am being strapped to the gurney, the EMS worker puts a neck brace on my neck. I look over to see Mister arguing with the EMS worker tending to him. "I don't want that fucking neck brace, ain't nothing wrong with my neck, it's my leg," Mister said. The worker explained to Mister that the neck brace was protocol. "If I gotta put this shit on, I don't want to go to the hospital, let me up," he said as he unstrapped himself.

I couldn't believe I had just wrecked Jamie's new car. He had just gotten it. I felt like a complete piece of shit. I could hear the officer asking Jamie to confirm if I was the driver as they lifted me into the ambulance. I looked over to try to make eye contact with him to give him my sad puppy dog face. He seen me, but it didn't work. He gave me the most disappointed look he had ever given me out of the many, many times I had done some stupid shit. I felt bad. Like really bad. The ambulance sped off and drove me to St. Luke's hospital.

After I received the nine stitches in my lip, along with my four or five traffic tickets, I was discharged from the hospital. Nobody had come with me to the hospital so I walked back to West Parmenter street by myself.

On the walk back, I made a promise to myself that I would pay Jamie back somehow. Even if it meant working in the weed spot for free until I paid it off. A little voice in my head was saying, "*Angela crashed your mother's car, so ya'll are kind of even.*" His sister had totaled my mother's little red Chevrolet hatchback about a year before.

That voice was quickly silenced as I turned the corner onto West Parmentar to see them all out in front of the house. The mood was totally different, but the drinking and smoking was still taking place. "Can I talk to you?" I asked Jamie. "No, I don't want to talk to you right now," he said and walked away. I walked into the house to find Buttercup sitting at the table with the gallon of the Seagram's Gin half full.

"You aight little nigga?" he asked. "Yeah, but this shit is starting to hurt," I said, pointing at my lip. "Here, you need some of this shit little nigga," he said, pushing the bottle over in my direction. "Nah, I'm good," I replied. "Drink the shit little nigga," he said, this time in a more demanding tone. I reached and grabbed the bottle and went to take a swig. When the alcohol hit the cut in my mouth, it felt as if someone were pinching my lip with a plier and twisting it. "Ahhhhhhhh, it burns man." I screamed out in pain. I tried to put the bottle down and he shoved it back into my hands. "Drink it nigga," he said again. I toughed it out and kept swigging as the burning sensation intensified. "Drink it," he continued. I wanted to stop, but this was Buttercup and with him, you did what he said.

In 2009, my cousin Onta Williams (who was riding in the backseat when I crashed Jamie's car) would be arrested along with 3 other men for an alleged terroristic plot to bomb a Jewish synagogue in the Bronx, N.Y., and to use stinger missiles to shoot down U.S. military cargo planes. He was coaxed into participating by an FBI informant who offered him $250,000 for his involvement. If you have been reading up until now, I have described the living conditions in Newburgh N.Y. It's beyond below the poverty level. For the U.S. government to concoct a trap by offering money to drastically change the lives of these poor individuals in exchange to commit a horrible crime was wrong and unjust. In 2014, H.B.O. did a documentary on the ordeal titled *The Newburgh Sting* which clearly shows entrapment by the government. Please watch this if you get that chance. Unfortunately, Onta was convicted October 2010 and ultimately sentenced to 25 years in prison in June 2011. I spoke to Onta recently and he is in great spirits and is looking forward to coming home soon on appeal. Now, back to my story.

Jamie had finally forgiven me for crashing his car. We decided we would just go harder with the hustling and get him a new even better one. He was doing well for himself and I was happy about that. My life was getting better as well because my legs and lip were healing.

My cousin Onta Williams circa 2015

Lesly and I had gotten a lot closer. We hadn't hung out yet, but we stayed up on the phone all the time. While on the telephone with Lesly one late summer night in June, she told me she wanted to invite me somewhere. "Have you ever been to the South Street Seaport?" she asked. I had heard of it from hanging out in the Lower East Side, but had never been. "Nah, I haven't," I replied. I had actually never been on a real date at this point, period. "Well, me, my girlfriend and her man are going there tomorrow, you're welcomed to come if you want."

I was nervous as hell. A double date? I had never been in that kind of setting. I had only gotten along with guys I grew up with up 'til then. Unless you count the kids I met in St. Cabrini. I didn't particularly like meeting new people. "Yeah, that would be cool, I guess."

I was too nervous to ask Lesly if her and I could just hang out, so I went with her suggestion. While on the phone with her, I get a call on the other line from Lesley Pierre and clicked over to talk to him. "Yo, you wanna come with us to the Rink tomorrow?" he asked excitedly. "Hell Yeah," I answered. The Rink was a skating Rink in northern NJ where all the cool kids hung out. I had never been and was dying to go. I don't remember if it was because I forgot Lesly had just invited me to the Seaport, or if I just decided Lesley Pierre's move was a better play, but I was now double booked.

The next day I decided that I wasn't going to pass up on this chance to hang out with Lesly. When she came to pick me up, it threw me off that she was driving. She was only 15, and that was too young to drive in New York City. She came to the spot on White

St. to get me and was aware that the place was a weed spot. We had talked a lot, but I never told her I pretty much lived at these weed spots. She would always tell me to go to my mother's, but that would be too much to explain.

When she got there, I noticed this light-skinned Spanish looking pretty boy in the back seat, and her female friend sitting up front with her. Right away, I regretted not choosing to go to The Rink with Lesley Pierre. "Yo, how you doing, I'm Juan," he said, reaching out his hand for a shake. "What's up, I'm B Lo," I said while offering him a fist bump instead. "His name is Brian," Lesly yelled back from the front seat. I didn't like the fact she did that, but I liked her so I let it slide.

While we were all four hanging out down by the water, whenever Juan and Lesly would engage in conversation, my blood would boil. It was all innocent and normal dialogue, but in my mind, they were flirting, and it was disrespectful to me. This was the first time I had experienced insecurity in this form. Anytime they talked to each other, and would smile or laugh. I chalked this up as her wanting to get with him.

"I want to go home," I said out of the blue. "What, but we just got here," Lesly replied. "I know, and I don't want to fucking be here," I said. I had just switched my whole demeanor up just like that. I always prided myself in having insight and telling myself I could see shit others couldn't. And this was one of those moments. "Can I talk to you for a second?" Lesly asked. She grabbed my hand and walked me over closer to the water. "What's the problem?" she asked. "You think I'm stupid, I see what the hell is going on, if you want to get with that fucking punk ass dude, go ahead," I said. "Are you crazy, that is my best friend's boyfriend," she said with a confused look on her face. "Just take me home," I said as I walked back toward where we had parked.

The car ride home had a very awkward silence. Lesly's friend would attempt to lighten the mood by telling a joke, or asking her to turn up certain songs on the radio. Lesly knew it would be a bad idea for me to sit next to him again on the ride back, so I sat in the front seat next to her. I just wanted to get out of that car and away from these people. I was now really regretting not going to the Rink with Lesley Pierre. Now, I was even trying to figure out what kind of girl Lesly really was. There was Amarr, the on and off boyfriend Mark Scott, and now, here she was hitting on her best friend's boyfriend. Was she "out there" I wondered.

That 30-minute ride home felt like forever. "Are you going to call me?" she asked as she dropped me off in front of the weed spot. "Yeah, whatever," I said as I got out and closed the door. That insecure, jealous feeling I had experienced that night was a feeling I hated. I knew I wanted to be around this girl, I knew I wanted to spend more time with her, but I had just cut it short because of what I assumed. She called me that night and even apologized if it came off as "flirting," but confirmed it as no such thing. We talked for hours after that and went to bed.

About three days later, I had somehow double-booked Lesly and Lesley Pierre on the same day yet again. Whenever Lesley Pierre would ask me to go somewhere, I would agree. He was a drug dealer with a lot of money, so he always paid for everything and I was just fine with that. He also knew all the cool places to go. Lesly and I had yet to go on a first official date, and this time, she had invited me out to a movie, but again with her friends in tow. She promised me there would be no other guys this time, just her close female friends, her and I. I agreed to go because I wanted to see her, but I kind of wasn't feeling the idea of me going to the movies with three females and just me. My plan was to ask her to come pick me up on White St, and stall her until Lesley Pierre showed up and roll with him.

Lesly and her friends showed up to White St. about 6:30 PM. The movie was scheduled for a 7:15 showing. Lesley Pierre was supposed to pick me up at 7:00 PM so I had mapped my move out perfectly. I went outside and told Lesly to park up so we could chat for a while before we left. She parked and got out and sat on the hood of her car while her friends remained inside her car. From where she had sat, she was facing the building that housed the weed spot. The only thing between her car and the building, was me, and the actual street. Any car that drove down the street behind me, was out of my view because I was facing her.

"Don't you think we should leave now?" she asked. "Nah, we got time, the movie technically won't start until 7:35 because of previews," I said. I was trying my best to stall her, she had opened her legs while she sat on the car and pulled me closer to her. Standing here between her legs was the closest I had ever been to this girl. I could smell her sweet perfume and it was driving my hormones wild. She kissed me on my neck slow and seductively. I felt my joint getting erect as she slowly slipped her tongue into my mouth. My heart was racing. I wanted to say screw the movie, screw Lesley Pierre, and just tell her to drop her friends off and come back so we could have sex. I was hot and bothered. If she had a skirt on, I probably would've tried her right there with her friends sitting in the car. This was getting to too heavy for me.

At around 6:57, as I am praying for Lesley Pierre to be on time, she looks down at her watch and says, "I think we should go now, we're cutting it close." I stepped out from between her legs, looked around for any signs of Lesley Pierre, and then back at her.

When I looked at her face, her eyes were following a dark vehicle driving down the street. The look on her face was as if she had seen the grim reaper driving this car. The car then came to a complete stop, and a tall dark-skinned guy got out and walked over to where we were. He reached his hand out and grabbed Lesly's arm and attempted to pull her off the car. When he grabbed her left arm, I grabbed her right arm, and now here we were literally playing tug of war with this girl. After about five seconds, I let her go.

"Yo, what the fuck you doing down here?" he screamed at her. I was confused as hell. Lesly had maintained that she was single, so who the hell was this guy?

As I turned to walk back inside the weed spot, I could hear the two having an intense conversation, but they weren't close enough for me to make out what was being said. I walked off and made it to the first step that lead to the door of the spot and turned back around. I had never felt this feeling in my life before. I was beginning to hate females because all the emotional pain I had ever gotten was coming from them. First Dawn, and now this. I decided I would take the high road and show Lesly I wasn't jealous or insecure. My plan was to actually tell the guy he could have her and to enjoy her. I made up my mind she was no good.

I calmly walked over to where they were now hugging and said, "No disrespect fam, I don't know you and I don't want any problems, if this is ya shorty, you can have her, she told me she...." before I could finish, he interjected. "Shut the fuck up and get the fuck out of my face," he said while looking at me as if I were a peasant. When he uttered those words, I immediately went to the place I was most comfortable. The place I knew more than any other place. I was going to punch him right there, but something said that wasn't enough. Now it wasn't about the girl at all. Or maybe it was. I just know I had tried for peaceful resolve, and he cursed me out, in front of our weed spot. I didn't say a word to him, I turned around and headed back toward the spot. As I'm walking, I felt a tear go down my face, and I started to bite my half-healed bottom lip. I knew what this meant.

When Jamie opened the door for me, I walked past him and walked right to the spot where I kept my little .25 with the one round in it. Jamie noticed me getting my gun and seen I was angry and jumped up. Koola had also jumped up. "Yo, what up you okay?" Jamie asked as I headed back out the door with the pistol. As I'm walking toward this guy, I was wishing I had the .9mm Amarr had given me, but that was still at Caesar's house. I know I only had one shot in this gun and would have to be accurate with it. I didn't know if this guy had a gun or not, but if he did, I was certainly at a disadvantage, unless I just kill him.

As I'm walking at a much faster pace over to where they are standing, I see Lesley Pierre and another guy I knew named Abe, getting out of a car. Lesley Pierre was smiling, walking toward me, oblivious to what was about to take place. I quickly pointed the gun at the tall guy and told her to move. She wouldn't move, she was seemingly willing to get shot for him. "Move Bitch!" I screamed. I then pointed the gun at the windshield of his car and shot it out. I then ran over to him, hit him with the small pistol and he fell with her landing on top of her. As I hit him with the pistol, Lesley Pierre, Abe, Jamie all stomped him out. I could tell they were trying to avoid hitting her, but she was catching some of these stomps as well. After about 35 seconds of them stomping and me pistol-whipping him, Koola came from out of nowhere with a 10 lb. curl bar and hit him directly in the face with it. The scream that came from his body was like nothing I had ever heard from a human being.

That was my cue that enough was enough. I wasn't fully healed from the first car accident yet, so although I could walk fast, I couldn't run.

I could hear sirens blaring in the background and I knew we all needed to get the fuck out of there. I saw a house with a small fence that led to a dark back block where I knew I could make an escape. I jumped the small fence, and as I'm walking towards another taller fence in the back of the house, I could hear the subtle growl of a dog getting louder. I looked back and seen a huge Rottweiler headed towards me.

As much as both my legs hurt, I started to run. I ran as fast as I could, jumped as high as I could and latched on the fence and began to climb it. I could actually feel the dog nipping at my sneaker soles. I made it to the top of that fence, and just fell and landed in the tall grass on the other side of it. My legs were in so much pain I couldn't stand up. I laid there thinking about how much of a mess I was making of my own life. I must've laid there for two hours, and if I had to judge by the sounds of the emergency vehicles I heard rushing to White St, I knew I had just made yet another really, really big stupid mistake.

"Don't you ever call me again in your life you asshole. You almost killed him and you broke my finger," Lesly screamed through the other end of the phone. I started to reply, but then just hung the phone up. *What am I calling for anyway*, I thought. I had asked her many times if she had a boyfriend and she always said no. Besides, I didn't start the fight, I tried to be civil with the guy. He had no business telling me to shut the fuck up.

Again, I was making excuses to myself to justify my behavior. What I wasn't realizing at the time was, even though it seemed I was the victor in the midst of hurting these people, I always lost in the end. My foolish pride was beginning to dominate my life. I once heard a saying that goes, *'pride kills more black men than guns, police, drugs and heart disease combined.'* Go figure.

Around 2:00 that same morning, I met up with Lesley Pierre on his block to catch up. "Yo, what was that all about, and who the hell was that dude?" he asked. "I have no clue, he just came on the block being disrespectful; You know I can't have that," I said. "Yo man, that shit was so crazy," he said excitedly. "I told my man J Scott about what happened, and now he wants to meet you." I had known of J Scott, but this guy was like urban legend. He was one of those guys you would hear about, but never ever see. I had also heard that Lesley Pierre was selling drugs for J Scott, and now everything started to make sense. All the cars and jewelry Lesley Pierre had couldn't just be coming from some 16-year-old High School student who worked at Shop Rite. "Set it up. I'll meet him," I said. Many things went through my mind about this, why would he want to meet me? I didn't know, but I was about to find out.

Lesley Pierre and I walked down a dark block behind a huge flea market. *Why are we walking*, I thought, but didn't say. Was this J Scott guy so mysterious you had to walk to him to meet him?

Not even two minutes later, a new, grey Mazda MPV pulls up, the door slides open and a semi chubby, light-skinned guy says, "get in" and we both hop in. J Scott looked nothing like I had expected him to look. He had long curly hair and bright blue eyes. By the way people talked about him, I was expecting a big Shaquille O' Neal looking type of character.

"I heard ya'll had to put in some work last night," he said to me. I downplayed the severity. "Yeah, a little something, kid lucky to be alive," I said nonchalantly.

My cousin Jamie had gotten word from someone who new Koola that the guy we beat up was in the hospital with a broken eye socket. As soon as I heard this, I knew it was the blow Koola had delivered with that curl bar that had did it. "Well, I could use some soldiers out here if you're interested," J Scott said looking back at me while trying to focus on the road. I felt I was past being anybody's soldier, even at 14. But I also knew that working with this guy would put me on another level. He made a lot of money and had a lot of territory he controlled. I would surpass any of my peers if I worked for J Scott. I tried not to show my excitement as I answered.

"Yeah, man, I'm with whatever." We parked in front of a laundromat, and he insisted we finish our talk in there. He explained that what he needed for me as of now was to go pick up work from Washington Heights, and bring it back up to Spring Valley. For every trip I would make $500. When he said he needed soldiers, I assumed he meant shooters. What Lesley Pierre had told him about me was that I was a shooter, nothing about drugs. Again, I had to conceal my excitement.

"That sounds good to me," I said. As we walked out to go marvel at the new MPV he had just got, he made a comment about wanting to put rims on it. "I know a guy on Atlantic Avenue in Brooklyn who got a dope rim shop," I said. "What you doing tomorrow?" he asked "Nothing, if you want, we can go," I replied. This meeting with J Scott was the start of a chapter of my life I didn't see coming. Meeting him would become the definition of a silver lining.

J Scott looked nervous as they lifted his new Mazda MPV and began removing the wheels one by one. "How well do you know these guys?" he asked me. I assured him he was in good hands and wasn't being taken. Mind you, this was a time when the Mazda MPV was one of the hottest cars on the road. Who would've thought a soccer mom van would win the affection of the Hip Hop community and be the #1 car to be cruising in.

The guys at the shop told us to leave and come back in a few hours and this made J Scott even more nervous. As we walked and talked, waiting for his new wheels, he explained some things about how Lesley Pierre had been messing up. He was looking to cut him off and find his replacement. I explained to him that while I had no problems transporting the drugs, selling drugs just wasn't my thing. When I told him my dream was to be a rapper, he looked at me like I had five heads. "Can you rap?" he asked. "I think I'm good," I said. "Well, then go for it," he added. "But you can't be out here shooting people AND be a rapper," he concluded. He was absolutely correct.

CHAPTER 18

Young and Sprung

It threw me for a total loop when I saw the name Lesly Rodriguez show on the caller I.D. I hadn't heard her voice since my attempt to call her and she told me to never call again. I was two for two with girls who had told me to never call again. I had some major bad luck with the ladies. Something told me to ignore the call, but then something else made me pick it up on the fourth ring.

"Hello," I said. "Brian, can we talk?" a soft voice said on the other end. "What is there to talk about?" I said. "You lied to me and could've put my life in jeopardy," I added. "Brian, that guy you all beat up was Mark Scott, the ex-boyfriend I told you about. I was trying to explain to him that him and I were done, and you just over-reacted," she said. "I'm sorry for it all, I want to talk, just in person and not over the phone," Lesly said. I wanted to talk to her too. I had missed her. I also remembered seeing her hugging that guy when I ran out with the gun. Maybe this was a setup. "If you want to meet in person, you gotta come to White St," I said.

I knew she wouldn't want to come back to the scene of the incident, and if she was willing to, maybe she cared for me after all. "I really don't wanna go back over there," she said. "But if that's the only way we can talk, I will."

While Jamie and I were in the weed spot watching TV, I notified him that Lesly was coming over to talk. He didn't think it was a good idea, but I talked him into letting her come.

When she got there, I walked her into a back room where she sat on the bed. I sat down next to her, and as soon as I smelled that perfume, it seemed we had picked up where we left off before the Mark Scott guy had interrupted us. We didn't get two words out before complete passion took over. I picked her up by her short, thick frame and laid her on her back. I then pulled down her shorts as I licked her belly button. After removing her shorts, I looked down to see her panties wedged in between perfectly shaven labia. Her vagina was so fat, it looked like a plump, juicy, ripe peach sitting perfectly in between her firm thighs. She took her hand and began to massage her own vagina slow and seductively. When I looked up, she was looking down at me as to say, "*impressive huh.*" Yes, it was most certainly impressive.

She then began to push my head slowly down toward her very moist mid-section. This was new ground for me. I was overwhelmed, yet eager at the same time. I began to go down on a woman for the first time in my life. We would make love multiple times throughout the course of the night. We didn't do much talking at all, but this night, I realized I liked her more than I even thought I did. I was sprung.

The next morning, while I was walking Lesly out, Koola was walking in. "Yo, what the fuck is this?" he yelled angrily. "What the fuck is this white bitch doing in my spot B Lo?" I had never seen him this hostile before. "Why is this fucking bitch in here? This girl is trouble and I never want to see this bitch here again." He screamed. "Yo Chill Koola, chill," I said trying to calm him down. "Fuck him, Brian, I'm leaving," she said as she walked away. I was furious, because even though I thought Lesly was deceitful and dishonest, I had fell for her. And I was as I said, sprung.

Over the next few weeks, my new order of operations with J Scott was going smooth. I would get Mike Boykin, the same kid who Nicky Aiken had convinced me to have a fight with years earlier, to be my driver. We would go to Washington Heights and pick up enough drugs to send both of our teenage asses to jail for many, many years. J Scott had also told me about a move he eventually wanted to make to Virginia, but for now, everything was running smooth here.

Lesley and me on a jail visit circa 1996

The new school year was scheduled to start in a few days and I couldn't wait. By this time, shoplifting was a thing of the past. This school year, I would be using some of the thousands of dollars I had made from transporting drugs for J Scott to buy all the clothes and supplies I would need. I still had the big chain Jamie had bought me from Mart 125, so my jewelry game was on point. I had even bought the same Timberland coat Tupac had on in the "Brenda's Got a Baby" video. I was super straight headed into the 10th grade.

Lesly and I had gotten much closer by now. I still didn't trust her enough to make her my official girlfriend, but the sex was so crazy it had me kind of strung out. She was also excited about the upcoming school year, but every time the topic would come up, she would say she didn't think it was a good idea for me to go to school. I never asked why she thought that, but it always stayed in the back of my mind.

About a week before the official first day of school, Adonis and Caesar had come with a proposal about us opening our own weed spot. I was now making money, but I wanted to make more so I listened. Although I was leery of selling crack or heroin, I would sell weed with no issues.

We put our money together and bought a whole pound of some good stuff. The only problem now was, we had no spot to sell it out of. I really didn't like Koola because he had talked down and played me in front of Lesly. I didn't react because I knew he was actually right. She had brought trouble there, and the police were called. This was his place of illegal business and she shouldn't have been in there. But, I was sprung so I took her side over his. I even suggested we sell our weed in front of White St as I had before, but Jamie politely asked that we didn't. Said it would cause more problems.

I called my cousin Mister up in Newburgh and he suggested we go up there to sell the weed. He claimed he had a spot where we could get that amount of weed off in no time. They grabbed the pound of weed, I grabbed the .9mm pistol Amarr loaned me, and us three headed up to Newburgh to make some extra money.

Everything Mister had told me was accurate. He had a spot up there where people came in droves to buy the weed. We had sold the whole pound in about four or five days.

The plan now was to take the money we made, go buy two more pounds and keep flipping it. The hardest part was keeping Mister and Adonis from arguing every day. On the day we were supposed to leave Newburgh to go get more weed from NYC, my cousin Arron was hosting a blackjack game in one of his gambling holes. Arron was a grown man trapped in a teenager's body. It's almost like he was born to be a hustler. I had about $350.00 on me when they first dealt me in.

Hand after hand, this one stocky black guy dealing would turn his cards up and have 19 or better. He was winning so much, I assumed he was cheating. But I knew Arron wouldn't allow me to be cheated.

As Arron, Adonis, Caesar and Mister looked on, they watched me losing hand after hand. After the $350.00 I had in my pocket was gone, I asked Caesar to let me hold whatever money he had to win my money back. He gave me about $60.00 and I quickly lost that. This guy was taking everybody's money. It was down to him and another player when I pulled Adonis to the side. I asked him to let me continue to gamble with the money we made to get more weed. "Come on Lo, that's everybody's bread, that's the re up, we can't lose that," he said. I decided to not listen to Adonis. I reached in the nap sack we kept the money in, and continued gambling.

In only a half an hour, I was back down to only $200 of the $1500 we had made selling the weed out there. He had almost won it all. I watched as Caesar, Adonis and even Mister looked at me in extreme disappointment. I wished I had listened to Adonis. This is why until this very day, I never really got into gambling after this. I felt really bad for losing mostly all the money we had all earned together.

"What you doing, you in?" the stocky guy asked as he shuffled the cards with a mischievous grin. *This guy has to be cheating*, I said to myself. "Nah, I'm out," I said as I got up gathering the $200 we had left. I felt like a complete asshole.

"C'mon man, you might as well lose it all," he said, smiling as everyone got up to leave. I looked at Caesar and Adonis again and I just couldn't let them take this loss for my action. I had to win this money back. "Fuck it, deal the cards," I said as I threw the $200 on the table. At this point, everyone looked at me like I was a complete idiot. Caesar shook his head and walked out the door. "You betting the whole $200.00?" he asked as he continued shuffling. "Yeah, it's down there, ain't it?" I replied.

He dealt us both two cards and he had a King of Diamond showing. *How is this fucking guy so lucky?* Now I was really convinced he was cheating. I looked at my cards and had a 7 of clubs, and an 8 of hearts. Probably the worse hand you can get when the dealer is showing a face card. "Hit me," I said. He threw a card face down in my direction, and I slowly lifted it up to see a 9 of spades. I was busted. In Blackjack, whoever gets closest to 21 without going over wins. I had 24. He had won yet another hand.

"It's been a fun time, gentlemen. Get home safely," he said sarcastically as he gathered his winnings. "Hold up, hold up," I said. "I ain't done yet, homie." His eyes lit up as if he were excited he would also be taking whatever money I had left. I motioned for Adonis to hand me the nap sack. This was the same nap sack he had seen me dig in to retrieve the $1500 he had just taken, so I know he assumed I was getting more money. He didn't realize this is also where I kept the .9mm handgun I had brought up there with me.

I reached in the bag and pulled out the gun and cocked it. Everyone who was still at the table put their hands in the air. "You know what this is," I said as I pointed the gun at the dealer. "Yo, Arron, what's up with this?" he said. Arron was half smiling while trying to be serious as he spoke. "Yo cuz, this ain't cool," Arron said. "Nah, I don't really be gambling like that A, I only do this shit for fun," I said. I looked back at the dealer, "Give me the fucking money, now," I said sternly. He passed all the money on the table, he then went in his pockets and pulled out more. I passed it all to Adonis. "How much did we have for the weed?" I asked Adonis. "$1500.00," he said, sounding excited. "Count out $1500.00 and give him the rest of his money back," I told Adonis. Adonis separated the two amounts, and threw a stack of bills back on the table. "Now *you* gentleman have a nice day," I said as we all got up and walked out. Once we exited the gambling hole, we piled into our vehicle and got the fuck up outta there. "Catch you later, Cuz," I yelled to Arron as we sped off.

School was a day away, and unlike the year when I had to play hooky the first day because of Dennis's over-sized Giorgio Brutini's, this year I had everything. I had money, jewelry, a new cell phone and the latest Polo gear that Ralph Lauren had released. Lesly and I attended different schools, so I knew I wouldn't see her, but I called her the night before to ask what she would be wearing. "Brian, I don't think you should go to school tomorrow," she said. Why was she so adamant about me not going to school? "In fact, if you don't go, I won't go and I'll come to pick you up and we could have some fun," she added. Her offer sounded very tempting, and by now, she knew she could control me with her fat vagina, but this was the first day. Any other day I would've happily cut school to be with her, but the first day of school was like the Met Gala. "I'm going to school Lesly, and so are you," I said. "But you really, really shouldn't," Lesly repeated.

I walked into Spring Valley High School, feeling like the man. Although I was barely 16, I felt like I was a man amongst children. By this time, I had been in all kinds of shit. I was sexually active. I had been in detention centers, shootings, robberies, drug trafficking. I had even tried my hand at pimping, but I had lost my only Hoe when I insisted we split the money *she* had been turning tricks for instead of me taking it all. Weird, I know.

In my mind, I was a certified gangster. My only real purpose for coming to school was to show out. I wanted to show up and show out. I walked into homeroom, surprised to be greeted by a beautiful African American school teacher. I immediately pulled out my grey Motorola flip phone and placed it on my desk. As the other students balked at me, the teacher asked me my name. "B Lo, I mean, Brian Carenard," I answered. "Great that you are here, Mr. Carenard.

They asked me to let them know upfront if you made it to school today," she said with a smile. She then picked up the phone and dialed. I didn't think twice about who "they" might've been, or even why "they" cared to know if I was there. "They" probably knew my history and I thought I wasn't coming in today I figured.

She hung up the phone and walked to the front of the classroom to introduce herself. I had opened up my new Polo P Wing jacket to expose the big gold chain I had dangling on my neck. I really felt out of place in a school setting. After all I was doing in the street, this place felt foreign. These same kids who were my same age and older, appeared to be children. I was growing up way too fast.

As I reached in my JanSport bookbag to take out my rap book, Vincent the school security guard had knocked on the door. Before the teacher could answer the door, it opened and Vincent stuck his head in.

"Carenard, can I see you for a moment?" he asked. I got up and walked out the door to be greeted by two plainclothes detectives, three uniformed officers, and the school principal. "Brian Carenard, put your hands behind your back, you have the right to remain silent, you're under arrest for Assault and Criminal Possession of a weapon," one detective said. As they handcuffed me, I noticed kids in the hallways staring at me, while other kids poked their heads out of classrooms to see what was going on.

If they were staring, I was going to play into it. I threw on the meanest face I could as I walked through the hallways staring back at the kids as to say, "This is that shit a real gangster goes through."

CHAPTER 19

Wild Animalescents

When they got me down to the police station, they fingerprinted me and took me into a small interrogation room for questioning. At this time, I didn't know that it's always best to exercise your Miranda rights. They asked me about the night in July where Mark Scott had been assaulted on White St. I was doing everything to avoid answering their questions, but they wouldn't let me leave, eat or anything until I did.

They promised me the easiest way out of this was to just tell them what happened. I told them him and I had a simple fistfight over a girl and that was it. "Who was shooting the gun, Brian?" the officer yelled. "What gun?" I asked. "We found a .25 shell casing and the guy's window was shout out and you did it," another officer screamed. "Yeah, and we picked your boy Troy

Campbell up the other day for this same charge, he told us everything," the officer said as he dropped a statement signed by Troy Campbell AKA Koola.

All the police cared about was who fired the gun. "You guys banged that kid up pretty badly, and he didn't even turn you guys in," he said. "You're going to jail for a long time buddy, and you can thank your pal, and your little girlfriend for it," the police said as he walked out.

Now it made sense. All I could hear was Lesly's voice telling me not to go to school. Now I see why she was suggesting I didn't go. She had gone to the Police Station the night of that incident and gave statements on all of us. The only name she didn't know was Jamie's, and I don't think she even realized Lesley Pierre and Abe were there. This bitch had sent me to jail for this dude. I was steaming mad. Beyond.

I got arraigned the next morning and was held on $10,000 bail. I tried calling every number I could remember collect, but the only person who didn't have a block on their phone was the same the person who put me in here. I wasn't about to call her. I was transported to Rockland County Jail where I was given an orange jumpsuit and a pair of imitation Pro-Keds. This wasn't Highland or St Cabrini. This was the real deal. Or at least that is what I was anticipating. As stupid as this may sound, I was hoping adult jail would be scary or intimidating. It wasn't at all.

As soon I walked into the pod, I seen old crackheads who had gained their weight back. A couple of people I hadn't seen in a while and had been wondering where they were. One of those people was my homie, Black.

Black was from Brooklyn too but had been living in Rockland County since a very young age. It was refreshing to see someone I knew. He had got caught with a Mac-10 over the winter. Police had found him hiding in a pile of snow as he tried to elude them after shooting up a party with the same gun.

"What you in here for B Lo?" Black asked as I looked for my cell. "Some bullshit," I replied. "Isn't today the first day of school?" he asked. "Yeah man, they got me in school," I replied. "But, I should be up outta here in no time," I continued. "I got a bullshit assault and weapons charge. This fucking dude Koola told on me," I ranted. "Koola told on you?" he asked, sounding surprised. "Yeah man, they showed me his statement," I said. "How much is your bail?" he asked? "It's 10 thousand," I replied.

Now I knew 10 thousand dollars was a lot of money, but I figured between Jamie, J Scott, Lesley Pierre, McGregor or maybe if even my father would contribute, I could bail out of here. All I needed now was someone I could call without a block on their phone. I tried every number I could think of. My next court date was in a month, and I just knew I wouldn't still be in here in a month.

About a month and half later, I got a letter from Lesly. I don't know if she had done it purposely or if it was just coincidence, but the letter made my cell reek of her perfume. It was the same smell I remembered from the day of the incident when we first kissed on her car. The same smell from when I invited her to White St. and we made love for the first time. This same beautiful, sweet smell from this foul fucked up person who up and gave the information that put me here. This was psychological torture. I tried everything to get that smell out of my cell. I wanted it out, yet every 20 minutes I would go fetch the letter and inhale it deeply.

I took about four days to even read the letter, but once I did, my level of confusion and uncertainty was killing me. In her letter, she apologized for making the statements. She said she was nervous and that the police coerced her to tell on me. I knew she was lying because I had seen the statements from her two friends, and they both claimed to not know who we were. She offered to visit me and asked me to please call her. I needed a visit badly. I needed a person to call who would make three-way calls for me so I could try and get the bail money up. She seemed sincere and super apologetic, but I couldn't get past the fact she told on me. This was a female who wasn't in the streets doing crime, yet I still expected her to live by the "No

Snitching" street code. Not only that, I felt she had chosen him over me and that was eating me. What was that saying about black men and pride? Yep, it's real.

Weeks had passed and I had not called or written Lesly back. Not because I didn't want to, but because my pride wouldn't allow it. I was cutting off my nose to spite my face once again. How was anybody supposed to know to come to try and get me if I wasn't calling or letting them know my situation? This was a new feeling for me and not a good one. I didn't feel heartbroken, I felt betrayed and this made me angry, sad and confused all at the same time.

Over the next few weeks, the letters from Lesly kept coming in. But I wouldn't reply to them. My stubbornness was now at an all-time high. I had engaged in the ultimate battle of war of wills with myself. My will was weakening because I needed help, but my Zodiac sign of Cancer was still winning. She told on me and how I grew up, we just don't fuck with rats, point-blank. Male, female, or otherwise.

On my next court appearance, my court-appointed attorney with the cheap suit and cheap cologne had filed a motion for a bail reduction. He gave the judge a whole spew about how I had just turned 16 and needed to be in school. The Judge's rebuttal was that I already had a pretty lengthy criminal history for my young age. He even mentioned me being arrested twice on the same day. He denied the motion, and offered me one year in the county jail, which I refused.

The system, these courtrooms and everything were taking a toll on my life. This was turning me into a bitter individual. I remember looking at the judge as he denied my motion, wishing I could cause him real harm. And I could tell he could tell what I was thinking. I came back from court ready to cause trouble. I needed to get out of here.

Every day we had to lock in from 3:00 PM to 6:00 P.M. This would be when I would write rhymes and study my craft. By now, I had filled up about four or five composition notebooks with raps. I had story raps, fun raps, battle raps, but the gangster raps were my specialty. I would kill about 17 people in a rap before the hook part even came in. I felt confident rapping about gangster shit because I was living it. This is also why they came out so good.

As many raps as I had been writing, I would still recite them only for three people. LaDedra, Caesar and Jamie. I would go out on the recreation yard and listen to all the jailhouse rappers rapping, and wouldn't say a word. I knew I was better than everyone, but I wouldn't rap a word. I would stand around and listen like everyone else. I don't know why I was so shy when rapping for people, but it was always the case.

There was one time Caesar was having a rap battle against this kid who called himself Alley Oop. The battle was neck and neck until a few of Alley Oop's rap partner started all verbally going in on him. Caesar would look over at me as to say, *Oh, I got a partner, too.* He summoned me to join in and help him, but I was too shy to rap in front of the crowd, so he took a bad L. He wouldn't let me live that down for months and months after that. My dreams of being a rapper were fading as I noticed a pattern that followed that of a career criminal. I was supposed to be in school, but here I was. Locked up again.

On this one quiet evening, while I sniffed one of Lesly's letters, my weak will had broken and I lost the battle. I found myself with a pen and paper in my hand, and it wasn't to write another rap song.

Dear Lesly, I hope this letter finds you and your family in the best of health......

I had written her to explain how betrayed I felt by her actions and she had only to tell me she was involved. I also let her know how much I missed her and wanted to see her. I knew she would need to get a permission slip to come visit me without a parent because of her age and I was damn sure her mother, Mrs. Rodriguez, would not accompany her. From what I had heard, her mother had really liked Mark Scott. And look what I had done to him. I gave her a time to be next to the phone and told her I would call. I felt weak as shit, but I needed some outside correspondence.

Aside from writing raps and playing spades, this place was the most boring place ever. That's one thing jail TV shows like *Lock Up Raw* and those other ones don't show or tell their audience; how fucking boring jail is. It's boredom to the point of torture. You do the same thing every day and it becomes so routine it absolutely begins to drive you crazy. That's why the day I seen my boy Quentin walk through that gate with his orange jumpsuit, I was ecstatic.

Quentin was a kid I knew since I was about 11 or 12 years old. My Aunt Celestine knew his mother so her son, my cousin Lance and I would go over to his house.

Quentin showed us our first porno movie when we were kids and the shit blew my mind. Well, here he was walking through the door on fresh drug charges.

"Yooooo Q!" I hollered as I seen him walk through with his super ice grill on. As soon as he noticed me, his mean stone face turned into a huge smile. "Yo, what's up Sun?" he screamed from across the pod. "Let me put my shit down. I'll be right there." Like me, Quentin wasn't a stranger to getting into trouble. But my charges were always violence, and his were always drugs. "What you in here for?" I asked almost certain I knew already. "I got a sealed indictment for a $50 drug sale," he replied. "How about you?" he asked. "Man, this nigga Koola told on me after we had to wash this kid," I replied.

I wondered why I always mentioned Koola telling, but not Lesly. Maybe because I would have to explain the visits later. "Yeah, I heard about that shit," he said, "It was that kid Mark Scott right? Ya'll fucked him up pretty bad," he added. "Why ya'll do that to that kid, man? He ain't even like that," Quentin said. This made me wish Mark Scott had just accepted me trying to be nice and moved on. Instead, he wanted to play tough. *Had to be the female,* I thought.

Now that Quentin was in here, I had someone to talk to every day. My boy Black had got sentenced to prison, and since he left, I was in there bored and alone. Now, instead of being bored by myself. I was bored with this guy every day. We would get so bored, we would sign up for Muslim service just to get out of the pod for a change of scenery. No disrespect to Allah, but even that got boring to us after a while.

One day, Quentin came to my cell and seen me rapping one of the raps I had written in my notebook. "This nigga come to jail now he thinks he a rapper," he said to no one but me. "I been a rapper nigga, fuck outta here," I said playfully. "So, let me hear something," he said. I was not accustomed to rapping for people at all. But I figured *what the hell, its only Quentin,* and started to pick out which rap I would say for him. As I flipped pages, I found one I really liked about racist police and began spitting.

Police is pushing Grand Marquis's and Chevy Caprice's stroll/Crimes in my soul, plus my heart piece is cold/ I leave a pig's vest pierced, I could tell by the smell of burnt chest hairs, If I get caught even death will be less years....... Fuck Police.

As soon as I was done, Quentin went silent for a second before he blurted out "Get the fuck outta here, you didn't write that shit," he yelled. "Then who the fuck handwriting is this nigga?" I replied, showing him my notebook.

It made me feel a sense of confidence that he thought my rap was so good I didn't write it. He made me prove it by spitting another one, and another one, and another one. I ended rapping for him for about two hours straight that day. He seemed amazed by my skillset. "Yo, man, you better than most of the guys on the radio," he said. I agreed.

From that day on, whenever there would be other rappers in a cipher, Quentin would go over to them and yell out, "All ya'll niggas is trash, can't none of ya'll fuck with my boy B Lo right here," and motion over to me. They seemed confused this guy was here saying I was so good, but I wouldn't ever rap; not even once. Some had even walked by and seen me writing raps so they had an idea I rapped. But I would never ever rap for anyone besides Quentin. Quentin would come to my cell at least once a day and say, "Let me hear that racist police joint again." and I would spit it...

It had been a day when the boredom was just really, really getting to us. We were in Muslim service and that wasn't enough to cure it. "Yo, we should go back to the pod and fuck somebody up," Quentin said. "I'm with it," I replied. "Who you don't like in there?" he asked.

I had had two fights with the guys I had issues with and won them both. I had no problems with anybody anymore. At least not in there. "Bro, it don't even matter at this point, just set it off and I'm going in." I replied. "Bet," he said looking excited.

I didn't know if Quentin was half-joking or not when he suggested we just start picking fights with random people, but my plan was to just follow his lead. We walked back into the pod from Muslim service and Quentin immediately walked over to a kid named Delano and said, "You a Bitch ass Nigga yo." The kid stood up and before he could reply, Quentin had punched him in his mouth.

Delano was a Jamaican drug dealer who should've had too much money to be in jail. I hate to play into the stereotype about Jamaicans, but as soon as Quentin punched him, Delano threw a weak ass kick that missed by a mile. Quentin then began beating the shit out of him. While they were squabbling, I see a fat kid named Dominick walking towards the action. I didn't have a problem with Dominick. As I had told Quentin,

I hadn't had a problem with anybody in there but I gave him my word if he set it off, I would go too.

As Dominick inched toward the action, I quickly wrapped my arm around his neck and threw him in a chokehold. I could feel the life leaving his body as his fat frame squirmed to get free. As soon as I knew he was out on his feet, I let go and watched his fat body hit the floor like a sack of potatoes. Within seconds, the officers rushed in, demanding everyone get on the floor. Quentin was still pounding on Delano and Dominick was laid out snoring.

They restrained Quentin, woke Dominick up and ordered everyone to their cells. About 20 minutes later, after they had restored order, they let people back out of their cells for recreation. Everyone's cell had opened besides Quentin's, Delano's, Dominick's and mine. What the hell were we thinking?

If we thought we were bored before. Now it was intensified by a hundred. Quentin and I each got 30 days keep locked, while Delano and Dominick got 15. When there was a fight in there, each participant got in trouble whether or not you started it. I felt kind of bad for Dominick because he didn't do shit. The only thing he did wrong was come to jail.

Being on keep lock was like the light version of being in the hole; or in solitary confinement. Actually, looking back, being on keep lock was worse because you're in your cell for 23 hours of the day on both, but when you're only on keep lock, you can still hear and see people enjoying their recreation time. At least in the hole or in solitary confinement, it's rather quiet down there, and you know everyone is in the same messed up position as you.

I decided I would use these next 30 days on keep lock to write even more raps. Lesly had somehow gotten permission from her mother to come see me so I had something to look forward to.

I pondered on what I was doing with my life. I didn't know anybody who made it as a rapper in real life, but I knew drug dealers and gangsters who lived well. That rapper shit was my dream, but it was far-fetched. The closest I had ever even got to a real rapper was at Special Ed's video shoot when I was 12, or when I would chase Marley Marl or Pete Rock's luxury cars down the street to get a glimpse. They had both hit it big and bought huge houses up in Rockland County.

I would lay on my back and stare at the ceiling and just ask God why he dealt me such a bad hand. And soon as I would question God, I would reel myself right back in and blame myself. I made my bed, I had to lay in it.

"Carenard, Cell 26, you got a visit," the officer screamed out. As soon as he did, my heart started pounding. I hadn't seen Lesly in 3 and half months now. I was nervous, excited and happy as hell to be getting out that cell for a few hours or so. I hadn't had a haircut so I was scruffy, but at this point, she knew that I had fought and was on keep lock. As I walked in the visiting room, I seen other inmates hugging their spouses and playing with their children. I looked around to see Lesly looking pretty as ever, waiting for me to come greet her. As soon as I gave her a hug, I could smell that same sweet perfume that seemed to hypnotize me. This time, it had a different effect. This time it reminded me of my cell and I let it be known. "You smell like my cell," I said smiling. "Stop spraying those letters with that perfume."

As we sat and talked, she asked me questions that made me really think. Things like, if I wanted to go to college, or if I wanted to ever have a family, even if I could see myself living to grow old someday. The saddest part was, as I thought about all of her questions, I realized my answer to each of her questions was no. I hadn't even known anyone who had went to college. In fact, I knew more people who had went to prison than had went to college. I had known more people who had gotten killed before they were of age to go to college, than people who had actually went to college. This was my life and that was that.

Her questions were starting to become irritating. The reality of my life had become hard to face. "Can you go to school in here?" she asked. "A C.O. told me about some G.E.D. shit they have in here, but I'm going home soon, Jamie is going to get me out," I said. "Do you think they'll let you back in school?" she asked. "If I were you, I would get my G.E.D. in here, and start looking for colleges when I got out," she continued. "I don't wanna talk about this," I said to her.

For years I had heard people make fun of other people who got G.E.Ds. They would say G.E.D. stood for "Good Effort Dummy," or "Getting Even Dumber." I even heard one proud guy call it a "Good Enough Diploma." I wasn't thinking about that shit. To me, my life was Rhyme or Crime. Either I would be a famous rapper, or an infamous gangster.

As they told us to wrap up our visit, she said, "Brian, there is something I see in you that is very special." The same thing Mama Sampson used to tell me. "Do you think I would be here after what you did if I didn't think you were special?" she added. "You and your friends could've killed me," she said with tears running down her eyes.

"Alright, visiting hours are over," a husky officer yelled from over my shoulder. I stood up and said my goodbyes and headed back to my cell, where I would be locked in for the rest of the day. On the way back, I asked the officer escorting me how I could get into the G.E.D. program. He said he would fill me in the next day and try to get me set up. I thanked him and went about the rest of my day.

My first day of the G.E.D. program was a breeze. I don't know if it was because of how easy the work was, or because I was happy to be off of keep lock. Thirty days of being locked in an 8x10' cell for 23 hours a day was beginning to take its toll on me. I made a mental note to never listen to Quentin's ideas on how to cure boredom again.

They moved the kid Dominick to another part of the facility, but I had made sure to get an apology over to him via another inmate. I had choked the kid out for absolutely nothing, and it weighed heavily on me. I never got to know if he accepted my apology or not, but I hoped he had.

Now that I was out of that cell, I could call Lesly and have her make three-way calls for me so I could try to get this bail money up. I had been in there three and a half months and really wanted to get out. The holidays were here and I didn't want to spend all of my second holiday season away from my friends and family. I called Lesly and had her dial Jamie's number for me. He picked up on the third ring.

"Hello," he answered. "Yo Fam, it's me, B Lo," I said. "I can't talk long because these collect calls are ridiculously expensive, but my bail is $10k and I need to get out of here." I continued. "You think you can get everybody together to come up with the money?" I asked desperately. "I don't know B, $10k is a lot of money, but I'll get on it and see what I could do, don't worry."

Him telling me this made me feel so much better. I knew if not anybody else, I could depend on Jamie. Lesly was listening in on the call and could hear the tone of my mood switch. "I told you I'll be out of here soon," I told her. "I won't even be here by the time they give the test." She stayed silent for a moment. "Oh yeah, I forgot to tell you, I signed up for the G.E.D. program," I said. If you could hear somebody smile, I definitely heard it that day. "That great, I'm so proud of you," she said. We talked a little longer and hung up.

"Carenard, you got a visit," a skinny female officer said while standing directly in front of my cell. This was rather confusing because it was a school day and Lesly only showed up on weekends. Who could this have been? Nobody else came to visit me. Maybe my mother came even after I wrote and asked her not to. I didn't want my mother to see me like this because I knew she would cry, and then I would cry, and jail ain't the place for other people to see you crying.

I quickly put on my jumpsuit and walked down to the visiting room. When I got there, I seen my court-appointed attorney and this suit he had on looked cheaper than the last one. He had a huge smile on his face, which made me curious. "Sit down, I got good news," he said. "I got the judge to grant our motion for a bail reduction, and he reduced your bail to $1000," he said, smiling from ear to ear.

I couldn't believe my ears. I was going home. I damn near hugged the guy. "It's always better to fight your case from the outside, so contact your family and let them know, and when you get out, come down to my office and we will figure out the next steps," he said. I thanked him and went back to the pod as excited as a mega millions lottery winner. Now all I needed to do was make a few calls and I was out.

As the G.E.D. teacher congratulated and passed out certificates to those who had passed the test. I waited patiently to hear my name. I knew I had passed it, but my goal was to get the highest score in the class. As soon as she said, "Carenard, 740," I knew nobody was beating that. I couldn't wait to go back to the pod so I could call Lesly and tell her. She was the one who even suggested I take the test, so she deserved to know first.

What didn't dawn on me at the time was, this GED equaled having an actual High School Diploma. That meant when I did get out of here, I wouldn't be able to go back to my high school. I had literally spent only 2 or 3 weeks in high school altogether and it was over already. There would be no prom, no homecoming, no graduation, none of those things. Not that I was into any of that shit anyway, but it would've been nice to have the option.

I called Lesly that night and asked her to call Jamie again. "Do you think you need to call him every day?"

she asked. "He knows your bail is only $1,000, Brian. You told him a thousand times already," she said.

Lesly herself had even been trying to get up some of the money to help, but her only income was a small weekly allowance. Besides, she had been catching hell from her parents about the high phone bill they accrued from my collect calls.

Jamie had told me he was gathering the money for almost a month now. When it was $10,000, I could understand the delay, but this was $1000. I watched these guys make that in a day. I wondered how between all these people who claimed to care about me, can they not come up with $1000 in all this time. I asked Lesly to dial my mother, who had made it clear that she was just as broke as she was when I got arrested. I had an idea. I kind of knew it was a long shot, but I was desperate.

My mother answered the phone sounding distressed but lightened up as soon as she heard my voice. "Hey baby, how you doing in there?" she asked. I let her know I was fine, asked about my siblings and got right to the point. I was so eager I forgot to even tell her about my G.E.D. "Hey Ma, do you think my father will help put up some of the money to get me out?" I asked. "Well, you know your father Brian, but I guess it can't hurt to ask him," she gave me his number and I told myself I'd call later in the week. I wanted to provide Jamie with more time before I asked my father for anything.

That evening, I walked around the pod showing off my G.E.D. to anybody who cared to see it. While I was making my rounds, one older gentleman by the name of Truman asked me to sit down and chat with him. Truman was probably in his late 40s and looked like he had lived a very hard life. "Have a seat, young mon," he said in a Jamaican accent. "I see you're showing off your ting there," he said. "Yeah man, I got my G.E.D. today," I replied. "I got the highest score in the class." He didn't seem impressed.

"You know I see when you and Quentin beat up the boy dem," he uttered. "You hang around with boy like Quentin, you going to trow ya whole life away," he continued. "I used to be like that boy when I was a youth, and look, I been in and out of prison my whole life," he said making direct eye contact. "You can use that ting in your hand and make a future for yourself, or you can end up like me, being in here when you're old with nothing." This wasn't the first time I heard this, but for some reason, this time, it hit me a little harder. I couldn't imagine being incarcerated in my 40s, having to live like an animal in a zoo. "I sit here in this bullshit jail, waiting to go upstate to prison so I can settle in and do my time," he said. I didn't understand what he meant by that and wouldn't until much later.

Most people don't know this, but being in jail and being in prison are two different things. Jail is where you are housed while you await trial if you can't make bail. Prison is where you go after you are convicted and sentenced by the judge. In NY State, they seem to make the conditions of jail so bad, it makes you want to plead guilty just to get to prison and live a little better. This helps them avoid spending money for trials, and keeps the conviction rates high. You would think when you're supposedly innocent until proven guilty, your living conditions would be a little better. They actually give you better-living conditions after they find you guilty, or get you to plead guilty. 97% of the people convicted of a crime never made it to trial. I don't think this is by chance at all. After hearing Truman give me the sermon about making better choices, I got up to walk away. "Aight old timer, I heard you and I'll keep it all in mind," I said. This shit was taking its toll on me and I needed to get out of here.

About a week went by before I walked over to the payphone and dialed my father's number. He picked up on the third or fourth ring and the operator started his pitch. "You have a collect call from an inmate blah blah blah... Press 9 to accept the charges."

I didn't expect my father to accept the charges, to be honest. The last time I had even seen my father, he had come to our house in Hyenga Lake, and tried to regulate one of me and LaDedra's sibling battles. I had cursed at him and offered for him to come outside and fight me. I had gotten so mad, I threw a pair of hair clippers I had in my hand through my mother's living room window. He was so frightened he somehow convinced my mother to call the police on me. I left before they would arrive.

I guess what made me so mad was him popping up out of the blue trying to play daddy to us, meanwhile, he had a whole other family at home he tended to every day.

On this day, I needed him to play daddy and come help his youngest son. I heard the tone of my father pressing the key to accept the call and immediately got excited. "Hey, Dad," I said before I was quickly interrupted. "Fuck you Bwian, and don't ever call my phone again." And then, Dial tone. That was another turning point of my life. I told myself I would never ask this guy for anything else. My resentment for him had just amplified tremendously.

Months had passed since I initially told Jamie and everyone else I knew that my bail was only $1,000, yet I was still sitting in there. I called Lesly's phone one evening only for the same guy, Mark Scott, to pick up and tell me to go fuck myself and to stop calling her.

I was becoming such a bitter kid and I started to harbor animosity for everyone. I even wrote my mother letters telling her she didn't love me and how if she did, my life wouldn't be this way. I felt like I just wanted to die and get it over with. It became an inside joke around the pod that I was the kid who couldn't get out of jail with a one-thousand-dollar bail. The only other people who couldn't get out of jail with that low of bail were the drug addicts, homeless people and the old mentally disturbed people who had nobody.

How did I end up in this category? All this was turning me more into a monster. I fought almost every time they would let me off keep lock. The C.O.s all hated me. I hated me. I hated life period.

I had been in there for seven and a half months on the day of what would be my last court date. I had stopped getting haircuts. I would only shower once or twice a week. I had given up on everything and everyone in my life. I even stopped caring about whatever happened to me in there. I was totally burnt out at 16 years old.

My lawyer pleaded to the judge about how I had obtained a G.E.D. and still had a chance to turn my life around despite all the disciplinary reports the facility had submitted, and that's when it happened. The district attorney and my lawyer had been called to the sidebar to have a discussion that was off the record. My lawyer then returned to his post next to me.

"May I have a brief word with my client?" he asked the judge. "Make it quick," the judge replied. "So, they have an offer for you; you can plead guilty and get six months with five years probation, which also means you would go home today," he said. "Or, you could plead to a county year, which means no state prison and you finish the time there in the county jail."

In NY State, you only had to do eight months of jail time for each county year. I had already done seven and a half months. That meant I could go home today, and have 5 more years of probation over my head. Or, I could go back inside that shitty jail for two more weeks, and go home with no probation at all. Of course, the wiser decision would've been to just finish out the two weeks and go home, but I just wanted out of this place.

"I wanna go home today," I said. I could feel the excitement of going home sneaking up on me. I couldn't believe it. I was getting out of there.

After I packed up all my raps and other belongings, said my fuck you's to everyone in the pod, I called Mrs. Dow, Caesar's mom, to come pick me up. I asked her not to tell anybody because I wanted to surprise everyone, especially Caesar and Jamie. I wanted to surprise them alright, just not in a typical fashion. I wanted them to see me as the ghost who they thought was buried, but had just been dug up out of his grave. I harbored so much ill will towards my former favorite people, and I would let them know it.

Caesar had still been in school when we got to the Dow residence. I immediately went to the spot where I had left the .9mm handgun I borrowed from Amarr many months ago. It was still there in the same position I had left it in. I thought to myself, *this punk motherfucker must've not been putting in no work if he hadn't touched the gun in seven months.* I grabbed it and quickly put it in my waistline.

I then called J Scott to see if my position was still open to transport his drugs. He assured me that not only was my position still open, but he had some other work for me if I wanted. We decided on a place to meet and I headed out.

I met J Scott in the alleyway behind the big flea market across town from Caesar's house. "Welcome home, Killer," he said with a grin. I see why this guy had so much mystique about him. He moved like a phantom of some sort, never wanting to be seen in public. He then explained that he had set up a big crack spot in Martinsville, Virginia, that made tons of money. He said he had a few soldiers down there already but could use me.

One guy he had down there was a guy named Sweets. Sweets was a kid from the Bronx who was in Lakeside, the same detention center Jamal "Shyne" Barrow had been in. We had crossed paths before but didn't know each other too well. "Before we get you down there, I need to check with Bishop first and make sure he is okay with it," he said, sounding concerned.

Bishop was a name I heard many times before. He was an older guy from East New York, Brooklyn, who had been known for being involved in numerous killings in Brooklyn. When people talked about Bishop, they spoke as if they were talking about the boogie man. "Once I tell him I'm bringing another guy down there, I can link you with Sweets and he'll teach you the operation," he said. "Lesley Pierre know you home?" he asked. "Nah, fuck that dude, them motherfuckers let me sit in jail for mad long with a thousand-dollar bail," I said. "Fuck all those guys."

J Scott knew Lesley Pierre was also involved the night we beat up Mark Scott. "He should've got you out simply for not implementing his bitch ass," he said. This made me think. Why would J Scott call Lesley Pierre a bitch ass? When I had left, Lesley Pierre had still been working for him and they were cool. I guess shit changed since then.

I finally decided it was time to go pay Jamie a visit over at White St, and just as I had anticipated, when he opened the door, he had looked like he seen a ghost. "Yo cuz, what's up man, when you get out?" he asked with his hand out. I ignored his hand and walked past him "Don't Yo Cuz me nigga," I said. "You motherfuckers let me sit in jail for all that time with a thousand-dollar bail?" I said loudly. "All the drugs you motherfuckers sell and the money ya'll be making?" I continued. "Ya'll motherfuckers don't love me so...." Jamie had cut me off before I could finish.

"You right cuz, but shit slowed up a lot out here. I think this nigga smoking that crack shit and all that," he said referring to Koola. "We ain't getting it like we was man," he said. "Man fuck all that, ya'll motherfuckers could've each put up $200 apiece and got me out. I don't want hear none of that shit cuz," I said. "Where is that bitch ass nigga Koola at anyway?" I asked. "You know that motherfucker told on me, right?" I said while fiddling with the gun on my waist. "What are you talking about?" he said, looking confused. "You heard me, he is the one who told the police it was me shooting that night," I said. I then pulled out the gun and pointed it at a picture on the wall and fired it. "Yo, what the fuck you doing?" Jamie yelled. "Tell that sucker ass nigga I'm going to see him," I said and walked out.

My mother had been telling me that my new probation officer had been calling her house for me to come in for my initial visit. I think my mother knew I had no intention of abiding by any probation rules. I would stop by her house to play with my younger siblings for a few minutes, pick on LaDedra, and I was back to the streets. My mother and I had the understanding she had lost the grip on me many years prior to this and we both seemed to accept it. She knew I could take care of myself. She had stopped worrying about me a long time ago.

J Scott called me and told me it was urgent I meet him in that same alleyway. When I got there, he confirmed that I would be going down on the next run to Virginia, but meanwhile, he had something he wanted me to handle for him. "Yo, this nigga Lesley Pierre been stepping on my toes out here," he said. "Ever since he started doing his own thing, he been trying to snatch my customers." Now I was certain J Scott and Lesley Pierre weren't on the same page. "I need this nigga dealt with," he said.

J Scott offered me $500 cash to shoot Lesley Pierre and I accepted it. He specified that he didn't want me to kill him, but to give him a leg shot or something. I had begun to tell myself that Lesley Pierre betrayed me by leaving me in jail all that time, so he deserved it. I wasn't the same person he had known before anyway, so I didn't care for him as I once did before. I assured J Scott it would be handled and we went about our separate ways.

Jamie had called me and told me Koola wanted to talk to me. I didn't think it was a good idea, so I declined. If we were going to ever speak again, it was going to be when I wanted to and I didn't want to right now. I was the man now. What I did ask Jamie was if he was still writing raps. I had let him know that I had gotten much better during my time in jail. As mad as I was at them, I still wanted the He-Menz to work. I told him even though I was mad at them, I would still get us into the studio to record our demo.

A week went by, and the night had come for me to carry out the hit on Lesley Pierre. I had called him a few times to make him think I still had no problem with him, but I was still very mad at him too. By this time, Lesley had went into business for himself and had his own workers. He was doing extremely well. Not as well as J Scott, but he was winning.

If he had it, why did he leave me in there, I wondered? This guy had almost crippled me before, and he participated in the crime I went down for. Getting me out was the least he could do. I figured I'd call first to make sure he was home and when I did, he apologized about not being there for me when I was locked up. He sounded sincere. It was almost like he knew something was up. The human being in me started to feel bad, but I had convinced myself I wasn't human anymore. Plus, I had already taken the money from J Scott so I listened to him, heard him out, but knew I would go through with it. My plan was to go to his house, get him to come out and just shoot his legs. I was just praying he didn't reach for anything or I'd be forced to kill him.

As I walked towards Lesley Pierre's house, I could feel my adrenaline rushing. I was about to shoot my ex-friend for $500. I had known this guy since 7th grade and this drug and street life shit had me ready to shoot him. I thought about the fun times we had playing Basketball; or when I convinced him to buy $1200 turntables because he would be my DJ.

I thought about our trips to Harlem after leaving school early. Even about his father making sure I would be compensated after the accident when nobody on my side even cared. I realized by the time I got to his house, that I couldn't go through with it. At least not for this reason. My new plan would've probably still left us enemies, but at least he wouldn't be hurt. I decided I would shoot, so I fulfilled my duty, but I planned to miss on purpose. Foolish logic I know, but this was the mind of a 16-year-old child.

When I got to his house, I knocked on the window to his basement floor bedroom. I would usually knock on the front door, but I didn't want to alert anybody else that I was there. He moved the curtain back and yelled, "Who's that?" "It's me, B Lo," I said. "Give me a second," he replied. I waited about 7 minutes before he came back to the window and said, "Yo B, I gotta catch you another day, I gotta do something for my pops." I was angry, yet relieved at the same time. Maybe I still had some human left in me after all.

CHAPTER 20

Southern Hospitality

J Scott was explaining the order of operations in Virginia as we cruised down the I-95 headed South. He had made it clear that it was Bishop's crack spot, and he paid Bishop a percentage of whatever money he made from being allowed to sell his own drugs there. He also made it clear that no matter what else happened, for this thing to keep going, Bishop needed to be paid, and paid on time.

I was to keep $20 from every $100 I sold, which was fine with me considering how much drugs we were going down there with. Sweets had some of J Scott's drugs, and some of his own drugs to sell. There also was a female named Theresa, who was Bishop's aunt, who would also be selling Bishop's drugs. All of this was out of this same spot.

When I inquired about how one drug spot could appease so many different people, they assured me there was more than enough to go around. "This shit could pull in about six or seven thousand dollars a day on a good day." Sweets said matter of factly. "Shit more than that," Theresa added. J Scott assured me I wouldn't be down there more than three or four days at a time because I would need to come back and re up, or get more drugs.

We pulled up in front a big house on Moss St. in Martinsville V.A. It took only seconds after we stepped out of the car before a crackhead had walked up asking for drugs. Within ten minutes, Sweets had made about $300. I had seen nothing like this in my life.

Now that J Scott had showed me how shit worked down there, he was headed back up to N.Y. He left me with the words, "B Lo, we are here to get money, and violence fucks up the money." I thought to myself, *Nigga, Bishop is the most violent guy in the world if the rumors are true,* but I just nodded my head in agreement. I had left my gun in NY anyway. I had it in my head I was attempting to be a drug dealer again, and the violence was behind me. This was a fresh start for me.

Right behind the crack spot, was a little hole in the wall bar called the Red Room. This would be the place that older folks would go drink, dance and party. There was a red light that would be lit up whenever the place was open for business. This is where Sweets and I had our first conversation. "We getting a lot of money out here," he said. "I know J Scott don't want niggas on no wild shit, but our reputation is getting around and they don't like NY niggas down here," he said while sipping a beer. He told me he had noticed a few cars circle the block a few times and speed off. "You got a gun down here?" I asked. "Everybody got a gun down here," he replied.

The next day I woke up to a line of 16 crackheads waiting to be served. I quickly ran outside and served them all. Sweets was still asleep so I figured this would be good for me to get my shit off as fast as I could.

The one thing that stood out to me was these crackheads weren't like crackheads in NY. These were like everyday people who looked clean and healthy. They had cars, nice clothes, and everything, yet were here buying crack.

A few minutes later, I noticed a group of teenagers walking to school. I immediately thought about my life and how bad I fucked it up. I should've been on my way to school, but here I was, 700 miles away from home, in a remote town in Virginia selling crack that wasn't even mine.

I noticed these kids walking in my direction. Were these stick up kids I thought? I automatically regretted being out here without a weapon on me. They all were walking rather slowly, and wearing bookbags, and a few were female so that kinda killed the notion of them coming to rob me. As they got closer, I put my hand behind my back as if I had a pistol back there. "Yo, can I get 6," one of the kids said. "I don't got no weed homie, sorry," I said to the kid. "No, I need 6 rocks," he said. "What the fuck you gonna do with 6 rocks?" I asked smiling at him. He smiled back and said, "I'm gonna smoke them motherfuckers, what you think?"

His friends had started laughing and nodding in agreeance. "How old are you?" I asked. "I'm 15," he replied. "And you about to smoke some crack?" I asked, looking bewildered. "Hell yeah, gonna put it in my weed and make Primos," he said confidently. "You don't smoke Primos?" he asked. "Hell no I don't smoke that shit, ya'll bugging," I said laughing hysterically. In all the years of my life, I had never met anybody that young that smoked crack. I sold it to them and sent them on their way.

As I'm posted up in the front of the spot, serving crackheads as quick as they come, I notice a skinny black older looking guy to my right looking suspicious. I had learned from being incarcerated to watch my surroundings very closely. I noticed every time I would look his way, he would turn his head. Sweets had warned me it was going around town that some guys from NY were down here making a lot of money, and some of the locals weren't happy about it. Was this one of the locals? I really knew I would be needing my gun if I was gonna be out here doing this shit.

"Come here," the skinny guy said to me. "Hell no, you come here," I replied. I had begun to get nervous. Was this a clean crackhead? A stick-up kid? A cop? I was about to run upstairs and ask Sweets for his gun when the guy spoke to me "Yo, your name B Lo right?" How the hell did this guy know my name? "Who the fuck are you?" I asked. "I'm asking the questions around this motherfucker," he replied.

Before I could say anything back to him, Sweets had come outside, walked past me and gave the skinny guy a fist bump, "When did you get down here, Bishop?" Sweets asked. He ignored Sweets. "Yo shorty, come here, let me talk to you," Bishop said. I walked over to officially greet the man, myth and legend known as Bishop. "J Scott told me you're from Brooklyn, what part of Brooklyn you from?" he asked. "I'm from all over Brooklyn," I replied. "You ain't from Brooklyn nigga," he said with a smirk. "Who you know in East New York if you from all over BK?" he asked. I began to name some of the people I knew. "Who you know in Flatbush?" he asked. "I lived in East Flatbush when I was a kid, on E. 58th St," I answered. "You know Barry from Seth Low.

Houses?" I asked him. I had only asked because I remember Barry telling us a story about a guy from East New York they called 'The Bishop" who used to terrorize the neighborhood. "Yeah, I know Barry, with the glasses," he answered. "I'm just fucking with you shorty, I know J Scott and Sweets are some Upstate niggas so I had to check," he said looking at Sweets. "I'm from the Bronx, nigga," Sweets said, laughing loudly. "I'm from Upstate too I said, I told you I'm from all over this motherfucker," I said confidently.

"Yo, ya'll wanna get some beers?" Bishop asked. "It's 9 A.M. in the morning Bish, it's too early to be drinking beer man," Sweets replied. "I'm with it," I said. "Let's go shorty, let this nigga Sweets sit here and sell everybody's drugs." "Yo Bishop, can you call me B Lo?" I asked him. "Oh, my bad B Lo," he said, smiling showing a mouth full of gold teeth. Bishop and I walked around the corner where a new shiny gold Sterling had been parked. "Hop in shorty...I mean, B Lo," he said as we sped off.

Bishop hardly stayed down in Virginia. He had his Aunt Theresa down there selling his drugs. He also was getting a percentage from J Scott, Sweets and this kid named Fat Chris. Fat Chris was a fat Puerto Rican kid from The Bronx who Bishop would also allow to sell his drugs there for a percentage. As we rode to the store to get the beer, he questioned me about what I wanted out of the drug game. "I honestly just want to make enough to get some studio time and pay for my group's demo," I said.

"To be honest, I usually rob drug dealers man, this really ain't my thing," I added. He laughed. "Well, don't rob the wrong drug dealer B Lo, you got drug dealers out here that will kill you, like me," Bishop said. "But you said you rap?" he asked. "Yeah man, I been rapping since I was a kid," I said. "I rap too; not on no trying to be a rapper shit, but I could spit," he said. "When we get this beer, we're going to go back to Moss St and kick some shit, you better not be wack shorty," he said. "It's B Lo," I replied, smiling.

We parked in front of the spot, Bishop turned the engine off and turned up the radio to a sound of hard boom bap beats blaring out the speakers. I expected Bishop to be wack, or average after his disclaimer, but he was surprisingly very good. After his verse, he looked at me as if he were expecting me to say an average 16-year-old's rap. Since he was from Brooklyn, I did one of my old Brooklyn verses I knew every Brooklyn nigga could appreciate.

Single handedly, my man and me we starting war/the A or the 4, to go hit up some damn department store/Two Lo's deep, Skell, Roke and J wanna stay/ but you know Brian I'mma' try and catch a chain on the way/ Jappy Lo, bust open la sacks to entice the heist/ he said 'its relevant we sell this shit for twice the price'/ Who you tell- ing, I'm 2 B Lo nigga you know my all day function/ I bet I catch a vic before we the Broadway Junction/punching screaming and scratching didn't get away though? I took the bitches earrings/ her dough, Lo hat and Figaro......

Before I could finish, Bishop was banging on his steering wheel "You didn't write that shit nigga," he said loudly. "That's my word to my mother I did," I assured him. "That's mad old, I got way better shit than that," I said. "You remind me of my friend Biggie Smalls, my boy is hot right now too," he said. "You ever heard of Biggie Smalls?" he asked. "Hell yeah I heard of Biggie Smalls. He got that song 'Unbelievable' out right now right?" I asked. "Yeah, that's my homeboy. I grew up with Fat Chris man, I know his Moms and all, we went to school together," he said, sounding excited "We went to Bishop Loughlin and Westinghouse together," he said. "That's where the name Bishop come from, it ain't from that 'Juice' shit." The mean, evil, unapproachable Bishop everyone seemed to spooked to even talk about, was nothing like the Bishop I was in this car talking to. We stayed in the car rapping until about noon, and then it was time to get back to the money.

From that day on, whenever Bishop was in Virginia, I didn't have to touch a drug. He actually believed if I got focused, I had what it took to make it as a rapper. The Notorious B.I.G. was blowing up fast and Bishop reminded me they were friends every day. "I'm trying to get in touch with this fat nigga," Bishop would say almost every time I seen him. I didn't know if I believed him about the magnitude of their relationship, but if he was lying, he was very convincing.

Sweets introduced me to a very nice older, heavyset lady named Debbie. Debbie was a lady who would come by and cook and clean for us whenever we needed. She would also drive us back and forth to NY to drop off money to Bishop, or pick up Drugs from J Scott. She was like the mother of our crew. The only problem with Debbie was she also had the habit of smoking crack.

Whenever we would close the shop for the night, we would go to the Red Room to get drinks, or go hang out in these projects called Koehler Hill. It would be in Koehler Hill where Sweets would introduce me to a chocolate brown 20-year-old female named KiKi. KiKi would ask me to speak just to balk at my NY accent. We were down in VA to get money, but when Sweets was around and Bishop wasn't, we were most certainly also going to have some fun.

Sweets had even recruited a crackhead he would ultimately name Eat Em Up. Eat Em Up's main job was to sell to anybody we thought may have been an undercover cop, but he got that nickname doing some other shit.

The guy's real name was Greg, but crazy ass Sweets thought it would be entertaining to get Greg, or Eat Em Up, to go down and give head to any willing female crackhead who would allow it. We would be sitting in front of the spot, hustling and bored, and an attractive female crackhead would come to buy drugs and Sweets would romantically whisper to them, "Sweetheart, you want your pussy ate tonight?" They would almost always automatically blush or giggle. "I'm serious," he would continue. And then he would say, "I'll give you two more rocks if you let my man Greg right here eat your pussy."

Crack must be a very strong drug, or getting head must feel really good to women, because at least four out of five of these crackheads would let Greg, AKA Eat Em Up go to work.

For the first couple of weeks or so, things were running pretty smoothly in Virginia. Everybody was making their quota so J Scott was happy, Sweets was happy, and most importantly, Bishop was happy. Me on the other hand, once I seen the amount of money that was being made, I realized I was taking a lot of the risk for a small portion of the reward. From then on, when I took the trips to NY to get more drugs, I would buy some of my own drugs to sell down there. Transactions were made so frequent at such a fast pace, it would be almost impossible to figure out whose drugs were whose.

I had also built up my own small arsenal of weapons. Whenever a crackhead would come with something other than cash, I would tell them to get lost; unless it was a firearm.

This was the interesting thing about crack addicts, when they ran out of money, they would come with some of the strangest things to try to trade for a rock. From kitchen appliances to car mufflers, you name it, they brought it. I think I must've seen it all. I even had a crackhead bring a case of Absolut Vodka that had been replaced with water. None of us realized it until after we unknowingly made watered-down fake cocktails disguised as Cranberry and Vodka. This same practice would be what would begin to slow things down for us in Virginia.

On one hot summer evening, two females had approached Sweets and I as we sold drugs in front of the spot. One of the females was light-skinned, thick and very attractive. Her friend, while also attractive, was a little more on the heavy side. I would've never guessed in a million years these girls were smokers, but Sweets seemed to know right away.

"Hey, do you guys listen to Hip Hop?" the prettier young lady asked as she approached us. "Hell Yeah, we love Hip Hop," I answered. She handed Sweets a plastic bag full of unopened CDs. He read the titles of the CDs out loud as he removed them from the bag. "*Coolio: It Takes a Thief, Shaq Fu: Da Return*." we like Hip Hop but not this corny shit," he said. "But how many you want for them?" he asked.

I had no idea these two young attractive females were looking for crack in exchange for the CDs, but Sweets knew right away. "How many you willing to give us?" the light-skinned female asked. "Give me a second," Sweets replied as he summoned me over to speak privately. "Yo you wanna take these chicks to the hotel and have some fun?" he asked. "We can probably get them to freak off with each other," he said.

I assured him I was down and we returned with a whole new proposition. "Why don't ya'll come hang out with us at our Hotel. We will give you as much as you want," Sweets said. These two young ladies now looked very excited. They agreed to join us and we all four hopped in a cab and headed towards the Holiday Inn.

I found it rather odd these females insisted they needed to get high before anything else went down. We initially rented two separate rooms. I started with the heavier friend, while Sweets went with the slim, thick friend. We would eventually trade places until we decided it made more sense to get one huge room with a Jacuzzi and let the girls go at it with each other.

It was my first time seeing two females together sexually in real life. Watching the heavier dark-skinned girl pleasing her friend was intense. It got even more intense when they switched places and the little one went down on her. The smaller light-skinned one seemed to be much more experienced with girl-on-girl action than her friend was.

As much as I enjoyed it, it also made me a bit uncomfortable at the same time. I can't actually say where the discomfort aspect came from, but I felt it. Maybe it was because even as good as they looked, I knew they were still crackheads. I laid in solitary confinement years later trying to replay those moments in my mind. The older I got, the more I wish I would've cherished those young explorative times of my life.

Sweets must've given these females about an ounce of crack over the next four days we were in that hotel. We would only leave for about two or three hours at a time to go back to the spot on Moss St and sell drugs. We had fallen far behind without even really noticing it.

By the time we got tired of all the drug-induced freak sessions we had going on in that hotel, we had lost thousands and thousands of dollars and J Scott and Bishop were pissed off. They hadn't known what Sweets and I had been up to for almost a week or so, but they knew the money had slowed up and shit wasn't running as it should've been.

When we finally got rid of those females and returned to the spot to hustle full time, we automatically realized something was very different. The money we would usually make in three hours, now took eight hours. We had only been gone for a few days and the clientele slowed up tremendously. We had taken trips back to NY to get more drugs that took longer than four days, and things had never slowed up this much.

There was something else going on. We sent Greg (AKA Eat Em Up) and Debbie to go out there and do some investigating and just as we assumed, there was much more to the decline in activity than us freaking off with those girls. We found out some of the locals had opened up a crack spot literally two blocks away from ours. They seemed to have had just as good, or even better drugs than we did because if not, the closeness of proximity wouldn't have mattered this much. Now we just needed to figure out who these guys were, and what we were going to do about it.

As clientele, customers, and profits continued to decline, the pressure from J Scott and Bishop began to build. My idea was to bring a few hitters from New York and begin putting pressure on the Virginia guys. Sweets just thought we needed more workers and to expand the operation up to the Kohler Hill projects.

We would go to Kohler Hill to hang out and fuck with females, but never to sell drugs. That was until we hit this snag. Selling drugs in Kohler Hill was more like how we did it in NY. We didn't stay in one place and wait for the addicts to come to us. We solicited the addicts and sometimes even raced other dealers to make sales. We were desperate, and it showed.

There was a smoker in Kohler Hill named Trina who would let us use her house to bag up drugs, stash weapons or whatever we needed it for. As long as we gave her enough drugs to supply her for the day, we had complete access to her apartment and it came in handy. Debbie and Trina were friends from the neighborhood so we knew that they had some sort of alliance. The Kohler Hill move was helping a little, but not nearly enough for Bishop's liking. He was used to pulling a certain amount a week and that's what he expected. We weren't even doing half of that.

I told myself I would express to Bishop the idea of robbing some of these drug dealers now competing against us. I told Sweets about it and he said in no way would Bishop be for my idea. He said if we did it, we should do it without telling J Scott or Bishop. He even got Fat Chris to agree this was the best way if we were going to do it.

A week had past and I finally got Sweets and Fat Chris to agree to my plan to rob the drug dealers who had opened up a spot two blocks away. The guys who opened this new spot had actually came by our spot a few weeks prior to introduce themselves, but never had they mentioned any plans of becoming competition.

I convinced Sweets and Fat Chris it was insulting for these guys to come map out our operation before opening up their own only two blocks away. I was trying to do everything I could to get Sweets and Fat Chris to be as amped as I was about robbing these guys. Dealing drugs was their thing, but robberies and shootings were mine.

I could sense their nervousness and uncertainty about the whole thing, but not only did we need the money, we needed to make a statement out there.

The plan was set and the robbery was scheduled for this specific evening. Sweets set it up so Fat Chris and I would go in and tie up whoever was in there, demand the money and drugs, and get back to where he would be waiting to drive us to safety. When Sweets remained adamant about his role being solely the getaway driver, it made me realize he wasn't as tough as people made him out to be. He had a reputation of being wild and crazy, but when I saw how reluctant and fearful he was about the potential danger of running up in a drug spot, I seen his true colors. And that was all I needed to see.

"Have Greg knock on the door and when they open the door for him, ya'll rush in and make sure there is nobody in the back rooms," Sweets said from behind the driver seat. "Once ya'll secure the area, then tie whoever is in there up, and make sure they tell you where everything is," he added.

He was giving a lot of orders for someone who was actually afraid to go in himself and it was pissing me off. "I'm going to be right here waiting for ya'll. Whatever you do, B Lo, don't shoot anybody unless it's absolutely necessary," he said.

In my mind, I was running the show. Anybody who was afraid to do dirty work could never have any say over what I did or didn't do and I was about to prove that.

"Make sure ya'll got those masks on when ya'll go up in there," Sweets yelled from the car as we approached the dimly lit walkway that led to the door. While Fat Chris was wrapping his bandana around his face, I pushed Greg to knock on the door so we could get the show on the road. At this point, my adrenaline was rushing and I wanted to get this over with.

"Who is it?" a deep voice asked from behind the door. "It's me Greg, I need one of those 20s," Greg replied. At that point, the door cracked open and I pushed Greg inside and pointed my .38 revolver at the shirtless man who had opened the door. I ordered him to get on the ground and to keep his hands where I can see them.

I looked back to notice Fat Chris hadn't even entered yet. Did he get cold feet? Did someone notice him? It didn't matter to me. It was too late for me to turn back now. I was on a mission and I was about to complete it. I noticed a stack of cash on the table and quickly put it in my pocket.

"Yo, get your fat ass in here," I yelled out loudly. I had called out to Fat Chris so he could watch the guy as I searched for drugs and money. A second after I did so, I notice a young lady coming from one of the back rooms holding a very small child. When she saw me with the gun standing over the guy I had ordered to the floor, she let out a loud scream and dropped the baby and ran towards wherever she had come from. I was about to chase her but decided against it. The baby started to scream and the guy was pleading with me to not shoot him. This robbery had went terribly wrong.

I wanted to go make sure the baby was okay, but something told me it was time to get the hell out of there. I was sure if the female had a phone in that back room, she had called 911 by now. I headed toward the door and as I'm rushing out, Fat Chris was just coming in. I had been inside this spot alone for at least a minute and half by then, and here he was coming in as I'm running out. "C'mon let's get the fuck out of here," I said as I ran toward Sweets in the waiting car.

While on our way back to Moss St., for the first time since I had been down in Virginia, Sweets and Fat Chris got to see my angry side. I called Fat Chris all kinds of fat ass punks for taking so long to enter the spot. I even told Sweets if he had been in there with me instead of opting to be a getaway driver, shit would've went much smoother. "I fucking could've shot a child because of your scary motherfuckers," I yelled at the both of them.

From that day on, there was a shift in how things ran down there. Once I realized Sweets and Fat Chris knew I was down for any and everything, I used their fears to my advantage. When Bishop or J Scott was up in NY, I decided I was going to be deciding how shit ran in Virginia.

Two days later, I was awakened by Bishop's voice yelling at Sweets and Fat Chris. "You motherfuckers are down here robbing niggas on some nickel and dime shit?" Bishop screamed. "And you can't tell me it wasn't ya'll because Fat Ass Chris dropped his I.D. outside the fucking spot," he added.

Apparently, the guys we robbed had reached out to Bishop and told him that we had robbed them. They were more worried about having issues with us than the little money we had taken. I was waiting for Sweets to tell Bishop that the robbery was my idea, but he didn't. Bishop let us know that we were starting to fuck up and things needed to change soon. And they most definitely would.

I had taken a trip up to NY to get more drugs and when I got back down to Virginia, I noticed Sweets had brought his then girlfriend Veronica down there. Veronica was a 16-year-old girl who Sweets had been dating since they were in Middle School. She was a very street smart, cool, level headed down to earth female. Her and Sweets were head over heels in love and now that it was summertime and she had no school, she came down to spend time with him in Virginia, which I thought was a horrible idea.

We were down there doing a lot of dirt and it made no sense for her to be down there. I wondered if Bishop knew she was there. This would be a decision that would come back to bite us all in the ass.

I had just bagged up $500.00 worth of crack to take to Kohler Hill to try and knock off. Since we had those two girls in the hotel, things had never quite gotten back to how they once were. The botched robbery didn't help. That just had us pegged as the out of town trouble makers. Sweets was with Veronica a lot so that left Fat Chris and I to handle the majority of the workload. I had made a goal to save up $5000 to invest into my rap career, and I was done with all of this street shit.

I had taken a cab to Trina's place in Kohler Hill housing projects. When I got there, I found Trina and Debbie in her kitchen playing cards. I had my .9mm pistol in my left pocket, and the $500 package in my left. I was very tired and told Trina I was going to take a nap on the chair in her living room. I specifically asked her to wake me if anyone other than the usuals came there.

I woke up about three hours later to find my gun still in my right pocket, but the $500.00 worth of drugs I had were nowhere to be found. "Trina, where the fuck is my shit at?" I yelled while looking under the seat cushions. "Where the fuck are my drugs at?" Trina seemed startled and scared and helped me look around for the package. "Who the hell was in this house?" I asked her. "Nobody but me, you and Debbie, I swear," she replied.

"Where the fuck is Debbie?" I asked her. "I don't know. She left about an hour ago," she said. I looked outside and seen Debbie's car was still parked outside, which I found to be weird. "If I don't find my shit, somebody is going to get hurt," I said. "Who else does Debbie know around here? Her car is still outside," I asked. "She probably over there getting high with Sharon and them," Trina stated. Apparently, Sharon was some other crackhead who had lived in these housing projects. "Can you bring me over there?" I asked her. "Yeah, give me a second, I'll walk you over there."

When Debbie came to the door, I could automatically tell she was high as a kite. She looked nervous and very uneasy as I asked her to walk with me back over to Trina's place. When we all three got back to Trina's place, I sat them down to get to the bottom of what happened to my drugs.

Trina maintained nobody else had been at her house and the only time she had seen anyone near me, was when Debbie was putting my gun back in my pocket. "Wait, *what*?" I said. "Yeah, Debbie said your gun was sticking out your pocket and she stuck it back down in there," Trina repeated. "Debbie, you was fucking around with my pockets?" I asked her. "Yeah, I said 'that boy got that gun on him' and I seen it sticking out your pocket," she said before I abruptly cut her off. "Why the fuck would you be going in my pockets Debbie?" I screamed. "How are you going to steal from ME after all the shit we do for you?" I said angrily.

At this point, I was 100% sure Debbie had stolen the package from me. She had stolen it and went and got high with some other smokers. She didn't even share any of the stolen drugs with Trina, which I could tell pissed her off. "I can't believe you would fucking steal from me, Debbie," I repeated. She automatically began to cry and demanded to be taken to see Sweets.

I held the gun on Debbie the whole ride over to where Sweets and Fat Chris were. When we walked in, I made her sit on the floor and yelled out for Sweets and Fat Chris. "Yo, this bitch Debbie stole my whole pack, yo!" I yelled. Debbie cursed. She had found a false sense of security because Sweets was present.

"Yo, I'm about to shoot this bitch, yo!" I yelled. "Yo, Sweets, Chris I swear I'm about to clap this bitch right now," I repeated. I could hear some audible mumbling coming from the bedroom Sweets was in. "You niggas got ten seconds to get out here or I'm killing this bitch," I said out loud.

I then put the gun to Debbie's head and she screamed. POW POW .... After the two shots rang off, Sweets came running out of his room in boxer shorts. "Yo why you shooting in the house man?" Sweets asked. "I told ya'll niggas to come deal with this bitch or I was going to deal with her." Debbie was on the ground grimacing in pain from the shots in her knees. I had moved the gun away from her head and shot her in both her legs. At that moment, I thought I was making an example. In hindsight, it was the most stupid thing I had ever done in my life.

Sweets had the brilliant idea of driving Debbie to the hospital and making sure Fat Chris stayed with her, so when the police came, we would know exactly what she told them. Whenever there is a victim of a gunshot, police are automatically called to the hospital to make a report.

Debbie told the police she was on her porch and someone shot from a car and she had been hit. The police knew she was lying because they saw powder burns on her pant legs. The officer let her know if she were shot from far away as she claimed, there would be no powder burns on her. She stuck to her story.

On the ride back from picking up Debbie at the hospital, she again pled with me about not having had stolen the drugs from me. She even said I should give her drugs for shooting her for nothing. Wanting to get high had just got her shot, and here she was, fresh out of the hospital on crutches looking to get high again.

Once Bishop and J Scott discovered I had shot Debbie, it seems they wanted me as far away from the drug selling aspect as possible. It was decided that my role was strictly shooter, and enforcer. I didn't have to sell any more drugs unless I wanted to.

Bishop and I began to out every day. Sweets would be with Veronica a lot, and Fat Chris just sold everybody's drugs all day.

Bishop knew how serious I had become about my music. I had made little tapes every chance I could get. He reminded me every day that Notorious B.I.G. was his close friend and whenever they linked back up, our lives would change forever. Our lives would change alright, but nothing like in the ways we had anticipated. Neither of us had the insight to foresee what would happen next! If only we did!!

This concludes Book One of Pain Peace and Prosperity. Stay Tuned for Book Two Coming Soon.

Brian D. Carenard

```
INMATE STATUS REPORT FOR PAROLE BOARD APPLARANCE
                        PART I

NAME: CARENARD, Brian           NYSID 77816371      DIN: 96A0549

                        CRIMINAL RECORD

Arrest Date    Arrest Charges              Place         Disposition

9-12-94        CPW 2nd (C) Fel.,           Rockland      3-15-95 - Adj. Y.O.:
               Assault 2nd (2 Counts),     Cty. Crt.     Assault 2nd (D) Fel. (2 Count
               Reckless Endang. 2nd,                     Reckless Endang. 2nd (A) Misd.
               CPW 4th                                   CPW 4th (A) Misd.,
               Crim. Mischief 4th                        Crim. Mischief 4th (A) Misd.
                                                         Sent.: 6 Mos./3 Yrs. Prob.

7-5-95         Assault 1st (C) Fel.,        "            1-23-96 - PG to:
               CPW 2nd,                                  Assault 1st (C) Fel.
               Assault 2nd,                              Sent.: 2-0/6-0
               CPW 3rd                                   (I.O.)

As a juvenile, Carenard was arrested twice on the same date (11-19-91), the first
for Assault 3rd to which he pled guilty to Att. Assault 3rd on 2-18-92, was
adjudicated a J.D. and placed on One (1) Year Probation on 8-4-92. On 12-14-92,
he was found to be in violation of his probation, and was placed in the custody
of DSS at St. Cabrini School for one (1) year. The second arrest on the same
date was for Assault 3rd and Reckless Endangerment 2nd, however, these charges
were covered by the above.
```

My Parole getting denied

www.ingramcontent.com/pod-product-compliance
Lightning Source LLC
Chambersburg PA
CBHW071802080526
44589CB00012B/653